Pimps, Players, and Baby-layers

Pimps, Players, and Baby-layers

James Henderson

Broke-Tooth Dog Press
P.O. Box 201
Morrilton, Arkansas 72110

Published 2002 by Broke-Tooth Dog Press,
P.O. Box 201, Morrilton, Arkansas 72110.

Printed in the United States of America

10 9 8 7 6 5 4 3 2 1

to Joyce Marie

Contents

Chapter 1
The Player

"He who pees in his own gene pool
shouldn't complain that it's contaminated."
H.H.

Look at Mac Daddy Ice. He's on television, doing his thang. Rapping. Notice the numerous gold and silver chains around his neck. Check out his bird-sized chest. It's a wonder he can hold his neck up. What's that emblazoned on his underwear, which hangs outside his pants? Must be profane because Top 10 Video blurs it out. Look at those beautiful women hanging on his jock. Wow! Gorgeous, curvaceous, bosomy, young, big-bootied women, of every race, creed, and nationality. Wow!...look at the brunette in the string bikini...She's bent over...her butt filling up the television screen...How—no, not how, where?...Where did she learn to shake her butt like that? Looks like electric Jell-O. Wow! The camera flips back to Mac Daddy. He seems mad about something; shaking his fist threateningly, making enigmatic hand signals—as if anyone besides him and his boys knows what the hell it all means. Listen for a moment ... The musical number sounds familiar, doesn't it? ... The Beverly Hillbilly theme song ...

Say what you will about Mac Daddy Ice, but he, unlike some rappers, has the creative present of mind to find good background material beyond outdated albums. In a husky voice, Mac Daddy Ice rhymes:

Listen to my story 'bout a punk named Ed
He tried to hump on my style, so I shot him in the head
Shotgun, that is ... twelve-gauge ... Remington ... Booyaaaa
My dogs said, Mac, you got to move away from there, Cali's the place to be,
Then I loaded up my Benz, dumped all my hoes, and moved to Beverlieeee...

Man, Mac Daddy Ice sure can rap. Now the women are in the picture again; but Mac Daddy Ice seems unconcerned about their presence. How nonchalant can a Brother be? He has all these scantily clad, beautiful women pushing and shoving each other just to rub his chest, and his biggest concern some dude named Ed, who had the audacity to copycat Mac Daddy Ice's style. Only a Player can afford such luxuries. A non-Player would be too concerned about which woman he would have first, and Ed would be the furthest from his mind. Hell, a non-Player probably couldn't remember the words to the song—even if he wrote it—with all those beauties around.

But a non-Player can dream, though. He can hope and wish and fantasize of being a Player like Mac Daddy Ice. He can even go so far as to emulate Mac Daddy Ice's style (as long as Mac Daddy Ice doesn't find out about it). To be a Player, you must act like a Player, right? Fake it till you make it, right?

Wrong!

Players, true Players, are born, not made. The idea that the majority of African-American men are Players or possess the potential to be Players is a myth—the result of age-old African-American male sexual stereotypes, including the one that all African-American men are well hung. How many Brothers wish that were true?

Yet unlike other myths, many African-American males try desperately to live up to the fallacy that all Brothers are notorious womanizers. How many Brothers wish that were true as well? How many Brothers have suffered, losing out on perfectly suited relationships because they were trying to be something they were not? There exist thousands, if not millions, of Brothers who wholeheartedly believe the lie, that they themselves are Players. So, finally, let's separate the true Players from the artificial Players.

What is a Player? Good question. A Player is a Brother who naturally charms women. It's that simple, but the key word here is *naturally*—which means "lacking in artificiality." Let's try an analogy for those Brothers who intend to hold on to their imitation Player cards until rheumatism sets in.

You like basketball, don't you? No doubt. Most red-blooded, O-type African-American males do. Now, can you play basketball? No doubt you said yes; in fact, ninety-two-point-nine percent of African-American males would answer yes. But go to any basketball court in America and you will find Brothers who, despite their best efforts to do so, cannot play basketball. Some can't jump, some can't dribble, millions can't shoot, and an equal number are lucky that they haven't had the shit knocked out of them yet. You've seen these types—jumping up and down like retards in a wind tunnel, tripping over their own feet, and shooting the ball every time it hits their hands.

But the damnedest thing, the most inexplicable thing, is that the wannabe basketball players who think they are talented but who are blatantly not are the most vociferous, most obnoxious, most pugnacious, and most selfish players on the court—as if they can bluff and bullshit their way to talent. They hog the ball, cry foul when their shots fall short—which happens quite often—and delay the game by either holding onto the ball or going home with the ball if a call doesn't go their way. In their minds, they are NBA material, despite never playing a minute of organized basketball in their life.

Now look at the truly gifted basketball players on the court. Their moves are fluid, graceful, effortless, and when they shoot, the ball actually goes inside the rim. Unless they are one of a large group of Brothers who could have played pro ball but didn't, they seldom brag. These Brothers were good at a very young age. They didn't suddenly develop skills, they improved on existing skills. Wannabe basketball players believe that one lucky shot per year proves their skill. They fail to see the logic.

Indisputable fact: All African-Americans have skills—the ability to effortlessly perform a given task. The key is to find out what skills you have, and then work very hard to improve on them. If you enjoy doing it, possess a passion for doing it, lose track of time while doing it, then you have discovered your true skill. Imagine if Allen Iverson had concentrated his efforts on wrestling in the WWF, or Tiger Woods had focused his dreams on playing in the NFL, or if Shaqulle O'Neal had desired to be a jockey. A colossal waste of time and skills, right?

As with the one-shot wonder on the basketball court, the artificial Player falsely believes in his skills. In time most wannabe basketball players eventually realize—usually after getting knocked on their butts—that their hearts are in the game but their ability to play isn't. But with artificial Players, this realization rarely takes root. No doubt you know an old geezer, well in his eighties, still thinking himself a Player, still hitting the nightspots and chasing women. A sad sight, isn't it?

An artificial Player may confuse being promiscuous

with being a Player; he thinks that sleeping with X number of women automatically qualifies him for Player status.

Wrong again.

By definition *promiscuous* means "having numerous sexual partners on a casual basis." A Sugar Daddy can accomplish that feat. A smelly, toothless, one-eyed giant with a moderate income can also accomplish that feat. So what? This definition does not define a Player. Fact: Many true Players (the smart ones), throughout their entire life, focus their attention on one woman.

So you're still not convinced, still entertaining illusions of Playerosity. Okay. Answer yes to any of the following questions, and, no doubt about it, you are a bona fide artificial Player.

1. Did you have trouble dating in high school?

2. Lacking options, have you ever taken a relative (second and third cousins and everyone on your daddy's side are relatives) to a prom, company party, or other social event?

3. Have you ever gone to a funeral or a family reunion ostensibly to find a date?

4. Do you utilize, or believe in, the mathematical approach (propositioning as many women as possible in the hope of increasing the chances that one will say yes)?

5. Have you ever written a pick-up line on the palm of your hand?

6. Did women finally start to notice you after one of the following events occurred:

   You purchased a car?

   You got a new job?

   You bought a new house?

   You or your friend got a record deal?

   You were initiated into a gang?

You won the lottery?

You were drafted by the NBA, WBA, NFL, CFL?

You sold drugs?

7. By way of introducing yourself to a woman, have you ever opened your billfold, flashed cash, or ostentatiously displayed the fake diamonds on your fingers?

8. On more than one occasion have you, for the purpose of having sex, paid a woman's rent, car note, utility bill(s), credit card bill(s), hair stylist bill?

If you answered yes to questions seven and eight, you may also be suffering from Sugar Daddyism. As you can see there's little difference between an artificial Player and a Sugar Daddy. Both types run the risk that when whatever they have that women are attracted to goes away, they themselves suddenly lose their sweetness. Money dries up, motors blow rods, houses burn down, knees buckle, dope wafts away, but a woman who's in it to win it possesses a remarkable prescience as to when to move her ass.

The Downside to Being a Player

Many actors, singers, celebrities, professional athletes, and even a few civil rights leaders will tell you that there are many negative aspects to fame, wealth, and glory: stalkers; lack of privacy; obnoxious fans; women who throw dirty underwear at them; women who steadfastly refuse to raise illegitimate children anonymously. Woe the celebrity.

On the other hand, a Player seldom talks about the negative aspects to being a Player. Why? Because the downside to being a Player is too damning, too self-deprecating, and far too stultifying. The Player talks at length about getting this sucked, getting that sucked, penetrating this and penetrating that, how many women were there, and on and on and on. While listening to the Player's often repeated spiel, you realize two things: one, you could never live up to his sexual exploits, and two, it's obvious that the Player enjoys talking about his sexual exploits as much as he enjoys making them. In the back of your mind, where common sense resides, you wonder about plausibility. If a certain woman could fellatiate as long as he claims she did, then why isn't she in the record books? If his stamina defies physics, as he purports, then why isn't he too in the record books? Also, isn't it rather amazing that He Who Has Bedded Millions of Women has never incurred a STD (Sexually Transmitted Disease).

When was the last time you heard Mr. Dick Hurts say, "I think she gave me syphilis," or "I've been itching ever since she left," or "She left me burning," or anything of that nature? No, you'll never hear the Player say that because that's the downside to being a Player. Gonorrhea, AIDS, chlamydia, trichomoniasis, herpes, genital warts, court-ordered child support, garnishment, DNA testing–these are also words that Players have tremendous difficulty pronouncing.

Wilt Chamberlain, God rest his soul, was without a doubt the Player above all Players. According to Wilt's autobiography, he sexually conquered 20,000 women. A remarkable number. Even more remarkable, Wilt claimed that there was not one quickie in the whole bunch; he took his time. Consider this: a year totals 365 days; a decade, 3,650 days; a half-century, 18,250 days. Mathematically this suggests…well, it suggests that Wilt either flunked math or started entertaining women while wearing a Huggie. It most certainly suggests that Wilt, despite his claim to the contrary, did not care one iota for the multitude of women he bedded. How could he? Outside of sexual performance, what possibly could have been the discerning difference between number 5 and number 19,999?

Women are human beings. To be a Player, a bona fide Player, this fact must somehow be overlooked.

Any Brother who enumerates his sexual conquests is not looking for a soulmate, and does not appreciate the simple fact that women are human beings–not objects merely to gratify a man's sexual pleasure.

The ingredients that sustain a Player—cockiness, indifference, a pinch of arrogance, and a dab of narcissism—are the same ingredients that keep a Player from ever truly connecting with a woman, truly loving a woman, truly loving himself. Talk to any old Player, and he will tell you in some form or fashion that "More isn't better." Being able to cite a high number of sexual conquests doesn't compare to being able to say, "I've maintained a long, healthy, monogamous relationship." Brothers who can say the latter say it proudly, loudly, publicly, and often. Outside of hushed conversations with the boys, Players rarely discuss their amorous abilities.

Truly loving one woman is an uncomforable if not frightening proposition for some Brothers because it entails taking chances: *What if, at some point, she dumps me? What if she finds out who I really am, just a man, with emotions, character flaws, problems—like everyone else? If I love her unconditionally, will I lose my Player's membership card?* Negative mental imaging, right? Yes, indeed. All relationships have certain risk factors built in. (But as you will see in Chapter 8, being a Player or attempting to be a Player also has dire consequences.) As old-fashioned as it may sound, loving one woman has tremendous benefits, two of which are having less to remember and less to pay out. Another tremendous benefit: not becoming jaded. A Brother who is fortunate to have only one woman in his lifetime does not complain that women can't be trusted, women are no good, and women only want your money. Talk to any Brother who has enjoyed a lengthy monogamous relationship, then talk to an old Player, and compare the difference. Who do you think will confess to enjoying a happy, healthy relationship? Who do you think will convey a more positive outlook on his life and his past? Who do you think is currently living alone?

True love doesn't come with every other relationship. As with gaining a true friend, you should consider yourself lucky if you accomplish one true love. Therefore, when true love comes, you should make the best of it; exploit it, or take it for granted, and you may never see it again.

Chapter 2
Sugar Daddy

"Having nice thangs is one thing; falling in love with nice thangs is something totally different." H.H.

He's old, lonely, pot-bellied, gray-haired, and when a young beautiful woman smiles at him, he instinctively pulls out his wallet. His name in street vernacular: Sugar Daddy. Though many old geezers can be labeled Sugar Daddy, the average Sugar Daddy is young, healthy, fair- to good-looking. Yet it is somewhat socially acceptable for an old geezer to play Sugar Daddy. If you're old, pot-bellied, and gray-haired, who can blame you for spending your hard-earned retirement on some young floozy? But if you're young, healthy, fair- to good-looking, and of sound mind, no way should you be giving up hard-earned money solely for the pleasure of having a floozy walk in step with you.

There are two reasons why young, able-bodied Brothers play Sugar Daddy: low elf-esteem and the Barbie Doll syndrome. Let's discuss the latter first.

The Barbie Doll Syndrome

As you know, Barbie is a long-legged plastic doll. She has the figure that men—mostly White men—would desire their woman to have, though on a smaller scale. Very few women, White or whatever, can match Barbie's standards. Nevertheless, millions of women—mostly White women—try desperately to emulate Barbie's figure. Across the board, in the African-American community, a Sister doll that epitomizes what every African-American woman should aspire to look like does not exist. Thank God. However, creative African-Americans don't need a doll to create a standard to which African-American women should aspire. In the minds of many African-American men, the almost perfect Sister should have a pleasant-looking face, a big butt, medium to large breasts, a big butt, short or longs legs, and a big butt.

Now, let's cut to the chase. Many Brothers judge beauty by looks alone. In today's culture a woman's looks is more important than ever—as characterized by the beauties sashaying across television screens. With the exception of, perhaps, Sandra Bernhart, a not-so-good-looking woman rarely makes the grade on television, the movies, or videos–unless, of course, she's being ridiculed.

Another fact: There are far more not-so-good-looking women in the world than there are good-looking women. A simple truth, but a surprising number of Brothers hold out for the so-called "10" to walk into their lives, and by doing so, pass up numerous women who are mature, self-confident, trustworthy, and available. Good looks and a big butt practically drive many Brothers crazy. Thus, the Barbie Doll syndrome.

Here's a classic example: Jack Offalot meets Jenny Talwarts at a party. Jenny is extremely attractive, with blue eyes (colored contact lenses), long hair (donated by a palomino), big breasts (silicone), and a large butt (maintained by an increase in food stamps and plenty of sitting around). Of course, Jack is smitten; he can't keep his eyes off her. After small talk and a couple of dances, Jack takes Jenny home, whereupon Jenny mentions, parenthetically, that her rent is due. She lets Jack kiss her, and they exchange phone numbers. The next day she calls Jack and again mentions her past-due rent. Being a gentleman, Jack asks how much she owes, and Jenny, being who she is, tells him an exorbitant amount. Of course, Jack doesn't have that much money—he doesn't make that much in one year. But Jack wants to see her again; he can still see those blue eyes and that big butt.

Jack has two options: He could tell Jenny to seek an investment counselor, or he could incorporate Jenny's problems as his own. If he chooses the latter, he has taken the first step to becoming a Sugar Daddy. Whatever Jack does financially on Jenny's behalf—from giving a portion of the amount needed to pay her rent to allowing her to move in with him—it will never be enough. Jenny will continuously beg him for financial assistance. Amazingly enough, many Brothers like Jack know they are being snickered, but they cannot stop themselves. It's like knowing something is red hot but having an irresistible urge to touch it.

Sugar Daddyism is simply a matter of not being able to feel the lice itching because of the gonorrhea burning. Yes, she's beautiful—but is she really worth it? Isn't being with her like leasing a car? You make the first balloon payment, you get to ride. To continue to ride, you must make subsequent payments. Miss a payment, and your riding days come to a screeching halt. Yes, you're right, people tend to get what they pay for.

But why make payments on something that will never be yours, truly yours? Not to mention the possibility that someone else may also be making payments.

An old saying goes, "Whatever you did to get her is what you need to do to keep her." Okay, simple enough, but what did she do to get you? Absolutely nothing—except flaunt her big butt in your face. Thus, all she needs to do to keep you is to continue flaunting her big butt in your face. What's wrong with this picture? You've bought yourself an expensive doll, albeit a doll with a big butt. As with dolls that you buy at Toy's R Us, human baby dolls offer very little in realistic social interaction. Try to get a doll to do anything but look pretty—ha! And notice that everything your doll does on your behalf seems mechanical, unimpassioned.

Nothing taints a relationship—any relationship—more than quid pro quo. In almost all quid pro quo relationships, somebody gets short-changed—usually the one who puts out first. Ask yourself, am I getting my money's worth? Better yet, ask yourself, *Am I so shallow, so unsure about my own self worth, that I must literally pay someone to be with me?*

Low Self-Esteem

Look at the Sugar Baby on the talk show ... She's clad in black leather pants, a red halter that barely contains her melon-sized breast, and red pumps ... and she's grinning from ear to ear. The talk-show host asks her how she gets men to pay her bills and provide her with all the luxuries her heart desires. With a meretricious chuckle, she stands up, pirouettes, and pats her expansive fanny. "That's how," she says before resuming her seat. The audience claps and guffaws, and a few boo.

While the Sugar Baby is having the time of her life on the telly, announcing to millions of people that she has the moral repertoire of a dead cat, one of her benefactors is sitting in front of a television set shaking his head, feeling as crunchy as a bag of Doritos underneath the wheels of an eighteen-wheeler.

To add a headache to an inexplicable, painful, purulent discharge, the Sugar Baby adds: "I don't give it up to nobody—uh-uh! My men, they'll tell you, they just enjoy the pleasure"—she pauses, and thrust her melons out even farther—"of having the opportunity to be near me."

You would think that any man remotely associated with this female Player would cut all strings and give her plenty of leaving alone. You would think that any man remotely associated with this woman would be so humiliated, so embarrassed, so chagrined, that he wouldn't consider another woman for decades. Yes, you would think! But you would be wrong. A man possessing a modicum of self-esteem would run from this woman, and he would run hard, deep, and long. On the other hand, a Sugar Daddy will swallow his pride, in the manner he's been doing since he met her, and stay the course.

What's one more humiliation in a long, extensive series of humiliations? In fact, many Sugar Daddies seem to delight in, to borrow a phrase, "looking like a damned fool."

The lower the Sugar Daddy's self-esteem, the uglier the woman he puts up with (uglier in this context is not limited to looks). Fact: An 8 or above—Tyra Banks' and Halle Berry's range—seldom adorn the arm of a Sugar Daddy who isn't a millionaire.

If she's an 8, or an 11, for that matter, you still shouldn't pay her simply to be with you—though most Brothers would prefer to be gypped by a Tyra Banks or a Halle Berry than a snaggle-toothed, fake-haired, loudmouth, gin- and juice-drinking Sugar Baby.

A good woman, a woman worth having, wouldn't dream of being some Sugar Daddy's Sugar Baby. Well, she might dream of it, but she certainly wouldn't do it, because she recognizes the courtesan quid pro quo factor involved in such a transaction. And she knows that a man who feels he must offer her remuneration for her time is a man who lacks confidence in himself, and has probably tried the same tactic with other women.

Unfortunately, good women are becoming harder and harder to find. In part because of a ballyhooed misconception that has infected the minds of women of all colors—"A woman should get paid!" Where, when, and how this ridiculous notion started, no one knows. Perhaps when women first realized how attracted men were to their butts. Maybe, maybe not, but the belief that "A woman should get paid!" is more pervasive now than it has ever been.

You have heard it in various forms: "You got to pay me for my time," or "I don't come cheap," or "I don't need a man who can't give me money," or "A broke man can't do nothing for me." You also hear the same motif in many songs: "Pay my telephone bill ... Pay my credit card bills..." "What have you done for me lately..." and "Don't come over until the check clears...."

Whatever happened to "Let's get together and get to know each other and maybe fall in love"? Can you recall Patti Labelle, Aretha Franklin, or Gladys Knight singing a song about waiting for the check to clear the bank before they stripped out of their underwear? Most importantly, just where in the hell are you supposed to live after you've paid someone else's rent and credit card bills? Outside? In a homeless shelter? Under a bridge? Can you imagine ... There you are, the munificent benefactor ... making do inside a cardboard box ... fending off mosquitoes in the summer and frostbite in the winter ... subsisting on a diet of sardines and Vienna sausages. Meanwhile, not too far away, there she is, the object of your altruistic affectations ... lying on a king-size bed, inside an overly furnished condominium ... eating truffles from a silver platter ... with a constant stream of lukewarm air blowing on her expensive fanny.

Before going further, let's correctify a misguided concept that many women believe is justification for their selfish behavior. Being stingy is one thing; being a damn fool is quite another. The two are worlds apart. A Brother who refuses to buy a date a two-piece special at Popeye's can be considered stingy. Some Brothers are just that parsimonious, and, for the most part, these Brothers spend an inordinate amount of time alone. Dining a woman to an expensive meal, or buying her gifts, doesn't make a Brother a Sugar Daddy; not at all. Also, if you're living with a woman, regardless of circumstances, and/or you have children by her, you shouldn't fear being or becoming a Sugar Daddy, nor should you fear assuming your responsibilities. Of course, there is no harm in a Brother offering financial assistance to a woman who truly needs help. The key word here: *truly*. A woman who needs financial assistance every time you get paid does not truly need help, but she may be tugging you into the dark world of Sugar Daddyville, populated by whiners with empty wallets. The moment you start doing things for a woman that she should and could do for herself—paying her bills, for instance—you have stepped smack-dab into Sugar Daddy doo-doo.

The majority of women do not desire a man with low self-esteem. No doubt many women will take everything you offer, but to gain a woman's respect, loyalty, and love, she must respect you as a man.

The concept of being a man confuses many people, but it's quite simple: A man respects himself, and he respects others—that's it in a nutshell. Kicking ass doesn't make you a man; accumulating toys doesn't make you a man; humping everything that moves doesn't make you a man; and reducing yourself to doormat status most certainly doesn't make you a man.

From Sugar to Shit

"I'm looking for a good man!" How many times have you heard a woman say that? Probably more than you care to remember. To the trained ear, *"I'm looking for a good man"* is a thinly veiled way of saying, *"I'm looking for a Sugar Daddy."* The majority of women who claim "I'm looking for a good man" are women who tend to have more problems than average. Of course she desires a "good man": her rent is five months past due, her gas is turned off, her electricity is bootlegged from a neighbor's house, and her five kids are desperately in need of a daddy. Instead of looking for a good man, she should be looking for a miracle worker.

Good men seek good women, and vice versa. How good can a man be if he desires someone who has more problems than virtues? But, you say, what about the men who have invested time, money, and hard work in women who were down on their luck, and in doing so, reaped the benefits of a loving, healthy, long-lasting relationship? Good point. But those cases are rare and quite against the norm. Telling a Sugar Daddy that one day his investments in a Sugar Baby may pay dividends is akin to telling a crackhead his smoking crack may one day cure his persistent coughing. For a Sugar Daddy to benefit from such a treacly relationship, a metamorphosis must occur: going from Sugar to Shit.

The moment a Sugar Daddy stops funding a Sugar Baby's expenditures, the dynamics of the relationship change dramatically—in other words, when the money stops flowing, she stops whoring. She'll probably stop coming around altogether, too.

By stopping the funds, the Sugar Daddy makes a definitive statement: *There's more to me than my billfold.* If—don't bank on it, though—the Sugar Baby hangs around, then maybe, just maybe, a meaningful relationship can emerge, one based on mutual respect.

Still, the almost-reformed Sugar Daddy should keep his antennae up. She may simply view his actions as a lump in front of the gravy train—in other words, she's holding out in the hope of receiving more before she hits the door.

In some cases stopping the succor suddenly and without warning isn't a viable option, especially in complex domestic situations, such as: "It's her place, but the utility bills are in my name." Under such circumstances the almost-reformed Sugar Daddy should plan his course of action. The worst-case scenario (also the most-likely-case scenario): The Sugar Daddy stops the funds because of some reason other than that he simply chooses to do so, such as loss of a job, or a hustle plays out, or an unexpected interruption in a government stipend. A sudden interruption in funds and your beloved Sugar Baby's jumping ship can be extremely heartbreaking. In fact, many Sugar Daddies never fully recover from such a traumatic experience. Thousands upon thousands of bereaved Sugar Daddies line the halls of many of our nation's psychiatric wards, and even more dot our nation's homeless shelters, highways, and libraries, shuffling mindlessly from place to place, mumbling incoherently the same phrase over and over again: "Iffa onwie I'd kep a teenie weenie bit uv what I gabe away!"

Chapter 3
The A-Hole

"The quintessential asshole:
He who bitterly complains that the top of
your shoe scuffed the bottom of his." H.H.

For convenience the word *A-Hole* will be used instead of the expletive. Interestingly enough, the expletive isn't a word widely uttered within the African-American community. In fact, the word sounds rather strange when an African-American says it: "You asshole!" How strange is that for a Brother? Yet the word, like no other in the dictionary, fully describes rude, obnoxious behavior. Rarely is the word used in jest. On occasion, the utterance of the word precedes violence.

So why this chapter in a book targeted at African-American males? A good question. To be blunt, the average A-Hole doesn't know he's an A-Hole, and, to be even more blunt, the African-American A-Hole ratio is about the same as the A-Hole ratio of other races. Call an A-Hole an A-Hole, and he doesn't have a clue to what you're talking about. Show an A-Hole, as attempted here, his personality warts, bumps, knots, and stretch marks, and maybe, just maybe, through an increase in awareness, the A-Hole might make an attempt to change his behavior.

A-Holism is not a disease in itself, but can be symptomatic of a plethora of diseases and some so-called diseases, such as alcoholism, drug addiction, senility, schizophrenia, depression, cancer, hemorrhoids, STDs, athlete's foot, halitosis, and ED (erectile dysfunction). Regardless of pathology, A-Holism can be classified into three groups: First-class A-Hole; Second-class A-Hole; and Third-class A-Hole.

Let's start with the latter, Third-class A-Hole, the most innocuous, and then work up.

The Third-class A-Hole

Basically, the Third-class A-Hole is a coward: he limits his A-Holism to situations and places where he can easily escape, as in the safe confines of his car. The Third-class A-Hole is what many people conjure in mind when considering an A-Hole, because they have encountered him a time or two. But of all three types of A-Holes, the Third-class A-Hole is the most prolific but the least threatening, because this type of A-Hole rarely confronts anyone. Yes, he will jump in front of a long line of waiting traffic, as if his schedule and time rank supreme. Yes, he will flip you the bird because he feels that you are impeding traffic. Yes, he will throw a hissy fit because you made a major driving error, not speeding off on a green light. And yes, he will tailgate you for several miles—an extremely aggravating experience to most people. But under no circumstances will the Third-class A-Hole stop his car and confront the subject of his ire.

Why mild-mannered men morph into Third-class A-Holes upon getting behind the wheel of a vehicle is a phenomenon sociologist and psychologist having been trying to understand for a long time. Ergo: Road Rage, an ambiguous term that actually encourages and excuses rude behavior on our nation's highways. Not everyone who has languished in an inch-per-hour stalled traffic suddenly becomes outraged to the point of getting out and kicking somebody's ass. Not everyone who has experienced a tailgater gets out waving a pistol. Why? Because many people, most people—thank God!—understand one simple rule: You can't solve a problem with another problem. But this simple concept is totally lost upon on all three types of A-Holes because they view life's problems and inconveniences as personal affronts: stalled traffic, to the A-Hole, isn't the result of construction but the result of all those idiots gawking at the workers.

Remember this: There's no argument between a wise man and an A-Hole. Although the Third-class A-Hole usually avoids face-to-face confrontation, he can wreak havoc and mass frustration with the best of them. He's the guy who breaks wind in a crowed elevator and then giggles about it. At work, he's the guy who hasn't the guts to come to you and tell you what you're doing wrong, but will run to management and tell them. When forced to confront, the Third-class A-Hole usually brings someone else along, just in case things get out of hand. At home, to his credit, the Third-class A-Hole, unlike the Second-class and First-class A-Hole, usually isn't a despot—possibly because even in his own home he fears face-to-face confrontation.

In an angry crowd, or with a hostile group, the Third-class A-Hole is at his best. Though obviously not a leader, the Third-class A-Hole cannot be matched in demonstrating public outrage...to any cause.

Third-class A-holes have been well chronicled in American history, though rarely on individual merit. Ninety-nine percent of the Ku Klux Klan, Third-class A-Holes; ninety-nine percent of participants in all lynchings, Third-class A-Holes; and ninety-nine percent of all gang members, Third-class A-Holes. The list could go on and on: men, all cowards, who lack the courage to stand on their own two feet and express their beliefs, regardless of how twisted, but more than willing to mingle within a crowd and shout over the din.

Unlike the other two A-Hole types, the Third-class A-Hole has the best chance for rehabilitation. His A-Holism isn't profound but the result of impatience and superficial superiority. The Third-class A-Hole doesn't view his family as inferior, incompetent, idiotic imbeciles who constantly impede his right of way, on the road and off. No, he sees them as human beings, human beings who have faults and character defects.

As the Third-class A-Hole grows older, his condition lessens. The older he gets, the more he realizes that the world doesn't revolve around him. No longer does he drive if he owns the road, no longer does he seethe with contempt and rage when someone else makes an honest mistake, and no longer does he ignore subordinates. This maturation process can happen overnight in some cases, often as a result of the Third-class A-Hole unintentionally interacting with an irate underling or motorist.

In street vernacular, somebody knocks some sense in his ass.

The Second-class A-Hole

Ethnic cleansing in Bosnia, Hitler's attempt to exterminate Jews, the caste system in India, slavery (including current slavery in Sudan), homophobia, racial profiling, and all manner of bigotry stem from Second-class A-Holism.

A Second-class A-Hole, unlike a Third-class A-Hole, doesn't simply thinks he's better than whomever, he knows he's better than whomever. In the mind of a

Second-class A-Hole, different means inferior. When apparent differences aren't obvious, the Second-class A-Hole will manufacture differences, such as the case in interracial prejudices involving light-skinned African-Americans and dark-skinned African-Americans. Surprised? You didn't think, or you don't agree, that African-Americans can be just as Second-class A-Holic as other races? Wrong!

In fact, African-Americans fear, mistreat, mistrust, malign, excoriate, maim, and murder other African-Americans more so than all other races combined.

Therefore, intensity is the only thing that separates one Second-class A-Hole from the other. Of course, if you take someone like Carl Casian, a pot-bellied, beer-guzzling mobile-home dweller, whose wife prefers crystal meth to home-cooked meals, his level of Second-class A-Holism against African-Americans will be more intense than someone like Jauna Bewite, an African-American woman who makes $80,000 per year and looks down on African-Americans who don't make the same. Juana's Second-class A-Holism started after she graduated from law school and was hired by large firm. Carl's Second-class A-Holism started at the tender age of five, when his stepfather, Shaun Allblacs, severely beat him for turning the television channel from Mid-South Wrestling to Soul Train.

Carl, and people like him who have been taught to hate, rarely change—conform, maybe, but rarely change—thus ensuring that this kind of hatred will survive time. For many African-Americans this fact is a hard pill to swallow; they believe that certain views can simply be turned on and off like a faucet, and that one day all races will come together and hold hands and joyfully sing the Coca Cola theme song. Idyllic, yes—but highly unlikely.

The need to feel superior (Second-class A-Holism) is

a secondary human need. It exists in all walks of life. Like its big brother Jealousy, Second-class A-Holism has affected everyone over the age of two. Lacking tangible evidence, or something legitimate to point to, a Second-class A-Hole can be very creative.

Thus: The athlete sneers at the maladroit, the maladroit sneers at the guy without a master's degree, the guy without a master's degree sneers at the guy who didn't attend college, the guy who didn't attend college sneers at the unemployed guy, the unemployed guy sneers at the unemployed guy who receives food stamps, the unemployed guy who receives food stamps sneers at the wino, the wino sneers at the pothead, the pothead sneers at the crackhead, the crackhead sneers at the homeless guy, the homeless guy sneers at Carl Casian, who sneers at everyone because his old lady is still smoking crystal meth.

Although everyone is brushed at some time or other by Second-class A-Holism, everyone doesn't dwell in it, wallow in it, and cultivate it. Those who do tend to be insecure, depressed, aggrieved, and shallow. Those who do make life miserable for so many people—especially family members.

Of all the cockamamie studies that have been conducted by eggheads across the country, from the study of how cow flatulence affects the ozone layer to the study of what role malt liquor plays in contracting gonorrhea, not one study has ever attempted to determine the long- and short-term effects of living with a Second-class A-Hole.

A short-term study of people who live with a Second-class A-Hole would probably reveal that simply living with a Second-class A-Hole for only a few short hours produces anxiety attacks, depression, suicidal thoughts, homicidal thoughts, bed-wetting, diarrhea, and constipation. A long-term study of people who live with, or have lived with, a Second-class A-Hole would undoubtedly show a marked increase in chemical addiction, depression, and other mental and physical illnesses.

Since the Second-class A-Hole constantly defines, redefines, invents, and re-invents reasons for his superiority, he can expatiate at length on every conceivable problem except his own. According to him, you are the problem. So deft, so convincing, so repeated—but so ludicrous—is the Second-class A-Hole's argument, that one can easily fall prey to actually believing its validity; after all, he does say it with passion. Stay with the Second-class A-Hole long enough, and not only will you view life as he does, but you will also do as he says. And you will be miserable!

Attempting to reason with or explain logic to a Second-class A-Hole is a waste of time. While you're talking, he's thinking of something you have done or said, or some situation you were/are in, that disqualifies your telling him any damn thing. Here are a few examples of how his mind works: "Yes, it's your TV but it's my cable, so I can watch any damn thing I want to!" "I don't give a damn what I did, you better not forget I'm a man!" "My house, my rules!"

On occasion, biblical references are utilized, though often misquoted, and always self-serving: "Apparently, you forgot the part about 'a woman shall obey her man.'"

"An eye for an eye!" "Spare the belt spoil the brat!" "A divided house cannot stand—so you need to shut up!" "Don't worry 'bout the chip in my eye when you have a log in yours!"

When confronted with a sexual contretemps, the universal Second-class A-Hole response is: "Hey, I'm a man!" This implies an innate inability to control one's self during any sexual encounter—basic BS when you consider that the Second-class A-Hole never lost sexual control with someone who doesn't fall within his parameters of sexual compatibility.

As the Second-class A-Hole grows older, his circle of friends diminishes and his family curtails their visits. Can you blame them? Bad feelings can last a lifetime, and the Second-class A-Hole doles out more than his share in one day.

Unlike the First-class A-Hole, the Second-class A-Hole understands and appreciates the concept of empathy, though fleetingly, because of a constant preoccupation of self and an uncanny ability to rationalize the most odious behavior. Bluntly: Why look at your own crap when the flush handle is so near?

Below are the top ten behavior characteristics of a Second-class A-Hole:

1. Regularly belittles someone, usually a family member, with no regard to person's feelings or well-being.

2. Professes undue antipathy toward a race, class, or ethnic group.

3. Tunes out during constructive criticism, or rejects it altogether, and often resorts to petty tit-for-tat.

4. Carps relentlessly and gloats over others' mistakes—citing mistake(s) as a confirmation of inferiority.

5. Insists on things—sweeping, eating, mopping, sleeping, breathing, etc.—being done his way, although another way is just as effective.

6. Rarely, if ever, offers praise or appreciation, unless money is concerned.

7. Fired frequently, but, according to him, employer(s) are always the A-Holes.

8. Borrows money from family and friends, then either develops amnesia or gets angry when time come to pay it back.

9. Yet when money is owed him, his memory is pinpoint accurate and his senses peak to bloodhound abilities, in order to track debtor down and hound him or her mercilessly.

10. Disrespects others' privacy and personal property, including, mail, diaries, e-mail, and telephone conversations.

Does any of the above fit? Are you sure? Occasionally committing one of the above offenses doesn't necessarily indicate Second-class A-Holism, but a repeated pattern, or commission of three or more offenses per week, suggests a serious problem.

This begs the question: Can a Second-class A-Hole change? Yes, he most certainly can. But, as with prescription addicts, he must first acknowledge he has a problem—a considerably difficult step: "I am an A-Hole!" Yet simply acknowledging those four words empowers the Second-class A-hole. Acknowledgment promotes awareness; awareness promotes intelligence; intelligence promotes compassion and sensitivity, which are the two ingredients most A-Holes lack.

If the Second-class A-Hole does not change—most don't—then he's almost guaranteed to live alone, isolated, without a friend in the world. A bleak picture, but a picture hard to imagine when you're under thirty years old. Keep it up, and the picture will slowly but surely materialize right before your eyes: You sitting alone in a empty house or apartment...rocking back and forth in a rocker...watching reruns of The Brady Bunch on a small black-and-white television set...with your one and only companion at your feet, an aging mongrel named Buddy, who only stays near because of the dog food.

The First-class A-Hole

What do you call a guy who beats his own mother? What do you call a guy who impregnates his girlfriend and then convinces his partners to shoot her to avoid paying child support? What do you call a guy who inveigles men to his apartment with the promise of free drinks, spikes their drinks, rapes and murder them, and then cuts them up in small pieces to be eaten later?

The answer to all three: First-class A-Hole, also known as sociopath. Roughly six percent of the male population are First-class A-Holes.

These individual lack conscience; they understand the concept of empathy, but they cannot grasp it on a personal level—because they have never experienced it. Thus, someone else's pain and suffering is of no importance to them.

Psychological eggheads have yet to figure exactly what makes a First-class A-Hole tick. Most come from dysfunctional homes where they were severely abused, mentally and physically, more often at the hands of their mother, but some come from stable, two-parent homes. And, since the First-class A-Hole usually does not complain of thought disorders, exhibit signs of depression, test positive for certain chemical imbalances, or demonstrate the inability to judge right from wrong, he cannot be diagnosed as mentally impaired.

To further complicate matters, the First-class A-Hole is extremely deft at mimicking normal behavior; in fact, most First-class A-Holes are slicker than snot on a door knob, unsurpassed in the art of manipulation, and unrivaled charmers. Yet, as with anyone who projects a false persona, the First-class A-Hole's deceptive performance seldom lasts for long. But by this time, the damage has been done: hearts broken, money stolen, and in some cases, lives taken.

By now you're wondering: Just what in the hell does this mean to me, an African-American male? Good question. It's hardly likely that a First-class A-Hole reading this will say, "Gee, I have an eerie feeling I'm being talked about here," and make an honest attempt to change his ways. However, you, an African-American male, a sane and stable man, will come into contact with a First-class A-Hole at some point in your life—a friend or a foe or a casual acquaintance. Each can be a major problem. Here's why…

African-Americans are a forgiving group of people. In addition to being overly magnanimous, many African-Americans honestly believe that only certain individuals are capable of committing certain crimes. As with the Orenthal debacle, many African-Americans could not imagine Orenthal using a knife to kill. In the same vein, many African-Americans cannot imagine a Brother being a sociopath, or, as called here, a First-class A-Hole—perhaps in part because Hollywood routinely depicts the sociopath as the Hannibal Lector type, the out-of-his-mind White guy who enjoys slicing and dicing people up for the sheer hell of it. In one area this characterization rings true: mutilating the dead; riding around with the dead; eating, or eating with, the dead; and having sex with the dead are activities in which African-Americans seldom engage. However, there are African-American serial killers, African-American serial rapists, African-American arsonists, and African-American First-class A-Holes; and their numbers are growing.

You're still wondering what all this has to do with you, right? Hold on, almost there.

Not all First-class A-Holes are nomadic hoboes who crisscross the country preying on unsuspecting women, nor bug-eyed perverts who remodel their vans and cellars into torture chambers, nor gasoline-smelling pinheads who masturbate at the sight of a conflagration or a firetruck. No, uh-uh! Many are uncles, brothers, fathers, stepfathers, cousins, and friends who have never spent a day in jail, and many pose the same threat as the three aforementioned. So it's important that you know a First-class A-Hole when you see a First-class A-Hole.

The First-class A-Hole develops slowly, over time, in stages. The first stage, NUTS (Nascent Unexplainable Tendencies Syndrome), starts at an early age. Below are classic symptoms of NUTS, but keep in mind that symptoms do not necessarily indicate NUTS in every case.

Bedwetting. Although bed-wetting can result from a wide range of legitimate physical and mental conditions, not one of which would be laziness, many sufferers are still stigmatized and humiliated (especially harsh in the African-American community, where bed-wetters are often called "Pissy"), which may be why many First-class A-Holes recall bed-wetting as a major problem during childhood.

Setting fires. Young children often experiment with fire; this is not usually a problem, but frequent fire-setting and the "glow in the eye" while watching a fire are good indicators of NUTS.

Cruelty to animals. Rats and mice don't count, of course. But anyone who becomes giddy with delight at the sight of an animal suffering or being killed is definitely NUTS.

Voyeurism. Peeping Toms are almost glorified on television, but anyone who crawls on his belly, climbs trees, hides in bushes, or uses telescopes or binoculars to gawk at someone has a serious problem, which can easily progress to stalking, rape, and murder.

The second stage to becoming a First-class A-Hole, XFL (Extreme Fantasy Land Syndrome), is marked by inordinate fantasizing—not normal fantasizing, such as scoring the winning touchdown, winning the lotto, or suddenly becoming a magnet for gorgeous women, but sick fantasies, involving bondage, torture, rape and murder. Manifestations of XFL usually begin to show during teen years. Entertaining bizarre fantasies often leads to acting out bizarre fantasies. Additional red flags are around-the-clock masturbation, extensive pornography collections, and miscellaneous sex toys.

The final stage is called Nutting Up, which occurs when the First-class A-Hole has grown tired of fantasizing and playing with sex toys, and acts out. Nutting Up varies from one First-class A-Hole to the next, but you can guarantee that the end results will injure or kill someone.

Now, finally, to the nut of the matter. Though it's rude to ask people for an in-depth mental history, it's beneficial to know exactly who you're dealing with. Today's mindset seems to be: *"As long as it or he or she doesn't hurt me or my family, I could care less."* Combine this apathetic mindset with a natural tendency by many African-Americans to forgive and forget, as long as the miscreant acts contrite, and you have a First-class A-Hole who actually thinks he's being rewarded for his antisocial behavior—a very dangerous mix.

This is apparent in the growing number of incidents involving First-class A-Holes who commit heinous crimes with a phalanx of damned fools supporting them. Witness the case of the First-class A-Hole who somehow convinced a trio of brain-dead Brothers, whom he allegedly paid fifty dollars each, to accompany him to beat up his pregnant girlfriend in an attempt to avoid paying child support—not the Rae Carruth incident, but a similar incident here in Little Rock, Arkansas. Another case, also in Little Rock, Arkansas, involved possibly two First-class A-Holes and a bevy of wanna-be A-Holes. The first two kidnapped an elderly woman, hog-tied her, put her in the trunk of her car, then rode around to several friends' houses and displayed her to demonstrate how adept they were in the art of kidnapping and car-jacking. Of all the guys—thirteen reportedly—who peered inside the trunk at an elderly woman tied up and undoubtedly frightened out of her wits, not one—Not A Single One!—thought: "Hmmm...what's wrong with this picture?"

Perhaps one did, but still, he wasn't compelled to do something as obscene as to call the police or something as heroic as to protest to his so-called friends and by doing so prevent a tragic ending to a tragic beginning.

This is inexcusable! When you refuse to confront outrageous, vile behavior—especially when it's right smack in your face—you condone it and allow it to flourish. You are a proud African-American man, borne of men who suffered years of slavery, oppression, and degradation, of men like the great Dr. Martin Luther King, Jr., who dreamed that his children, and no doubt all men, "be judged not by the color of their skin but the content of their character."

Irrespective of skin color, the First-class A-Hole is totally void of character. Always keep in mind that the First-class A-Hole *modus operandi* is manipulating people to gratify his sick needs. To do this he must make an emotional connection. If you look closely you can see this behavior in many of today's politicians and leaders. This is not to say that most are innate First-class A-Holes; a good number of them have been corrupted by power and money. But the behavior is the same: taking advantage of others to gratify sick needs. Remember this: People, regardless of position or status, who truly desire to help others, look for solutions, not emotional connections. Think about it, can you feel his pain? So how in the hell can he feel yours?

Chapter 4
Friends

"Flea-bitten: He whose best friend is actually his dog." H.H.

Scenario number one: You and your homeboy, Hot Forty, are sitting in his apartment watching WWF and putting a serious dent in a thirty-pack of Milwaukee Best. Hot Forty's live-in girlfriend, Tina Fedup, passes in front of the television—her sixth pass—looking not too happy about the many beer cans strewn all over the floor and coffee table. She grunts to punctuate her displeasure. Suddenly, Hot Forty pounces on her, grabs her in a headlock, similar to the one The Mangler used on The Nutcase moments before on WWF, lifts her up high in the air, with her screaming all the while for you to do something, then drops her headfirst onto the floor and starts pummeling her with his fist. What do you do? Stop the brute? Burp and pretend you don't see anything? Or raise your homeboy's hand in victory?

Scenario number two: Your dog, Mac Daddy, in a pique of rage, comes over to your place and informs you that's he's just been seriously aggrieved. Apparently a punk named Ed had the audacity to duplicate Mac Daddy's rapping style. Mac Daddy, brandishing a large pistol, tells you he wants revenge. One minor problem: Mac Daddy's Benz has been impounded. "No such thing as a walk-by," he tells you after asking for a ride. What do you do? Tell him, "Hell no!"? Toss him the keys and tell him to go alone? Or grab your keys and your pistol—

just in case—and say: "Let's go!"

Scenario number three: You and your partner since the third grade, Roger Roguish, are on your third work day at Soy Burger and Shakes. During a routine trip to the dumpster, the restaurant manager spots a case of soy burgers in the back seat of Roger's late-model Plymouth Horizon. Summarily fired and unjustifiably insulted, Roger kicks over the deep-fry machine and tells you: "Let's get the hell out of here!" What do you do? Stay put? Or kick the shake machine and storm out with Roger?

All three scenarios are classic examples of Friendship Taxation, which means placing undue burden on a friend. Though these three scenarios seem rather silly and obvious, similar real-life scenarios, just as silly and just as obvious, occur each day, and because of making the wrong choice, thousands of Brothers find themselves in prison, on drugs, and in graveyards. Take the real-life case of Gutt Les Wonder (not his real name), a timid pimple-faced nerd who stood by silently as his First-class A-Hole best bud entered a Nevada casino restroom behind a small girl, raped her, and then strangled her. When asked why he didn't so much as lift a finger during the ride home with the First-class A-Hole, Gutt Les Wonder said: "Hey, he's my friend."

The urge to excoriate such a weak, pitiful, spineless, yellow-bellied coward is almost irresistible, but let's take the high road and focus on why the timorous, sissified, chicken-livered coward did what he did. Without a doubt, and based on the thousand-and-one acne bumps per square inch on his face, Gutt had one friend in the world. Rather than upset his friend and risk losing him by reporting the incident to the police, Gutt did nothing. A conscious decision was made: *"Tell the police, and lose my friend, my only friend? Forget that! I'll say nothing, and keep my only friend."* Though in the end Gutt's friend deservedly went to prison.

Of course, you say, I would never stoop so low as Gutt did. Are you sure? Think back to any moment where you put friendship before common sense...Do you see any Gutt Les Wonder tendencies? If you're honest, sure you do.

Whether you call friends associates, acquaintances, homeboys, partners, dogs, troops, soldiers, my niggas, padres, or bosom buddies, you cannot deny the major influence these people have in your life. Many Brothers will sacrifice their life for these people. Many Brothers put these people before family, including children. Why? In the words of George Jetson's dog, Astro, "Unnn no!" No doubt people have an inherent need for companionship, a need to share with others, a need to connect with others, and a need to feel important to others—but what a price people sometimes pay for such needs. So, perhaps, the answer is that those in desperate need of friendship are also most willing to do anything to keep friendship.

Here's a fact: You are responsible for your friends, or whatever you prefer to call them, and their actions. *"Uh-uh,"* you say, shaking your head. *"I'm only responsible for my damn self!"* Kinda figured you would say that, so let's take a ride on a ship called *Proselytized.*

Before boarding, let's at least agree that you choose your friends. In fact, if someone else tried to do that for you, you would be livid. Mama, daddy, brother, sister, children, cousin, wife, girlfriend, and friends—all might as well shut up, because you choose your friends. Even in the face of sage advice—"That dude you runnin' with is bad news. I saw him beating on an old, blind woman on forty-second street. If I were you I'd cut him loose" —no matter. Amazingly, the more negatives comments made about so-and-so, the tighter so-and-so and you get. This phenomenon is called A-Hole Retentive

Syndrome.

Now that you have your boarding pass consider this: You choose a like-minded person who can benefit you in some way or other as a friend—a symbiotic agreement, because, of course, the other person chooses you as a friend for the same reason. Granted that friends are chosen for a myriad of reasons, some good, some bad, and some horrendous. Let's take a brief look at the worst of the worst reasons to choose a friend.

Money: This is the #1 reason friendships are initiated, maintained, and endured; it is also the #1 reason why friendships end. Regardless of what side of the coin you are on, the giving side or the receiving side, a friendship—or any relationship, for that matter—based on money almost always bankrupts.

Notoriety: Choosing a friend to increase one's status is the trademark of high schoolers, hangers-on, and idol worshippers. Almost always the object of one's affections takes advantage of the situation. Think about it: If you're fetching, toting, fixing, cleaning, and working for someone who never reciprocates, how much of a friend do you have? In other words, just because you've become accustomed to the smell doesn't excuse the fact you're kissing an A-Hole.

Protection: If you're in jail and worried about the four-hundred pound Carl Casian in the next cell who blows kisses at you and calls you Sweet Cheeks, then, maybe, you need a friend for protection. This is also the reason why so many Brothers rationalize gang affiliations. Yet even in the most crime-plagued, gang-dominated neighborhoods, there reside Brothers who keep to themselves, mind their own business, and stand on their own two feet. Also, whether in jail or out, the individual you choose for protection always winds up as your tormentor.

Drugs and Alcohol: The greater-later clause is

always at work when initiating a friendship with alcohol and drugs—especially drugs. Fact: Non-problem drinkers and non-drug addicts don't seek friendships with drunks and drug addicts. A drunk or a drug addict isn't giving you freebies because he's attracted to your award-winning personality, but he's expecting greater later—much greater—when you're hooked and buying whatever he's giving freely now.

Okay, you've received your boarding pass, been given a tour of the ship, and been shown to your quarters. Good. Let's finally get ready to set sail. While the ship's motors are revving up, think about the people you DFW (Don't Fuck With). As passionate as you are about choosing your own friends, you are far more passionate about steering clear of the people you DFW. In fact, you, like most people, maintain a DFW list .(Don't confuse a Shit list with a DFW list: a Shit list, like a menu, changes daily, but a DFW list, like a politician's lies, increases in number but seldom changes). Let's take a look at the people who comprise your DFW list.

The Did-nothings: Roughly twenty percent of the people on your list, these people have never offended you in any way. You simply do not like them! If asked why, you really don't know. Perhaps it's their constant inhaling and exhaling of air, or the rhythmic thump thump thump of their grimy hearts. Nevertheless, you make it your business to avoid them.

The Misdemeanors: This group makes up sixty to seventy percent of your list. These are the people who had the gall to look at you funny, or forgot to say hello, or interrupted you while talking, or, worst, offended a friend or family member. Also included in this group are the people who offended you way back when, including the guy who thirteen years ago briefly dated your ex-girlfriend, Paula Putout, after you and she broke up.

The Cretins: This group makes up ten to fifteen

percent of your list; the smallest group, but always the most despised. These are the people whose names are like manure in your mouth—and you prefer that your name is like manure in their mouth as well. Most of the people in this group have committed one or more of the following four African-American Male Cardinal Rules:

Debt Defalcation: Unlike banks and credit lenders, Brothers don't view bankruptcy, unexpected unemployment, and catastrophic illnesses as sufficient reasons not to pay outstanding loans. In other words, Brothers will hurt you over their money. Of utmost importance is the amount of money in arrears. Most Brothers overlook two's and fews—any amount less than five dollars. Ten to twenty dollars—not so bad, unless owed to a drug dealer. Any amount over twenty dollars—major problem.

Personal Perfidy: As with debt defalcation, many Brothers view personal perfidy, also called backstabbing, as a capital offense. Yet ninety-nine times out of a hundred when a Brother's main man winds up with his main woman, the Brother facilitated the love connection. In other words, kissing and telling can easily lead to losing.

Voluntary Volubility: Brothers do not only view voluntary volubility, also called snitching, in police matters as an unforgivable offense but they also hold an even dimmer view of voluntary volubility in personal matters. For example, you enter your partner's bathroom and find him skin-popping heroin, and, in an act of uncharacteristic concern, you run tell his mother. In Carl Casian's world this act of concerned interposition is called "Intervention," "Tough Love," and "Being a True Friend"; however, in the African-American community this is called "Getting Your Head Busted Wide Open."

Purloined Property: How many times have you heard someone say, "I'd give you the shirt off my back, anything you want, all you have to do is ask, 'cause if I got it, it's yours, but if I catch you stealing from me...I'll kill you!" Usually the first part, the altruistic part, is a lie; but make no bones about it, the second part, the explicit threat, is the truth. In the African-American community, in any matter concerning purloined property, the bit about "being innocent until proven guilty" doesn't apply. If you're a thief, thought to be a thief, a drug addict or an associate of a thief or a drug addict, then you're guilty of purloining said item in question, regardless if a million people other than you had an opportunity to purloin said item.

Most of the people on your DFW list know where they stand, and a good number of them have you on their DFW list. Actually this eliminates strife and confusion. You don't go to their house; they don't come to yours. You don't hop in their car; they don't hop in yours. You don't say anything to them; they don't say anything to you.

(Most people intuit when someone considers them distasteful: they've detected the negative facial expressions—nose twisted, lips turned downward, eyes squinted, etc.—and they've picked up on the snide remarks and the direct and indirect put-downs. But a small group of people, usually drug addicts, drunks, and A-Holes, constantly misread or fail to read well-marked signs indicating *persona non grata*—which is why they are forever getting their heads busted wide open.)

So what, you ask, does this have to do with sailing on a ship called Proselytized? Just hold on to your life jacket.

Now let's juxtapose the people you DFW to the people you call friends, associates, or whatever. If a person you DFW gets hit by a train, you ask, "Was the train dented?" Falls out of a plane, you ask, "Didn't land on anybody, did he?" Chokes on a Vienna sausage, you ask, "Barbecue or plain?"

So no way in hell will someone you DFW stash his drug paraphernalia in-between the seats after you and him are stopped by the police. No way in hell will someone you DFW shoplift while you and he are standing in line to be checked out. No way in hell will someone you DFW hit on your wife, girlfriend, whatever, while you go take a leak.

A friend can commit these same acts hundred of times, and nothing is said. When your friend comes over and stops up the commode, eats all the food, drinks all the liquor, puts an indelible stain on the coffee table by resting his size 18 clodhoppers on it, who does your wife, girlfriend, whatever, blame? Who winds up paying for it? When your friend or whatever has a bad reputation in the neighborhood, or a bad reputation with the police, who else shares the same bad reputation?

Are you starting to feel seasick now? No problem, no law against throwing up in the sea. Even when you're not around, when your friend hurts himself or hurts someone else, you are affected by his actions. You'll go to the hospital when he's hurt. You'll look his mother in the eye and shake your head at his funeral. You'll be there for him because you expect him to be there for you. This implicit agreement is the underpinning of all friendships, regardless if the friendship is superficial or genuine. A-Holes know this, people who expect greater later from you know this, people who skin and grin in your face know this, and you know this.

By assuming responsibility for your friends' actions you can control what they do or, more specifically, what they do to you. And you will never utter the pitiful phrase: "I thought you were my friend!" Well, you thought wrong! But where were your thoughts when you saw first-hand your friend doing the exact same thing to others?

A key ingredient to assuming responsibility is Setting Standards. Your standards are your own, of course, but by all means, stick to them. If you don't steal, then your friends shouldn't steal. If you don't get angry and put your wife, girlfriend, whatever, in a headlock, then your friends shouldn't do so either. Believe it or not, when a man sets standards in his life, others tend to follow suit. (If they do not, you should strongly consider cutting them loose.)

Take for example, the Honorable Dr. Martin Luther King actions during the Civil Rights Movement. As you know, Dr. Martin Luther King promulgated nonviolence to awake this nation to the perils of segregation and disenfranchisement. But did you know that he was stabbed, spit upon, hit in the neck with a brick? And not once did he raise his hand in defense or did he strike back—which, by the way, is the exact opposite human response. Not only did Dr. Martin Luther King catch hell with angry segregationists, violent white mobs, Bull Connor's waterhoses and police dogs, but he also caught hell with his own people, African-Americans, who threw rocks and booed, shouting and demanding a more combative approach to racial antiquities. But not once did Dr. Martin Luther King waver from his commitment to nonviolence. And, as you know, his lead, his indomitable spirit, change the course of an entire nation.

Think about it: If one man can change the course of an entire nation, you, an upstanding African-American man, can surely change the course of an entire neighborhood. No, you do not have to preach, you do not have to scream or shout. All you have to do is walk and talk like a man, which simply means respect yourself and respect others. Doing so engenders true admiration, and doing so eliminates a tremendous amount of BS. People who are full of BS don't implore a man who isn't, nor do they commit BS in his face. A man who respects himself and others sets a pattern to which the people around him strive to adhere, because they respect him not for what he has, who he knows, but for who he is. A Man!

Skinning and Grinning

What do you call people who show up after you've made a million dollars? *Relatives?* Well yes, but specifically the people who are not related to you? *My old lady's relatives?*

Perhaps. But here the term is Skinners and Grinners, people who show up skinning and grinning after the news has spread that you "have it going on." Of course, you don't necessarily have to have a million dollars to "have it going on," you just need enough to make Skinners and Grinners think you have more than you need and an irresistible urge to give large chunks of it away.

The nouveau rich are skinned and grinned all the time, and many are skinned and grinned right back to the poorhouse. A classic example is the case of...Well, perhaps his true name shouldn't be used. Here's a clue to his identity: His stage name represents a tool that is used to bang nails and rhymes with Bammer. Got it now? No? Well hell, let's just call him MC. Anyway, MC, like so many newly rich and famous, had a passion for surrounding himself with Skinners and Grinners, many of whom he paid a salary.

When the money dried up, the Skinners and Grinners got ghost; a few disappeared shortly before the money dried up, just before the IRS came knocking. Fact: Many Skinners and Grinners posses an almost psychic awareness as to when someone else's money is starting to get low. When all was said and done, MC appeared on television looking rather morose and explained what happened. Basically he expressed shock at the fact that everyone got ghost when his money dried up. And—get this shocker—he more or less stated that the only people—not enough to count on one hand—who remained were the ones who were around before he "blew up," a phrase meaning hit it big time.

Of course you couldn't help but feel sympathetic toward MC, an exceptional talent, and arguably one of the world's greatest dancers. His fans also contributed to his fall. A segment of his fan base decided he was too soft to be a rapper, a sellout—whatever the hell that means—so he changed, adopting a hardcore rap image; then lo and behold, another segment of his fan base accused him of being too hard. Either way he couldn't win. Maybe, just maybe, if he had ignored his critics, followed his instincts, continued doing that which had propelled him to the top, then he could have spent more time watching all those Skinners and Grinners who were dipping into the kitty.

Whether you get skinned and grinned out of millions or hundreds, it still hurts. Your money is gone, the phone stops ringing, the doorbell stops chiming, and you might as well sell that cell phone—no one is going to call you. Who's to blame? Well, can you really blame the Skinners and Grinners? After all, they did find your jokes exceptionally funny and they did think, though briefly, you were greatest thing since the disposable diaper. So ... well ... uh ... you know ...uh... that leaves you.

Remember that little maxim your mother told you as you were going out the door, something about your friends running out on you when you were down? It doesn't matter, you probably weren't listening. You see, skinning and grinning isn't something new—uh-uh! It's been around for a long time. The faces, the fads, and the clothes will change, but the techniques Skinners and Grinners utilize to worm their way into other people's pocket will never change. Here are a few techniques that Skinners and Grinners employ.

The Anal Smoke Approach. The favorite technique of a Skinner and Grinner is fatuous flattery. Flattery almost always works, and a professional Skinner and Grinner knows exactly how much to apply and when. Remember this: Any compliment coming right before or right after you spend your money is not a true compliment. Also, be honest with yourself: If you were, uh, less than attractive when you were broke, by no means did you suddenly metamorphose into a handsome prince when you blew up, regardless who says so.

Beg High But Accept Low Approach. What makes this ploy work is the fact that most people feel uncomfortable letting other people down. No one knows this better than a Skinner and Grinner. For example: Freddie Freeloader tells you he needs a favor. His son needs surgery to remove an alien growth from the side of his head (his ear). So, could you let him borrow five thousand dollars? "Aw man!" you say. "I don't have that kind of money." So Freddie waits a couple days, then comes back seeking a smaller amount, five hundred dollars. "Sure," you say, "I can do that."

Back in the Day Approach. Amateur Skinners and Grinners use this approach, which is based on flimsy connections. He knows you from Back In The Day, when you and he were either in college, high school, junior high, kindergarten, preschool, or sperm cells in a Petri dish. Of course you can't remember any of it, and if you think about it, even if it were true, why the hell do you owe him money?

The Back Door Approach. This approach is used by Skinners and Grinners who sense that you have your guards up. They know somebody you know, one of your family members or one of your associates, and attempt to get to you through them. (On occasion one Skinner and Grinner will invite another Skinner and Grinner along. This is called Doubling-Up, which can open the door to dual, complex skinning and grinning. A favorite tactic in Doubling-Up is Take-Yur-Pik, which involves one Skinner and Grinner ratting out another Skinner and Grinner to gain the target's confidence.)

The Gopher Approach. In Skinner and Grinner circles this approach is also called The A-Hole Wipe Approach—probably because mostly on-their-last-leg drug addicts and drunks utilize it. This approach requires less skinning and grinning and more work. The Skinner and Grinner insinuates himself into the target's world by performing small tasks, usually household chores, washing the car, cutting the lawn, or installing aluminum siding—for free initially, then for a small fee. As you can see, the likelihood of being treated like tissue is almost guaranteed here. The Skinner and Grinner in this position is always the last to know when the money has dried up. It's not unusual to find this type of Skinner and Grinner cutting the grass or paving the driveway or cleaning gutter pipes long after the occupant has been evicted and the IRS has seized the property.

Image

Image to friendship is like jalapeño peppers to hemorrhoids. Maybe that's not a fair comparison. Jalapeño peppers might set your hemorrhoids ablaze but will not kill you—though you certainly feel like you're dying. An image, however, can get you KISSed (Killed, Incarcerated, Shot, or Stabbed). If you remember only one thing after reading this book, let it be this: Gunshot wounds, knife wounds, and all wounds in general are a helluva lot harder to recover from than a sullied image. In almost 99.8 percent of violent altercations over something petty and frivolous, image was the impetus.

Here's a fictitious but classic example: During a friendly domino game at a local club, Chilly Chiseler accuses his old friend, Slick Willie, of cheating. Incensed, Slick Willie casts doubt on Chilly's paternity. "I know he didn't!" a patron shouts. "Yes, he did!" shouts another. "I wouldn't take that!" yet another declares. Suddenly, Chilly slaps Slick—*pow!* Now the patrons recapitulate, this time aiming their taunts at Slick. Rubbing his face, Slick starts for the door. "I'm going home to get something to put on your ass," Slick says before leaving.

Shortly afterwards, Chilly reenacts the slap to the delight of the club patrons. "What you gon' do if he comes back?" someone asks Chilly. "I've got something, too," Chilly says. "Hell…he get his shit, I'll get mine! He ain't the only one with some shit. Got mine out in the car…in the trunk…behind the—" Just then the door swings open and you-know-who is standing there with his shit/"something to put on your ass"—a double-barreled shotgun, at the ready.

There are a million and one possible scenarios that could follow. But in all likelihood both Chilly and Slick are about to be KISSed in one way or the other. One or both men will look back in retrospect at the incident for what it truly was: Bullshit, with a capital *B.* You can't help but think Chilly and Slick would have settled their disagreement diplomatically but for the onlookers lugging the thing up. Another factor depends on the gender of the onlookers: One or more women looking on can incite a simple disagreement to apocalyptic proportions.

On paper, particularly in the newspaper, these type incidences appear trite, childish even. Well, they are. But to the Brother who is in a situation where he feels slighted, dissed, wronged, embarrassed, made to look like a fool—and a group of onlookers is in attendance—appearing childish is the last thing on his mind. His face is growing hotter by the second, his heart is palpitating, his muscles are tensing, his eyes are focusing intently on his persecutor, and his emotions have short-circuited his ability to think reasonably.

Terms such as "flooding" and "emotional hijacking" describe this state of mental impairment, but here the term is called "clicking," or "clicked," which will be discussed further in Chapter 11. Clicking can get you KISSed quicker than a midnight stroll through Jasper, Texas. To avoid clicking, first recognize your hair triggers—the emotional buttons that make you click—and then imagine yourself reacting differently to a hair trigger; then practice, practice, practice! Yes, it is easier said than done, but it is doable. Brothers who click easily click often. In part because nothing delights some sick-minded individuals more than to watch someone click, and once they know what hair trigger to push to set a Brother off, they'll push it at every opportunity.

Another example, again fictitious but applicable: Johnny Davis lost his father, whom Johnny was very fond of, at an early age in a car accident. Aware of the life-threatening possibilities of speaking ill of an African American male's mother, several people opted to make an ill-advised comment about Johnny's father. Big mistake. Each time Johnny clicked. Badly. And on every occasion Johnny went to jail. The last incident, the most violent, made Johnny realize he had to control himself when someone made a comment about his father, or he would spend a good portion of his life in jail.

Looking back at each incident, Johnny discovered that he was practically waiting for someone to make a comment about his father, and a few people were more than willing to oblige him. Johnny decided to flip the switch. Instead of attempting to beat the dog shit out of anyone who said something directly or indirectly about his father, Johnny decided to simply say, "Hey, my father, who I loved very much, is dead. And I'd really appreciate it if you didn't mention his name." This worked beautifully. Many apologized. Anyone, you might agree, who would press the matter after hearing Johnny's statement deserves to have the dogshit beat out of him.

Fact: Once you put the remote control to your actions in someone else's hand, you can almost guarantee that the channel chosen is not the one you want to watch.

Johnny's problem wasn't exactly image-related, but what he did—assessing his situation, and choosing to conduct himself differently—can be used in almost all image-related situations. In the African-American community, images are almost par for the course, though not all are self-destructive. A Brother who imagines himself starting his own business or advancing his education has a better chance of doing so than a Brother who never considers the possibility.

The following are four image-related syndromes, one of which is dormant but still demands attention.

PMS: The acronym for Penitentiary Mentality Syndrome. In prison, inmates are locked in small cells, fed poorly cooked food, and given only the basic accouterments—soap, toothbrush, toothpaste, shaving kit, and prison-issue shirt, pants, and shoes. Although the inmate has very little worldly possessions, he is extremely protective of the little he does have. Therefore he might hurt or kill someone over his soap, toothbrush, toothpaste, shaving kit, prison-issue clothes, and his closet-sized cell, which he calls "his house." Not only that, he might hurt or kill someone over real or imaginary slights—a hard look, name-calling, an incidental bump. If he doesn't respond aggressively, he risks having his sexual orientation changed suddenly and without benefit of counseling. In prison, as in the animal kingdom, the weak supply nourishment to the strong. A Brother projecting a predator image in prison may be simply trying to survive.

Let's flip the script. The free world, as called by inmates, is not prison, regardless of how crime-plagued the neighborhood is. Yet somehow PMS has actually become more prevalent out on the streets than in prison, which leads to a daily increase in the prison population. Incidental contact, he-said/she-said (always negative), a lingering stare, putdowns, and petty theft are all legitimate reasons to injure or kill to someone suffering from PMS.

Low self-esteem is the lungs of PMS. The fear of being perceived a coward is the heart of PMS. Believe it or not, most people think about themselves more than they think about anybody else. Which means you or whatever you do isn't fractionally as important to them as you might think. Think about it, how often do you think about the guy who backed down from an argument two days ago? Chances are you haven't given the incident much thought at all. Now put yourself in his shoes. What's the difference? How many people in attendance do you think can't continue life because you didn't click?

ADDS: The acronym for Acting Demented and Dangerous Syndrome. This syndrome may have started with the antics of one Shackolee (considered apocryphal by some historians), a pugnacious slave who whooped his master's ass and then whooped a few other slave owners' asses for good measure—and, unlike Nat Turner, lived to tell about it. For his rebellious deeds Shackolee was considered a hero by his contemporaries. Songs were made about him. Yet very few slaves followed his lead. To do what Shackolee did, one had to be, what was then called a "crazy nigga."

In the '60s, '70s, and early '80s, quasi-Shackolees resided in almost every African-American neighborhood. These Brothers were purported to have beaten up not one but three or more policemen at the same time. Interestingly enough, no one knows what happened to these Brothers. Nevertheless they too, for a brief moment, before they disappeared off the face of the earth, were considered "crazy niggas."

Being considered a "crazy nigga" had several benefits, including deference, because only a crazy person would mess with someone who was publicly known to be crazy. So naturally, "a crazy nigga" was given wide berth. He was also a *cause celèbre*. This led to the emergence of many wannabe "crazy niggas," Brothers who sought the same infamous notoriety associated with being a "crazy nigga" by doing—yes, you're right—something crazy, which got many of them KISSed.

Crack cocaine has virtually eliminated this syndrome. Acting Demented and Dangerous looks very similar to acting high on crack. To many, being called a crackhead while attempting to gain a "crazy nigga" moniker is apparently not worth the trouble.

So why mention this syndrome at all? Excellent question. The need for recognition, infamous or praiseworthy, is so innate to the human condition that people will attempt self-destructive leaps and bounds to obtain or keep such recognition. So why in God's name would anyone suggest to a young, developing mind that a problem exists? But that's not the half of it: Not only is an inscrutable disorder implied, but, as if to give credence to the condition, medication is also prescribed.

The Pimp: You may or may not remember the movie Superfly, a rather successful blaxploitation film, which gave African-American males in the '70s the blueprint to becoming a pimp. John Wayne's heroic feats in innumerable war movies may have sent thousands of young Carl Casians to an early death, under the guise that bullets have a way of bypassing gung ho, heavyweight, Anglo-Saxon patriots. But, without a doubt, Ron O'Neal's performance in Superfly KISSed thousands of African-American males, under the guise that pimping women, selling drugs, and indiscriminately kicking Whitey's ass would be ignored by the law.

The Pimp image, the true Pimp image—a prestigious purveyor of prostitution—is moribund, or at least on its last leg. The decline of the image is due to two reasons: One, many African-American males realized that being a pimp, like so many images on television, isn't easy as it looks; and two, cocaine—a drug hardly conducive to sharing—persuaded millions of courtesans to maverick, that is to go it alone.

These vicissitudes defecated a pathetic creature, more disturbing and despicable than the pimp—the "tennis shoe pimp," also called "the Kool-Aid pimp," and sometimes "the flatfoot fool." He does not have a vehicle and he has only one pro, usually his wife or girlfriend, to proffer. Even to pimps this character is a joke.

Today's Player image may have in part spawned from the pimp image, but there's a distinct difference between the two. The Player image seeks notoriety from being a lady's man, while the pimp image seeks not only notoriety from being a lady's man but also a reputation as a savvy street businessman. To this end the pimp will maim, hurt, and sometimes kill women to ensure his pay, to which he feels he's entitled. This self-centered idolatry is proof positive of a First-class A-hole.

The Thug: Here it would be easy to attribute "The Thug" image to rappers and their lyrics, and be done with it, but let's take a closer look. At a glance, rapping seems rather easy...You come up with a couple rhymes and add background music, then you're set, right? Wrong.

To be a rap star, a successful rap star, one must have talent, a willingness to work hard, and a degree of luck. Lack any one of the three, and, as the old saying goes, "Don't quit your day job." Of course you could produce your own album, but still, if you lack talent and a hard work ethic, chances are you won't produce anything marketable. In the music industry, this type of work is called musical masturbation, which means only one person has gotten off on it—the producer. (Don't feel bad, there's also a term called literary masturbation.) All those rap stars you see on videos have overcome tremendous odds. The competition is fierce; the marketing base is fickle and has an extremely short attention span; and the level of throatcutting and backstabbing within the music industry is ten times higher than five episodes of *Survivor* combined.

The music industry is simply a business, and all businesses exist for one thing and one thing only: to make a profit. Given this tidbit of info, logic strongly suggests that no one (besides Suge Knight) has ever gotten into the music industry simply by "knocking a motherfucker out," though some hip hop lyrics suggest otherwise. This is where the confusion starts, the lyrics say one thing while logic says another. Logic also says that a Brother who has busted his butt to get into the music industry isn't spending an inordinate amount of time "spraying haters and their cohorts with AK47s and Uzis," "sexually servicing five or six women simultaneously," and "throwing lavish forty-ounce parties for everyone in the 'hood." No doubt an elite few have done such and also produced hit records, but for the majority, "The life we rap about isn't the life we're living."

The majority of Brothers get it; that is, they know what's being presented to them—a fantasy, a fantasy tailor-made to a Brother's dreams. Most Brothers know that dressing like a Thug, talking like a Thug, and listening to Thug music are a hell of a lot different than actually being a Thug. However, as with a small percentage of Carl Casians who play heavy-metal records backward and somehow hear "Go choke the shit out of thyself" and go do so, there exists a small percentage of Brothers who take rap music to heart and wind up getting KISSed.

One small fact many of these Brothers overlook: A million-dollar Thug has access to a million-dollar lawyer, but a slightly-above-minimum-wage Thug or a habitually unemployed Thug doesn't. What rhymes with disinterested public defender? So who's to blame when life attempts to emulate art and results in tragedy? Let's see...The artist is still performing, still making music and videos, still getting paid, while the mimicking malefactor is either dead, in ICU, or sitting in a jail cell reflecting on the virtues of gospel music.

Other Bad Apples

It's a colossal waste of time to tell someone what friends to pick and what friends to cut loose, but it never hurts to hold someone else's friends to a light and peek inside. The following list delineates the characteristics of a few so-called friends, or whatever you call them. See if you recognize any of these guys within your circle.

Grover Getover—Grover, like his first cousin Freddie Freeloader, is a relentless beggar. Though unlike Freddie, Grover has money to buy the things he need. Grover's motto: "Beg before being begged." Grover is the guy who chips in fifty cents on a thirty-pack and then drinks twenty-nine cans.

Telly Tellall—Telly's motto is: "I speak my mind!" Yes, he does, most certainly. He's loud and bombastic. But Telly never speaks his mind about his own personal affairs. Yet in any matter, no matter how embarrassing or personal, involving someone else's business, Telly is better than CNN.

Peter Peevert—Men talk about sex, no doubt, but Peter talks about sex all the time. He can steer any topic of conversation back to sex. His favorite subject: the proportions of his phallus. Peter rudely and lewdly shouts lame pick-up lines at any woman passing within his view. Think about this: If Peter reacts rabidly at the sight of any woman, what do you think he's thinking when he's around your woman, your sister, or your daughter?

Pedro Pedantic—Pedro is an authority on every subject, from analingus to zoology. Often no one else is able to get a word in edgewise because Pedro monopolizes the conversation. Yet you can't help but wonder if Pedro were really so damn smart, why is he always hanging around with Brothers who can't figure out what the hell he's talking about?

Sammy Slapjack—Sammy obviously delights in having his ass whooped. Rarely does a week go by without him getting his ass whooped in some shape, form, or fashion. He weighs a buck fifty, but his mouth is that of a much bigger man. Of course you are used to his childish taunts and empty threats, but everyone else—uh-uh! Thus the numerous knots upside his head.

Harry Hydrophobe—Apparently during early childhood, Harry either nearly drowned or was scalded with hot water. Whichever, the incident left Harry with a morbid fear of water, especially soapy water. So traumatic was Harry's ordeal he's also deathly afraid of anything associated with water—soap, toothbrush, and, due to its water content, deodorant. Harry can't connect his inability to attract a woman to his effluvium.

An aversion to water may have also affected his hearing, because he doesn't pick up on all the snide remarks about his ability to funk up the great outdoors.

Sandy Sanctimonious—What makes Sandy and his ilk so aggravating is their timing. No one with a forty-ounce at his lips wants to hear the gospel according to Sandy, no matter how relevant. Another annoying aspect to Sandy and his ilk is their incessant association of the divine with the simplistic. In other words, in a world where thousands of children starve to death each week, do they really and truly believe that their purchase of a new car is due to divine intervention?

Captain Morgan, TW Samuel, Bud Light, and EJ Brandy—These guys live up to their namesakes. These guy don't mind if you don't indulge, they mind if you don't buy. Notice how these guys never, ever think about eating—you suggest picking up a bucket of chicken on the way to the liquor store, and these guys will look at you like you just said something about their mothers. The next chapter includes more discussion about these guys, but take a good look at 'em: Are you looking in a mirror?

Pokey Pothead—Amazingly, Pokey keeps a modest supply of marijuana without having a source of income. And amazingly, despite all the marijuana that Pokey smokes—and he certainly smokes a lot—he doesn't seem fazed by the drug. As with the preceding four, Pokey lives for his namesake. But look closer...Pokey can't find a job because Pokey can't pass a drug test...and Pokey, well over thirty, still lives with his mother.

Brad Braggart—Brad monopolizes conversations with how much he has and how much he paid to get it. Ask Brad who he thinks will make the playoffs, and he will dive into a long narrative about how much he paid for his big-screen television. In any category—clothes, food, cars, houses—Brad has or had better than you or knows someone who has or had better than you. Brad is the guy who owns a truck but would rather be pistol-whipped than haul anything in it.

Weird Willie—Like a certain discolored, emaciated, disfigured-nose pop star, Weird Willie has an unnatural predilection for the company of prepubescent boys. Weird Willie appears to enjoy playing with kids and kid games, which makes it hard to determine if he has ulterior motives. Still, where children are concerned, it's best to err on the side of caution.

Henry Henpecked—Henry can't sit down for two minutes without calling home to check in with his better half. He rarely stays away from home long periods of time, which is rather amazing because his better half treats him like a puppy with explosive diarrhea. Of course, Henry's personal problems are not your problem. But don't you get tired of him bitching and whining about his situation?

Cory Cockstrong—To tell the truth, but for Cory's massive size, his tremendous biceps, triceps, quadriceps, and deltoids, you would have kicked his ass a long time ago. Cory's impertinent behavior—using his friends as punching bags—often makes you rethink your position on gun control. To your astonishment, Cory calls you his best friend.

Dan Daily—Not a day goes by without Dan paying you a visit, and he often comes by when he knows you are away. Notice how wonderfully Dan gets along with your significant other. Also notice how Dan listens intently when you tell him about your problems with your significant other. Perhaps, you think, Dan might be taking notes to use to his advantage? Nah!

Women Friends

When a woman says, "I think we should just be friends," most Brothers know this is the short version of: "I know that you want some in a bad way, which is why you've been hanging around, why you helped me catch up on a few bills, and I know I've been dangling it in your face like a carrot on a stick, putting it so close that you could practically taste it, but to be honest with you, I never intended to give you some, never, not once, not in a million years."

Most men prefer not to have a woman friend unless some semblance of sex is involved, which is why women use the above deflection technique. But a woman can make for a wonderful friendship, especially if no underlying sexual tension exists. With a woman as a good friend you don't get the petty competition that almost always exists between men. Usually a woman is more sensitive to personal problems. You can tell her things you wouldn't dare tell a man, such as your fears, feelings, and dreams.

Many men have described their best friendships with erstwhile girlfriends and ex-wives. "We couldn't stand each other's guts when we were together," many men have said, "but when we broke up, we became the best of friends." This is rather interesting, and it reinforces the wisdom of taking the time to become friends before becoming bed buddies.

The same wisdom can and should be applied to all relationships. In order to form a meaningful friendship that might last a lifetime, three cards must fall together—the first being reasonable trust, the second being responsibility, and the third being forgiveness. Trust is a unique word bandied about all the time. But the key to trust is trusting yourself. This sounds rather namby-pamby, but it most certainly applies. How can you expect someone to reasonably trust you if you can't trust yourself? How can you expect someone to reasonably trust you if you enter a relationship with an ulterior motive? As the old saying goes, "You can't expect to get more out of it than you put into it."

Chapter 5
Alcohol

"Telling a drunk to 'drink responsibly' is akin to telling a suicidal person, 'If once you don't succeed try again.'" H.H.

"Tastes great!"
"Less filling!"
"Tastes great!"
"Less filling!"

You remember the television commercial...One group of pot-bellied, has-been sport players shouted that a certain beer "tastes great!" while another group of pot-bellied, has-been sport players demanded that the beer was "less filling!" One aspect of this commercial resonated realism—give any group of pot-bellies free beer and enough time and they will find the most damnedest thing to argue about.

Kool-Aid tastes great, soda tastes great, fruit drinks taste great, but beer tastes like piss—and don't ask how this conclusion was reached. And as far as "less filling" is concerned, many beer drinkers claim that is their least concern, and cite diuresis and gastric disorders as more important beer-drinking concerns.

Although beer companies' blatantly false and patently ridiculous advertisements push common sense to the brink, the liquor industry's advertisements push common sense over the cliff, along with the heart and soul of many African-American men.

By the appearance of the countless liquor ads within

African-American dominated neighborhoods, the liquor industry, after self-banishment from advertising on radio and television, said, "Hey, let's concentrate the bulk of our advertising budget in socioeconomically disadvantaged Black neighborhoods."

Yes, the liquor industry also advertises in magazines and billboards along the interstate, but where else other than socioeconomically disadvantaged African-American neighborhoods do you see liquor advertisements on billboards, buses, benches, cabs, building facades, and liquor stores? Nowhere. The number of ads in itself is appalling, but the subliminal and flagrant messages border on criminality.

Let's take a look at the ubiquitous billboard featuring the svelte Brother in the thousand-dollar velvet suit. He's handsome. Muscular. His hair is cut in a neat trim. He's wearing an expensive watch, his facial expression deadpan. The velvet suit he's wearing fits to a tee. To his right, staring at the side of his head, a beautiful Sister, wearing a beige silk dress with a slit that goes way up to here. In her right hand, with its manicured, candy-apple-red painted fingernails, rests a large wineglass, a quarter filled. It's hard to tell if she's handing the Brother the glass or if she's showing him what she's drinking. Yet it is rather obvious that they are either preparing to go out or just arriving back from a night on the town.

In the right-hand corner is the object that appears out of place, obscenely incongruous to this scene. A whiskey bottle. Bigger than life. Not a high-dollar brand of whiskey, which is what you would expect these two African-American sophisticates to be sipping but a cheap, rotgut, buy-one-get-two-on-Tuesday brand. In smaller print on the bottle's neck, the words *With Ginseng*. Now ask yourself, what possible benefit ginseng offers in rotgut whiskey. Perhaps the peace of mind that your liver and kidney will rot with an oriental twang?

Where else have you seen this particular brand of whiskey? In mountainous heaps of trash. In liquor stores, though unlike the billboard's depiction, in half-pint size. In the hands of the neighborhood drunk, though usually wrapped in a brown paper bag.

The ad more or less says, "Not only do Skid Row, piss-smelling drunks prefer our brand of whiskey, but Brothers and Sisters of esteemed social status prefer our brand of whiskey as well." Since when? Go to a liquor store in another neighborhood and you'll discover this particular brand isn't even in stock. Now imagine this billboard in another neighborhood where similar socioeconomic problems exist, say, for example, near or on a Native American reservation, with Native Americans portrayed as connoisseurs of cheap whiskey. How mad do you think MADD would get?

These ads ignore the fact that African-Americans' alcohol consumption is less than other groups, including Carl Casian's. Of course the liquor and beer companies know this. So why the prodigious propaganda proliferation of liquor ads in socioeconomically disadvantaged African-American neighborhoods, where alcohol-related problems compound intrinsically?

Because African-Americans allow them to do so!

The Forty-Ounce

A beer company executive looked out the window of his high-rise building at a liquor store several miles away in an African-American neighborhood. What he saw disturbed him. Several distinguished citizens loitered outside the store, begging and hustling paying customers for change... *This isn't fair,* he thought, *No, this isn't fair at all.*

At the next board meeting, he said, "A man who supplicates assiduously through rain or shine should not be denied our product because of penurious complications."

Thus the forty-ounce bottle.

The executive could not have known how a big a hit the forty-ounce would become with African-Americans males. Consider this: A six-pack costs four bucks (rough average), while a forty-ounce costs two bucks and fifty cents (rough average). At this rate, the six-pack cost about 57 cents an ounce, while the forty-ounce costs about 62 cents an ounce, which makes a difference of 5 cents an ounce. Not exactly an amount to quibble over, right. But a nickel here and a nickel there adds up to a fair amount of money, and an even larger amount if you factor in the thousands upon thousands of forty-ounce bottles sold each day. And you thought Grover Getover was greedy.

While you're pondering how many nickels it takes to buy a keg, take a brief moment to consider what's the least preferred object besides a steering wheel or a gun you would like to see in the hands of an angry drunk. Yes, you're cooking with hot grease now—a forty-ounce bottle, empty or full. In the movies when a guy gets popped over the head with an empty bottle, the bottle shatters, the guy looks goofy for a second and then falls unconscious. Well, that's not quite how it works in real life. Getting popped upside the head, over the head, around the head, or anywhere near the head with an empty bottle, forty-ounce or not, can kill you, or leave you physically unable to shoo a fly from your face. This happens more often than you think, possibly daily. Unless the person popped with a forty-ounce bottle is seriously injured or killed, the incident rarely makes a crime report.

For those drunks who prefer not to pop someone

upside the head with a half-full forty-ounce bottle, an empty forty-ounce bottle can easily be broken and used as an effective stabbing device.

Then, just as the forty-ounce bottle was losing it appeal, lo and behold a forty-ounce appears in a rap video...and then another...and another...and—*blam!*—the forty-ounce bottle popularity peaks to all new heights. "Oh the joy!" many beer executives exclaimed. Other beer companies that had previously shunned the forty-ounce market quickly jumped on board, including a few foreign beer companies. Is there a more unnerving sight and sound at a grocery checkout line than a Brother struggling to tote twenty to thirty forty-ounce bottles? And why is it that malt liquor forty-ounce bottles clang louder than regular forty-ounce bottles?

Liquid Nuts Syndrome

What makes a guy who weighs a buck and a quarter, wet, whose own shadow sometimes startles him, who wouldn't dream of busting a grape with a sledgehammer, suddenly belligerent and violent with a man twice his size? What makes a guy who is usually easygoing and taciturn, who would rather let a roach live than kill it, suddenly profane and irascible? What makes a guy who generally treats his wife or girlfriend kindly, who would rather take a walk than engage in an argument, verbally and physically abusive?

The answer to all three questions: Liquid Nuts Syndrome, a phantom feeling of having gonads caused by alcohol overindulgence.

Before going further, let's highlight a few facts. Alcohol is a drug, a depressant; it has no stimulant value whatsoever. Alcohol does not promote aggression. Why alcohol brings out certain negative behavior characteristics in some people but not others is not fully understood.

Okay. Now let's highlight a few observations obtained by streetology, the scientific study of all manner of public A-Holism. Nine times out of ten, people who literally show their ass while under the influence of alcohol wanted to show their ass when sober, but were either too afraid or too embarrassed to do so. People tend to act drunker than they really are. *"Hey, I was drunk!"* Many people think this is an acceptable excuse for stupid behavior.

However, alcohol does diminish motor skills and clear and reasonable thinking. This explain why drunks get their asses whooped ten times the national average. In the drunks' mind he's ready to raise hell, but the rest of his body—arms, legs, fists—is dead tired, staunchly against any physical exertion and begging for rest. He ignores the warning and gets his ass whooped.

Drunk behavior is often learned behavior. Often, a guy whose father regularly got his ass whooped while drunk will act out the same behavior. Others learn their behavior from television and Hollywood movies, wherein drunks also get their ass whooped.

(To their credit, television higher-ups finally realized that portraying drunks as anything other than drunks was an egregious affront to the million of families living with a drunk. The television drunks were lovable, happy-go-lucky, funny men like Foster Brooks, Otus of The Andy Griffith Show, and Dean Martin. Meanwhile, real-life drunks were staggering and falling down, pissing in closets and flowerpots, trying to be funny, cooking and burning at ungodly hours, and disrupting the peace and quiet of entire neighborhoods.)

Liquid Nuts Syndrome can get you KISSed in a heartbeat. A word to the wise: If you must drink, Think

Before You Drink! Why wait till you're intoxicated, when your thinking is impaired. By preplanning what activities you will do or not do while drinking before drinking, you can prevent a tremendous amount of pain and frustration and embarrassment. Here are seven easy-to-follow steps that will work if adhered to.

Step 1. Determine your Alcohol Buzz Limit—the amount of alcohol it takes to give you a buzz, which is, hopefully, why you're drinking, isn't it? (Any amount of alcohol consumed pass the Buzz Limit becomes drinking to get drunk; more on that later.) An unusually high Buzz Limit, such as a six-pack of beer, a pint of any distilled liquor, or a quart of wine, suggests an upwardly moving alcohol tolerance level, which is not good.

Step 2. Before taking the first sip of whatever, think about why you're drinking. To relax? To socialize? To relieve pain (not exactly a good reason to drink)?

Step 3. Take a long, hard look at the people with whom you are drinking. What are their drinking habits? How do their drinking habits influence you?

Step 4. Make a mental list of the things you plan to do while drinking. Watch a ball game? A card game? Sit around and chat with friends?

Step 5. Make a mental list of the things you do not plan to do while drinking, such as the following:

Attempt to kick Cory Cockstrong's ass.
Complete and file tax forms.
Play detective with the old lady to test her loyalty.
Drive or operate heavy equipment.
Ask the boss for a raise.
Hash out an old grudge with anyone.
Discipline the kids.
Make any decision requiring careful consideration.

Step 6. Ensure that you eat before consuming any

amount of alcohol. Food helps your body metabolize alcohol. Drinking on an empty stomach increases your blood alcohol level preternaturally and increases the time it takes your body to metabolize alcohol.

Step 7. Now that you know your Buzz Limit, decide whether or not you intend to surpass it. If so, rehash your mental list of things you will not do while drinking. If not, stick to it.

Everyone has a mental clock—but each individual has to set it. Tell yourself before going to sleep, "I can only sleep for a few hours or I'll be late for work," and your mental clock will wake you in time. By presetting your drinking limit before actually drinking, your mind will warn you once you've met the limit. But, as with the mental clock, you must respond to the bell.

Numb Nuts Syndrome

To fully explain Numb Nuts Syndrome, a few egghead argots will be used, though sparingly. As stated before, alcohol is a depressant, which suppresses or inhibits a rather amazing number of human functions, one of which is a man's ability to produce testosterone. The more alcohol a man consumes, the more compromised his testosterone level, which controls not only male hair growth and the bass pitch in voice but also his ability to get his Johnson to come to attention. Among other things this tells us that TW Samuel and a few of his drinking buddies are more talk than action.

Now here's the kicker: Testosterone is produced inside the testes, which is controlled by the pituitary gland, which is controlled by the brain. When TW Samuel's testosterone level is low, a red light comes on (so to speak) and signals the pituitary gland to crank out more hormones that will stimulate production of more testosterone. Not wanting to assume full responsibility for this emergency request for more hormones, the pituitary gland sends an interoffice memorandum to the brain, which is dealing with more than enough alcohol-related problems of its own. All of this signaling back and forth between the brain and the pituitary gland, to get the other to go to work, causes a significant increase in a hormone called LH or luteinizing hormone, which promotes sexual arousal.

Therein lies the problem. Numb Nuts Syndrome. It's sorta like being anxious as hell to play ball only to discover that you left all your equipment at the house. Of course, TW Samuel isn't thinking about pituitary glands, testosterone levels, and all that other jazz; he only knows that he has an irrepressible desire to get it going on.

This explains why an ogress looks an appealing prospect at closing time. This explains why he who lacks the confidence to approach a woman sober will stagger, pitch and roll twenty feet across the dance floor to a pretty woman sitting at her table to slur: "May I have a..*hic*...dance?" When she shakes her head, clearly signaling, *No way, José!* he grabs her arm and attempts to pull her out on the dance floor. This also explains why so many men awake after a night of merriment and mirth and discover Miss Whothehellareyou in their bed—and also discover no condom packages in sight.

An increase in sexual desire, minus a decrease in sexual performance, multiplied by alcohol-impaired thinking, equals a major fuck-up to the tenth power. DWI (driving while intoxicated) or DUI (driving under the influence) is considered by many as the most tragic ramification of irresponsible drinking, in part because of the tragic loss of life and catastrophic injuries associated with alcohol-related car accidents. However, rape, date rape, child abuse, and the transmission of many STDs, including AIDS, are just as tragic and catastrophic, and, more often than not, alcohol-related. Think Before You Drink!

Disease or Mental Freeze?

Is alcoholism a disease? The answer depends on who you ask—although you will never hear this question being pondered by the guys warming their hands near the barrel fire and passing a half-pint around. In response to this question, many claim that "some people are simply allergic to alcohol—one drink can trigger a biological craving that demands more drinks." Others claim that "alcoholism is like cancer, diabetes, and heart disease," in that each can be lethal if left untreated.

Here, alcoholism is not a disease. If cancer and heart disease could be packaged into bottles and sold, you can guarantee that very few people would be in line to purchase them (this view does not deny that alcoholism is a serious problem and causes sickness and suffering and death to millions of people).

Tell a Brother that his drinking is due to alcoholism, a disease, which he cannot control, and watch the victimization process take place before your very eyes: *"I'm not responsible, I have a disease—pass the bottle."* He's exonerated from drinking responsibly, and he's exonerated from the foolish behavior resulting from his drinking.

This luxury is one which an African-American male can ill-afford. Although African-Americans consume less alcohol than other groups, they incur higher levels of alcohol-related illnesses such as cirrhosis, cancer, hypertension, and other medical problems—plus higher incidence of alcohol-related homicides, assaults, and injuries.

Hang around the barrel fire long enough, and you will eventually hear the words that are supposedly the first step to alcohol recovery: "I am an alcoholic." Then watch the guy turn the bottle up and drain it dry. Knowing you have a drinking problem is one thing; doing something about your drinking problem is another. Today, many people know they have a drinking problem, and many have no compunction openly stating the fact, but instead of this awareness acting as an impetus to change drinking habits, it has somehow made it easier to justify poor drinking habits. Of course, *"I am an alcoholic"* sounds more pleasant than *"I am a piss-poe drunk."* But which declaration do you think will excite someone to take a serious look at his drinking behavior?

Exactly. Which is why here alcoholism will not be considered a disease but a debilitating piss-poe condition, stemming from a history of irresponsible drinking.

How to Become a Piss-poe Drunk

In order to receive a Piss-poe Drunk master's degree you must first attend Problem Drinking School, which accepts all applicants, the only requirement being a fondness for drink. Upon graduating from Problem Drinking School—a lot easier than you think—you can take the next step to receiving a Piss-poe Drunk degree by matriculating into Drunk College, which also accepts all applicants. Note: Drunk College allows those who test high on an ACT (Alcohol Consumption Test) examination and those who report experiencing one or more blackouts a week to enter as graduate students. The moment you exhibit signs of DTs (*delirium tremens*) or Rum Fits (a *grand mal* seizure caused by alcohol withdrawal) is the moment you graduate to a full-fledged Piss-poe Drunk. Now let's take a closer look at each institution.

Problem Drinker

By definition, anyone who drinks and incurs a problem, any problem, is a problem drinker. People who drink responsibly or abstain from drinking do not have problems with drinking. You're shaking your head again. Okay. Say, for example, after taking the first drink of your life you're headed home in your car and Mickey Myopic steps out in your path. *Bam! Pop! Crunch! Shit!* But—thank God!—Mickey lives. He's seriously injured, of course. Meanwhile, you fail a field sobriety test and go to jail.

Do you think the judge will feel sympathetic to your case when you tell him this was your first time drinking, and, after all, Mickey Myopic did step into your path? Fat chance!

But, you say, this could happen to anybody who drinks. Not exactly. A responsible drinker wouldn't get behind the wheel of the car after drinking because he has already decided what he will do and will not do, which includes driving, before taking the first drink. A problem drinker doesn't anticipate problems, which, combined with alcohol-impaired thinking, is why the problem drinker incurs more problems than average.

To add strange hickies to a hangover, problem drinkers surround themselves with other problem drinkers, or drunks, or piss-poe drunks, which exponentially creates more problems. What's more pathetic than two drunks fighting over spilt whiskey?

Have you ever eaten something that made you sick?

Chances are you now steer clear of whatever it was. A natural human response. However, alcohol makes some people sick every time they take a drink, but still they go back to drink again and again. No one fully understands why this happens. Heredity, alcoholic genes, peer pressure, stress, emotional disorders, and billboards advertising rotgut whiskey have all been cited as potential origins of this phenomenon, but no consensus has been reached.

Perhaps what trips up many problem drinkers, drunks, and piss-poe drunks is the "Moe Better" concept, the belief that the more of a good thing or feeling one has, the better. This concept trips up many a pothead, too. No doubt you've seen a pothead roll up and smoke one joint right after the other, or roll up and smoke one fat, humongous joint. Logic escapes him but tells you that he can only go so high, and the rest is a waste, which he could have saved for a smokeless day. Many problem drinkers, drunks, and piss-poe drunks identify with the pothead's logic. They falsely believe that if three drinks stimulate joviality and jocularity, then a keg of beer, or a barrel of wine, or a bathtub of whiskey should send them to the moon. Well, it doesn't quite work that way.

Anyone who has ever taken a drink or two knows about the alcohol buzz—a warm, feel-good sensation—associated with drinking. What is not commonly known is that this buzz can be easily obtained but cannot be expanded on. Basically: You can not increase the buzz by drinking more. Drinking more actually reverses the buzz, which is why you often see grown men, drunk, crying and sniveling and blowing snot like two-year-olds. Drinking more increases your tolerance level, which requires more liquor to achieve the buzz the next time around (an extremely high buzz level is a blinking red light). And drinking more increases the chance of mental and physical alcohol addiction. It's somewhat analogous to attempting to have sex with a wild animal: The harder you attempt to reach your goal, the more tore up you get. The next time you go somewhere where people are drinking, take a good look at what you see. Notice the people who are drinking responsibly. Notice the people who are drunk or close to it. Then ask yourself, which group of people appears to be truly enjoying themselves? Which group of people will likely feel like shit the next day? Which group of people will be able to honestly say, "Had a great time last night"?

Another indicator of problem drinking: drinking for the wrong reason. People drink for many reasons, and 99.9 percent of them are the wrong reasons to drink. For example, drinking to achieve a good night's rest. Yes, alcohol promotes sleep, but alcohol does not promote good sleep, the kind of sleep you awake from feeling refreshed and motivated. Alcohol suppresses REM (rapid eye movement) sleep, which is when dreams occur and is imperative to a good night's sleep. This is why one single drink before sleep can cause you to feel lousy the next morning.

Another bad reason: drinking to overcome melancholia, despondency, or depression. This type of drinking is considered by many eggheads as the root of alcoholism. This type of drinking is similar to having someone knock you unconscious to alleviate a toothache—an inane attempt to solve a problem with another problem. Possibly what makes this type of drinking attractive is the transference of pain. The guy who is knocked unconscious to alleviate a toothache is no longer concerned with a toothache, even when he wakes up; a black eye or a busted nose is often more painful than most toothaches. However, he now has two problems: a facial injury and a toothache. When the effects of alcohol diminish, the problems one sought to mask are still there. So to relieve the problem once again more drinking is needed. Repeat these steps often enough—*bam!*—you have a dependence for alcohol.

The Drunk

All the guys you see hanging around the barrel fire and passing a half-pint bottle around are not drunks—losers maybe, but not drunks. Let's say there are a total of ten guys near the barrel fire. One of the ten has a mental disorder, possibly schizophrenia or depression. Two of the ten are problem drinkers, as described previously. Two of the ten are "situational drunks," someone who seldom drinks alone but lacks the guts to tell friends and associates no to drinking. One of the ten doesn't drink whatsoever; he's there because he's cold and homeless. The last four are either drunks or piss-poe drunks. (Do not attempt to make these distinction on your own—can cause severe head trauma from being popped upside the head with a half-pint bottle.)

There is a thin line between a drunk and a piss-poe drunk. A drunk's chances of rehabilitation are slightly higher than a piss-poe drunk's chances. A drunk is basically someone in training to become a piss-poe drunk. An obvious indicator of being a drunk is the shakes—trembling hands—a minor form of alcohol withdrawal, and an early sign of alcohol dependency. The shakes says it all. Regardless of what you drink—*"I only drink beer!"*—regardless of when you drink—*"I only drink on days ending with Y!"*—regardless of how you drink—*"I sip, never guzzle!"*—and regardless of how long you've been drinking—*"I've only been drinking two months!"*—the shakes says, *"You have a serious drinking problem!"* Don't think because you don't shake, you couldn't possibly be a drunk. Any time you need a reason to confirm what you are not, chances are you are just that.

Fact: Many people who are dead or in prison because of alcohol-related problems never shook one day in their life.

The shakes are revealing, but the best indicator of being a drunk is an increasing pattern of drinking. This also confuses many people because of the prevalent misguided notion that drunks drink every day. But many drunks drink every other day or only on weekends, which can also produce the shakes and blackouts and often leads to everyday drinking. Remember, the more you drink the more your buzz level increases, the more your tolerance level increases, and the closer you get to alcohol dependency.

Below are classic symptoms of being a drunk:

Hiding liquor or hiding drinking. Often a drunk will hide his liquor and forget where, then get angry and accuse others of stealing.

Morning drinking. It takes a certain kind of stomach to handle continuous morning drinking—a rotgut stomach.

Blackouts. Blackouts, the inability to recall periods of time while drunk, can also occur with problem drinkers. Blackouts are caused by a high blood alcohol level, not how often you drink. Drunks and piss-poe drunks, however, suffer an inordinate number of blackouts.

Physical deterioration. Because of the drunk's liquid diet, his physical appearance will show obvious signs of deterioration, rheumy eyes, bags underneath eyes, rubbery skin. Also because of a liquid diet, drunks tend to incur an above average of boils, bumps, keloids, knots, cuts, sores, scratches, moles, rashes, pockmarks, holes, dents, indentations, and inexplicable swelling of entire body parts, usually the neck and head.

Lying. But for crackheads and pathological liars, the drunk would be the world's greatest liar. However, drunks are inarguably the world's worst liars. Often they lie because of guilt feelings associated with drinking. *"I'm not drunk!" "I can stop drinking whenever—though now is not a good time."* These statements would sound remotely credible but for the drunk being drunk.

Not all drunks go on to becoming piss-poe drunks. Some drunks rehabilitate through medical treatment (Antabuse and other drugs, aversion therapy, and hypnosis), AA (Alcoholics Anonymous), religious affiliations, or treatment centers; a modest percentage of drunks successfully rehabilitate on their own accord. The classification of people who incur drinking problems is simply a classification—whether you prefer *alcoholic* to *drunk,* it's still your responsibility to control your drinking, and if you see your drinking as problematic, it probably is. Early treatment is the best treatment.

Any of the aforementioned treatment plans can adumbrate a road to recovery, though do-it-yourself rehabilitation is…well, not for everybody. You should be able to find an Alcoholics Anonymous group within your neighborhood. AA has a long history of successfully treating alcoholism. Of course their views differ than those presented here, but why get mired in semantics when your goal is recovery? Various church organizations, though not generally associated with alcohol recovery, have also played a significant role in helping many a man get back on the wagon.

The church seems the ideal route for many African-Americans males. In fact many churches respond favorably to AA meetings on site. One Brother with a desire to help others is all it takes to start an AA group. Many treatment centers are expensive, but more and more companies are offering addiction benefits in group insurance plans, so if you need it, use it. Those Brothers whose alcohol recovery plan is spiritually anchored tend to stay sober at a much higher rate, and many report living a more peaceful, enjoyable life.

The Piss-poe Drunk

This is the end of the road. What lies beyond is insanity, prison, and death. Don't let the name fool you. This condition has nothing to do with piss or being poor. You can be a millionaire and still be a piss-poe drunk. The following are indisputable proof of being a piss-poe drunk:

Drinking to make the day. Before doing anything, the overwhelming physical dependence for alcohol must be addressed.

I'll-be-damned drinking. Drinking despite doctors'warnings to the contrary. Or drinking in spite of alcohol-related health problems, including cirrhosis.

Outrageous tolerance levels. Measuring one's tolerance level in gallons. It takes a tremendous amount of drinking to achieve ridiculously high alcohol tolerance levels.

Whatever-is-handy drinking. This includes rubbing alcohol, shaving lotion, antifreeze, ammonia, and other cleaning products. (Of course, anyone who puts a jug of Clorox to his lip probably doesn't realize he has a problem.)

Binge drinking. Suicide attempt, short and simple. Sadly, this type of drinking also ensnares—and kills—a large number of beginning drinkers, due to foolish drinking games and BS bravado.

DTs (Delirium tremens). This brings to mind pink elephants dancing on their toes, but it's a lot more than that and can be deadly. DTs result from profound alcohol withdrawal. Symptoms can include one or more of the following: fever, hand trembling, profound confusion and disorientation, sweating, vivid hallucinations, and tachycardia (rapid heartbeat).

A piss-poe drunk is not a pretty sight. Drinking has definitely made his life unmanageable. He will indeed need a miracle. If he doesn't seek help, more than likely his drinking will kill him. The ideal method to recover from this level of drinking is to never reach this level of drinking. The majority of piss-poe drunks are middle-aged men and older, the forty-plus crowd, but a growing number of young men, including teenagers, are making the grade. Achieving piss-poe drunk status at an early age isn't anything to be proud of—it's on the same level of proudly displaying a genital wart.

The piss-poe drunk cannot recall when his drinking faded into an obsession with alcohol, but his immediate family, specifically his wife and kids, can give a detailed account as to when the man of the house crawled inside a beer can or liquor bottle and never crawled out. The following is a testimonial from a Brother who requested his name not be used.

"At first my daddy only drank beer on weekends. Not much, you know, a six-pack at the most. Milwaukee Best, that was his favorite. I can't tell you how many cans of Milwaukee Best I've seen in my life. But he wasn't the type of man, you know, that would get drunk and want to fight. He'd get his drunk on and watch TV…wouldn't bother nobody or nothin, just sit there and drink, with a big ole grin on his face.

"Next day there'd be twenty or more beer cans scattered about with him in the middle. One night a couple of his friends came over to watch a fight. Sugar Ray was fighting somebody, Hagler, I believe. One of his friends brought a big bottle of Canadian Mist with him, and he told me to go get three glasses. I told him, 'My daddy don't drink nothin but beer.' They all laughed at that, and he [his daddy] went and got the glasses. The next day I went to use the bathroom and found him face-down between the commode and the tub, his pants down. Vomit was everywhere, on the wall, on the tub, on the sink, on the shower curtain, all over the floor—everywhere. And the stench! A sickly, sweet stench, you know, kinda like rotten plums with a twist of alcohol mixed in. So I called Momma—well, I screamed, really. Hell, I didn't know. I thought he was dead…or dying.

"That woke him up. He had a large Adam's apple, you know, and I remember trying to focus on that because dried-up vomit was caked all over the side of his face and he stank. Then when he saw me, he smiled and winked at me, you know, as if to say, 'I'm al'ight, son. I'm al'ight. A little drunk, but I'm al'ight.' Momma came and pushed me out and slammed the door in my face. Somehow he managed to go to work that day. I don't know how he did it, but he did. But I had a strong feeling—I guess you could call it a premonition—that that was the beginning of the end. I could feel it, you know.

"And it was. He started drinking Canadian Mist every day, and Momma hollered and shouted at him all the time, but it did no good. He had an old baby-blue deuce and a quarter in the front yard. The motor was shot. It still had a good body, though. Anyway, he'd hide his liquor under the hood and make like he was fixin' on the motor. Everybody in the neighborhood knew what he was doing—he wasn't foolin nobody.

One time he passed out under the hood, with a wrench in one hand and an empty half-pint of Canadian Mist bottle in the other. The woman next door called Momma, and she told me to go out and get him. A buncha people were standing around laughing at him, a few of my friends, too. I started crying. I wasn't crying cause everyone was laughing at him; I was crying because of the wrench.

"That wrench in his hand told me he really thought he was foolin' somebody. He really believed he was. That hurt more than anything else. Then, Momma started holding family prayer meetings. She'd call her sisters and some people over and they would pray and shout while Daddy lay stretched out on the floor, passed out. His oldest brother, Luke, came over and roughed him up a little bit and told him to get his shit together. I know my daddy would have whooped him if he hadn't been drunk. Luke was a lot smaller than Daddy. None of it did no good, though. He started going to work when he felt like it. One day his boss come over and asked him for the keys to something or 'nother where he worked. I remembered his hand was shaking when he handed over the keys. His boss told him, 'Come on back when you feel better.' But I could tell by the look on his face that he knew my daddy wasn't coming back. After that, I guess he said, 'Fuck it!' you know. Momma talked him into going to the VA a couple times. He'd come back, grinning, fat, lookin' his old self, then two or three days later it was the same ole same ole, back to making a hundred trips to the car before passing out on the living room floor.

"I guess Momma just got tired, you know. She was starting to look like she was drinking herself. So we moved...while he was passed out. I kinda hated her for doing him like that, but I was young. Now I realize what she was going through. Then after that, you know, I

sorta lost track of him. Momma remarried. But I didn't forget about him or nothing like that, you know. I-I...you know what I'm saying?

"When I went to the funeral, I didn't feel, you know, I didn't feel devastated. I mean, I felt bad, but in a way, I was sorta glad—not glad—but, you know, I was glad he wasn't suffering no more. He'd thinned out since last time I'd seen him, and I don't know where they got that cheap suit from. He never wore green in his life. But he was smiling, as if to say, 'I'm al'ight, son. I'm al'ight.'"

Chapter 6
Drugs

"Hell hath no fury to he or she who has fallen in love with a crackhead." H.H.

Soaking your shorts because you can't make it to the bathroom in time? No problem, there's a drug for that. Losing your hair on top? No problem, there's a drug for that. Too dry or too wet in a certain area? No problem, there's a drug for that. Erector won't erect? No problem, there's a cure for that as well. Nowadays it seems as if there is a drug to cure almost everything but the big two, cancer and AIDS. Don't you often think if scientists didnt spend as much time and energy concocting cures for maladies most people didn't know existed, they would have come up with a cure for the big two a long time ago.

For example, take ED (erectile dysfunction), and keep it if you like. Since when is this a legitimate medical condition? Yes, you're right—when the drug industry said it was. Can you once recall some old geezer saying, "Man oh man! This damn erectile dysfunction is killing me. I sho' be glad when they come up with something to cure this shit"? Maybe, quite possibly, just maybe, the Big Guy upstairs intended a certain age, perhaps sixty-five—seventy most definitely!—for men to find somewhere and sit down and play with the grandkids instead of trying to tiptoe through the tulips.

The ads for erectile dysfunction medicine are almost as unsettling and just as ridiculous as rotgut whiskey ads. Aunt Bea stares fondly at the side of her old man's head, her eyes aglow, smiling, as if to say, "I saw it but I don't believe it, and I'm sure I don't want to see it again!" Her old man, white-haired, wizened, looking on the wrong side of eighty, is also smiling, though sheepishly, as if he'd just gotten away with filing a false dependent on his income tax. Below their picture, above the drug's name and the gazillion and one possible adverse side effects, reads the caption: *He did it for me!*

Right off, you know that's an out-and-out lie. You can imagine, though painfully, that by the time Grandpa took the drug, started toward the bedroom where Granny lay waiting, stopped to take a leak, then remembered he'd left the faucet on, went and turned it off, then suddenly needed to take another leak and went and did that, forgot what he'd intended to do in the first place, suddenly remembered, started on his way to the bedroom again, and finally eased out his clothes, Granny was fast asleep, and the drug had lost its effectiveness.

Someone should tell these ol' boys, "Any ol' thing can prime a motor, ether, drugs, whatever, but you still need gas to get it a rockin and a rollin."

Now, the tragedy.

Don't See None, Must Not Be None!

Before President Bill Clinton signed the Welfare Reform Bill, Carl Casian and his cohorts had been clamoring for years that the welfare cheats and welfare queens were draining the federal budget. Such was their furor over those who they claimed were sitting on their butts reaping the fat from their hard-earned tax dollars, you wondered if they ever went to sleep. At the heart of their derision was the welfare queen. Oh, such hatred and contempt! This project dweller!...sitting on her ass, watching soap operas...*damned soap operas!*...having one baby right after the other by God knows who...to increase her welfare check...while hardworking, taxpaying Anglo-Saxon Americans foot the bill. Oh, the indolence!

If you were paying attention, you noticed that every so-called welfare queen dragged out onto a talk show stage or highlighted in a newspaper under such headings as WELFARE QUEEN RECEIVES CHECKS IN FRENCH ALPS was an African-American woman. And in every live footage or photo of a welfare office, food stamps office, and commodity cheese and two-year-old pork office, all the women standing in line were women of color.

If you were paying attention statistically to who was on welfare and who wasn't, you knew that Carl Casian and his clan made up the majority of welfare recipients—even though, as it was often pointed out, African-Americans comprised a larger ratio by race. So how come Carl Casian's people never showed up in any footage or photos of people standing in line at any welfare office? Surely there existed one or two of Carl Casian's girlfriends who could fall under the category of welfare queen? It didn't make sense. The dominant number, the unseen number?

This mysterious phenomenon of a disappearing majority but an overrepresented minority transfers to other areas as well, specifically America's drug problem. The overwhelming majority of this country's drug users—including, believe it or not, crack—are Carl Casian and his clan. Crack? *The so-called Black drug? Uh-uh!*

Another astonishing fact: Roughly, for every one African-American drug user there are four to five Carl Casian drug users. Most hospital emergency room reports and many crime studies clearly show this. So how come almost every news report on drugs, almost every documentary on drugs, and all police campaigns to combat drugs, are centered in or on African-American dominated neighborhoods? How come not one mobile-home park was raided by police under the guise of "get tough on drugs," ostensibly to weed out meth-heads, and everyone, the young and the old, harassed and treated like criminals? And how come young Carl Casians living in suburbia are not routinely stopped, harassed, made to spread-eagle on the pavement, and searched, because they allegedly fit the description of two guys who were reportedly selling drugs?

If you're an African-American male, you know how come. No one has to tell you, because you've either experienced it or seen it. Is it right? No. Is it fair? No. Is it the way things have been for a very long time? Yes. Is it the way it's going to be for an even longer time, despite the recent attention on racial profiling and the disparity in African-American drug sentencing laws? Yes.

Therefore, the African-American male, the Black man, the Brother, has a larger responsibility, a larger burden than his Carl Casian counterpart where drugs are concerned. Which is one reason among many why African-American males cannot silently acquiesce to drug use within their ranks. How is he your Brother if you do not let him know you frown on drug use? How is he your Brother if you silently stand by while he sells poison to his *own people?* "If I don't do it," he says, "someone else will." Perhaps, but *he* doesn't *have to* do it. A word of caution: It may not be prudent to confront strangers about illicit drug use or drug sales; however, those Brothers within your circle of association, friends, and family members, should definitely know that you disapprove of illicit drugs. Another word of caution: Even with Brothers within your circle of association use caution and common sense—a Brother who is high, combative, or in clear possession of a weapon isn't in a receptive state of mind to hear your views about the perils of drugs in the African-American community.

But you will be surprised at the number of younger Brothers, the seven- to twelve-year-olds you *can* reach by your words and your actions—especially your actions.

"Say What, Kemosabe?"

African-Americans were/are not the only minority group pitifully characterized on television and in the movies. Chinese, Mexicans, Japanese, Italians, and other ethnic groups are included, but without a doubt, the Native American should receive the runner-up award for the Most Maligned By Negative Imaging Award. Even with Lone Ranger's sidekick Tonto you couldn't help but think Tonto was hired help who never got paid. "Tonto, go get this!" "Tonto, go get that!" "Tonto, pull these bad guys off my ass!" Never, not once: "Here's your pay, Tonto." Didn't you long for the day for Tonto to retort, "Go get it your damned self, Kemosabe!"

In ninety-nine westerns out of a hundred, totally out of sync with history, Native Americans were defeated in battle. How convincing were these movies, so much so that unless you were a Native American—and even a few of them may have been won over by the convincing Hollywood version—you cheered for the cowboys, who were simply trying to claim all the land for themselves, despite the fact that the Native Americans were there long before Paleface arrived. (Also, though rather embarrassing, it was easier to cheer for Tarzan than those pesky native Africans who, though terribly and collectively afraid of one chimpanzee-hugging White man, kept up a tremendous amount of racket with their rituals and ceremonies.)

The Hollywood version of the conflict with the Native Americans did align truthfully with history in portraying the Native American as the savage. Think about it this way: Someone moves into your house, entices you to sign a contract enabling him to share your space, a duplex so to speak, then he breaks the contract, calls you a savage, goes to war with you, and less-than-subtly suggests you move somewhere more compatible, perhaps a reservation.

The frontiersmen, hunters, and pioneers of the time knew that kicking the Native American out his native land onto reservations and then claiming the lands as their own looked shitty to even the most avid Native American-hater, so they had to make the Native American appear as sinister as possible. Simply labeling him a savage didn't quite fill the bill. A prophetic hunter suggested malt liquor in a forty-ounce bottle, but that was shot down because of obvious transportation issues. Whiskey, however, was in abundance. Thus, the Native American was not only a savage, but even more a savage after drinking whiskey, which by the way he didn't manufacture. Paleface, on the other hand, did manufacture whiskey and could, due to his superiority, control its effects—despite an occasional bar fight and killing.

As you know, this worked out quite well. To this very day Native American reservations prohibit alcohol. And Paleface occupies the land and still has an occasional bar fight and killing. You see where this is going, don't you? Alcohol, a drug, was used to control and manipulate a group of people. Each time an African-American dings out big-time—kills a family member for drug money, sells children for drug money, etc.—Carl Casian can crank up his diatribe and be heard: "More laws! The death penalty! Tougher police! The second amendment!"

Notice, however, when one of Carl Casian's family members dings out big-time—shooting schoolmates because someone had the audacity to count his pimples—the clamor changes: "Liberal gun laws are killing our children! Taunting, name-calling, and bully tactics have no place in our schools! Safety locks on guns!"

What's Hot, What's Not

Anyone over the age of seven has heard volumes on drugs and drug abuse from teachers, parents, television, and other sources. Who doesn't know that heroin, morphine, and many pain-killing drugs such as Codeine, Demerol, and Percodan are the true narcotics? Who doesn't know that cocaine is derived from coca plants in South America? But what about other facts that are seldom if ever mentioned, such as the drugs that have never made the African-American drug-of-choice list. Below is a list of such drugs, and possible reasons why most African-American drug users consider them *non grata:*

Gasoline, Paint, Lacquer, and Glue: This is the drug of choice for many young Carl Casians who apparently don't mind looking high and smelling like premium unleaded at the same time. Sniffing, or huffing, these chemicals can cause severe brain damage and sudden death. Even before gasoline prices skyrocketed, African-Americans generally steered clear of sniffing.

Designer Drugs: Primarily a drug named Ecstasy, which has hallucinogenic and amphetamine-like properties. Rapidly becoming the drug of choice for high schoolers. Can raise body temperature and induce overheating. Many users claim the drug enhances orgasms, which may be the reason why many African-Americans avoid it. After all, if it ain't broke why try to get a refund for it.

Methamphetamine: Also known as crystal meth, a stimulant, which can be manufactured with a few store-bought ingredients. The high is similar to cocaine but lasts longer. African-Americans hold a dim view of make-it-yourself-at-home drugs, and a dimmer view of make-it-yourself-at-home drugs associated with mobile-home dwelling Carl Casians.

LSD: Lysergic acid diethylamide, a hallucinogen, popular in the '60s. Extremely potent and causes severe, unpredictable side effects, including bizarre hallucinations. This is one drug African-Americans run from, citing, in one Brother's words, "A dislike for seeing shit that ain't there."

Anabolic Steroids: A synthetic form of the male hormone testosterone. Primarily used by bodybuilders and athletes to increase power and endurance. Can cause breasts to grow and genitals to shrink in healthy men. No further explanation needed.

An ASS

"Peer pressure" is a pussy compound noun. No one likes to think he was pressured into doing anything, let alone pressured by peers. The term evokes memories of early childhood warnings: "If Billie Blisters sticks a needle in his arm, will you stick a needle in your arm, too?" Nonetheless this is exactly why roughly ninety to ninety-five percent of first-time drug users try drugs. Someone offers, someone accepts. An Act of Simple

Seduction, or ASS for short. Facts: (1) Physically forcing someone to take drugs against his or her will rarely happens and is an act of torture, not seduction. (2) An infinitesimally small number of first-time drug users suddenly decide to try drugs all on their lonesome.

Friends, associates, acquaintances, whatever, proffer drugs for many reasons, not one of them good. Here are the top three reasons:

"I'm expecting greater later." This is seldom stated but often implied. With hardcore drugs this is almost always the case. The first time is usually the last time many people are offered drugs freely; another rare occasion for free drugs is completion of a drug rehabilitation program. The Giver-of-free-drugs knows if you get hooked you will soon buy your own supply and feel obligated to share. After all, he turned you on.

"Really tastes great!" This is the Giver-of-free-drugs who has yet to experience drug-related problems and honestly believes that drugs are great, groovy, a trip, a blast, and other goofy terms for drug euphoria.

"I'm fucked up, you're fucked up." You would think that this Giver-of-free-drugs would be easy to detect, but he's not. This person has evil intentions; he knows the consequences of drug use because he's currently experiencing drug-related problems. He's hurting and the only answer to his hurt—he thinks—is to hurt someone else.

Any Giver-of-free-drugs knows that a would-be drug user has reservations about trying drugs that he has been told again and again were dangerous and addictive. So a negative must be turned into a positive. By example, the Giver-of-free-drugs says, "Hey, look at me! I've been doing drugs for years, and I'm just fine." Coercion and threats will not work. Usually drugs are offered without a single word spoken. If you don't take it the first time, there's always the next time. Why else are you hanging around? The more people indulging, the greater the temptation. Which segues to the top three reasons why people accept drugs.

"Get in where you fit in." No one likes to be the odd man out. If the majority of the crowd you run with gets high, it's only a matter of time until you will too. If not, why in the hell are you running around with them? Remember crowd contagion: committing acts within a group that you wouldn't do on your own. On the other hand, your self-esteem is so low, the thin space between a slug's underbelly and the ground, that you wouldn't dare hurt somebody's feelings by saying no to drugs.

"Hear this!" Many people who are in pain lack the ability to express their pain in normal mediums, such as a letter, a phone call, or straightforward conversation. So to let the world know, or someone specific know, they act out in ways sure to draw attention, such as doing drugs—another example of attempting to solve a problem with a problem. Here, the accepting of drugs is a plaintive cry for help, but is as effective as calling a plumber to respond to a heart attack victim.

"If you can do it, I can do it!" If Billy Blisters can stick a needle in his arm and live to talk about it, he who has big balls but no brains can do it too. This is almost always a case of blind hero worship. One moron looks up to another moron because of a plethora of infantile reasons—sports, cars, women, money, clothes, etc.

An ASS takes two, one to penetrate, and one to bend over and accept. If you say no to a friend who offers drugs, guess what? Nothing! Absolutely nothing. What could happen? A cold stare? So-and-so might not play with you anymore? This sounds childish, doesn't it? But daily, Brothers acquiesce to drugs for the above reasons and many other silly-assed ones. If a friend doesn't let a friend drive drunk, what the hell is a friend who offers drugs? Remember this: Problems, no matter how severe or how overwhelming they may seem, have a shelf life.

Nothing comes free. Look for the ulterior motive in the offer of free anything. Ask yourself, is this something that will make me a better person, or worse? Is this something I would like my parents, my kids, my grandkids to see me doing? Is this something I could list favorably on my resumé? Is this something I can proudly say I do?

Marijuana

The trip here is, an overwhelming number of people, young and old, have tried marijuana, including the guy who lied about inhaling. So, to tell someone marijuana is harmful...well, that smoke won't float, will it? Okay. Let's take a look at marijuana's good points:

> The high is usually mild and pleasant, often producing the giggles or a good mood.
>
> Doesn't induce an addiction, thus eliminating the desire to steal, rob, cheat, and murder to support habit.
>
> Slows time to a standstill.
>
> Enhances the quality of music.
>
> Cheaper than other drugs.
>
> Promotes deeper thinking.
>
> Stimulates an appetite in individuals wasting from illnesses, including AIDS.
>
> Has no physical side effects.

With this many benefits, you can't help but wonder why marijuana isn't legal. But hold on. Let's take a look at marijuana's bad points:

The high intensifies the present mood. Happy becomes happier. Sad becomes sadder.

Doesn't induce addiction, but long-term use can produce a psychological dependency, which produces an I-prefer-to-live-with-Mom-and-Dad-until-they-die effect. Short-term memory adversely affected.

He who's over forty and still lives with Mom and Dad prefers that time slows down a bit.

Music ten years or older has a unique sound quality of its own.

Elmer's Glue and regular unleaded gas are also cheap ways to get high.

Promotes deeper thinking, but promotes deeper thinking about BS, such as the complicated process to manufacture perforated toilet tissue.

Causes voracious appetites in many can't-live-without-Mom-and-Dad types who refuse to help pay for food.

Red eyes can be cured with eye drops, but a marijuana scent permeates clothes and is easily detected.

The above applies to everyone who smokes marijuana. But again, the African-American male pays a bigger price where drugs are concerned—not only with the police, but in the job market.

Therefore, the African-American male cannot afford the luxuries of a cheap marijuana high. If you're in school, high school, college, or planning to go to school, marijuana use will disrupt your ability to concentrate, thus jeopardize your ability to excel in your studies and graduate. If you're currently employed, planning to move up the company ladder, and still smoking marijuana, a random drug test, or a newly initiated drug-testing program, or an accident on the job, which usually calls for a drug test, can cost you your job.

Remember: Marijuana can linger in the body for weeks, even longer in hair follicles, and no quack remedy—vinegar, Golden Seal, cranberry juice—can eliminate it from the body—only time can do that. On the other hand, if you enjoy washing dishes, mopping floors, or performing chores for the nouveau riche with a big, wide grin on your face, with no concern for a pay raise, then roll up another fatty, take a big hit, and let the good times roll.

Pharmaceuticals

When you think pill-popper, or prescription addict, Elvis usually comes to mind. Allegedly, the king popped enough uppers and downers to keep one half of a herd of elephants asleep for months and the other half dancing on their toes for weeks at a time.

Notice when a beloved celebrity pops one million pills too many, the public looks elsewhere for a culprit: "If not for that quack prescribing all those pills, he'd be alive today!" Whatever, but who is pushing up daisies, the doctor who prescribed the pills or the fat boy who took them?

Regardless of your situation—living with a drug addict, in love with a drug addict, living in a drug-infested neighborhood—your deciding to do or not to do drugs is your personal responsibility. Yes, your situation may be conducive to drug use, but there may not be enough room on your tombstone to explain all that.

Drug addicts are in constant pain—from guilt, depression, and resentments. To alleviate this pain, the addict takes more drugs, which exacerbates and compounds the pain, which calls for more drugs. A vicious and often deadly circle.

Americans in general possess an utter fascination with drugs. Pain (minor or major), diseases, anxiety, stress, depression—many believe these can easily be alleviated or cured with some kind of a drug. No doubt many wonder drugs, like penicillin, have saved the lives of millions, and many other drugs have enormous psychological and physiological benefits. But do you really need a drug each time your head hurts or each time you experience gastric indigestion? No, you do not. Imagine how hard it is for kids to grasp the concept of "drugs are bad but the countless drugs grownups take are good." The following is a video-recorded conversation with a father, Mario Cooper, and his six-year-old daughter, Kimberly Cooper.

> MARIO: Now, Kim, tell me, what would you do if someone offers you drugs?
> KIMBERLY: I'd say, "No, I don't do drugs."
> MARIO: Good girl! And you would come home and tell me or your mother, right?
> KIMBERLY: Yeah.
> MARIO: Good girl.
> KIMBERLY *(puts finger in her mouth)*: Daddy…is cigarettes a drug?
> MARIO: Sort of…well, yes.
> KIMBERLY: Then why you smoke 'em?
> MARIO: Because…because—tell you what, you just let Daddy worry about cigarettes, and don't you ever try them.
> KIMBERLY: How come, Daddy?
> MARIO *(laughing)*: Cause I'll whoop your butt, and cigarettes will stunt your growth and give you cancer.
> KIMBERLY: Cancer can kill you, can it, Daddy?
> MARIO: Yes.
> KIMBERLY: Then how come you smoke 'em, Daddy?
> *Mario sighs.*

> KIMBERLY: Cigarettes can kill you, Daddy, you just said that?
> MARIO: I did, and they can, but that's not what we're talking—
> KIMBERLY: Then how come you smoke 'em, Daddy?
> MARIO *(angry expression)*: 'Cause I'm grown!
> KIMBERLY: When you're grown you can do stuff that'll kill you?
> MARIO: You ask too many damn questions, did you know that? (walks out of the room)

Mario did what many people do when forced to look at their own personal behavior: get angry and exit the scene. Cigarettes, as you already know, kill thousands each year. But many smokers classify cigarettes as an extremely low DEF (Dying Extremely Fast) risk. Rationalization is the heartbeat of all drug addictions, though with prescription drug addicts this heartbeat is almost always tachyarrhythmic.

One of the reasons why prescription drug addicts find it so easy to rationalize their drug use is the fact that opprobrium to prescription drug use is practically non-existent, especially in the African-American community. Of course, you would prefer Bennie Barbiturates, Vinny Valium, and Dennie Demerol to live next door to you than Christopher Crackhead. But Vinnie, Bennie, and Dennie can be just as pernicious as Christopher, and all four have an equally high DEF risk.

Vinnie, Bennie, and Dennie, however, have a lower chance of rehabilitation than Christopher, who runs the risk with each drug buy of being caught, jailed, and sent to drug rehab. The pill-popping trio avoids jail by obtaining their drugs from sympathetic hacks who claim that "you can't judge someone else's pain and suffering." Maybe so, but it is rather obvious when someone has crossed the threshold into prescription addiction, especially to someone who has witnessed a loved one waste away and then die because of it. All drug addictions, including alcohol, point in one direction: downward, about six feet deep. Alcohol affords a longer fall, but even that can be sped up with a combo of other drugs. With prescription drugs and other hardcore drugs the header to the six-foot hole is about the same rate of speed—fast. Whether sedatives—Valium, Xanax, Librium, clonazepem—or painkillers—Demerol, Talwin, Darvon, Dilaudid—the moment you start to depend on them for anything other than the reason prescribed is the moment you have stepped into prescription addiction.

With most prescript addicts, the substantive need for the drug blends in with the imaginary need for the drug, which makes it just that much harder to kick a prescription addiction. Often, friends and family members see through the haze, and therefore should not hesitate to voice their concerns. Until the addict accepts the fact that he has an addiction, the condition cannot be treated—and, untreated, his addiction will likely kill him.

If you think you can survive the pain or the stress or the anxiety without medication, then by all means do so. You know your body better than anyone else does, and therefore you and only you should decide what goes in it. Note of caution: By no means should you endure pain needlessly; use sound judgment.

Many people do not ask their doctor questions, thinking they might appear obtuse in the eyes of a professional. You don't have to go to a family planning clinic to know that some doctors are in the profession primarily for money. So ask questions. If you don't like the answers, get another opinion. And don't just follow the prescription to the letter, but also find out exactly what you're taking. The Internet, or a PDR (Physician Desk Reference), which can be obtained at any library, can provide you with needed info.

Cocaine

Save for alcohol, no other drug has destroyed the lives of thousands upon thousands of African-Americans. But by comparison, alcohol doesn't have shit on cocaine. Unlike cocaine, alcohol will at least talk kindly to you as it walks you to the grave, and will often take the long road to get there. Cocaine, however, will scream, "You ain't shit! Your family ain't shit! Your friends ain't shit! Your kids ain't shit!" as it hurries you to the grave—and it takes the shortcut! This is true whether you smoke it, eat it, snort it, drink it, inject it, or go the suppository route.

Rather harsh, isn't it? But what drug other than cocaine have you seen that turns able-bodied, intelligent, civic-minded, law-abiding, young African-American men into crippled, brain-dead, nefarious First-class A-Holes in the span of a few short weeks? What drug other than cocaine have you seen that turns beautiful, intelligent, aspiring young African-American women into ugly, bug-eyed, puerile prostitutes? If the shoe fits, you might as well put the other one on.

The abject condemnation toward crackheads (a term that encapsulates all cocaine addicts) within the African-American community has weakened tremendously. Perhaps the emaciated, ghost-like figures— and their constant begging and willingness to steal from family and friends—have faded into the immoral background many have grown accustomed to seeing. After all, this problem has been going on for some time now. Many a mother, a father, a spouse, a child have pleaded, begged, and prayed for the family member they once knew to finally come clean, but to no avail.

So what do you do when someone you love continues to practically kill himself? You never stop letting them know: *"If you don't get help now, you will die!"*

Because no matter how hard they pretend to ignore you, how often they walk away, how imperviously they react to your words, they do feel you.

Cocaine addiction hurts—all the time, high or sober. A tremendous amount of guilt accompanies a cocaine addiction, which often leads to an overwhelming sense of depression. And the sad fact is, tragedy is the one thing that animates most crackheads toward recovery. Therefore indifference or a glib "Gee, Harold, you're down to three rocks a day—not bad!" does the crackhead little good. Constructive condemnation sparks guilt, anger, and indignation, which occasionally sparks introspection, which occasionally sparks a desire to change.

Cocaine Politics

What better rallying cry for an African-American leader than the drug problem within African-American communities? Not since the days of segregation has one issue robbed the soul and spirit of so many young African-Americans. Perhaps a young African-American leader will rise from the smoke of political affiliations and outdated'60s mentality and motivate young African-Americans to strive to achieve their maximum potential. (Irrespective of what you may think about Reverend Louis Farrakhan and the Nation of Islam, their religious doctrines and teachings have motivated and helped many a young African-American man to recover from drug and alcohol addiction.) For every young African-American hooked on drugs and heading toward an inevitable fall, a future, a family, a neighborhood, a people follow right behind him.

This fact shoots high over the crackhead's head; he

believes that it's his life to mess up and no one else is affected by his decision. Actually this would be a good thing if it were true.

Remember, shortly after crack hit the streets it was suddenly a black drug. It was, as reported by eggheads of various yolks, the most potent form of cocaine, which, naturally, demanded stiffer prison sentences. However, if you were to ask any crackhead from Seattle, Washington, to Miami, Florida, just how potent crack is, the answer would be the same: *"It varies!"* Think about it: How can a gram of powder cocaine be made more potent by adding baking powder or whathaveyou and cooking it?

Yet this logic has sent thousands of African-Americans to prison for inordinate long periods of time—while the talks continue about disparate drugs sentencing guidelines for African-American. This strongly suggests that if African-Americans showed an interest in crystal meth, a homemade facsimile of cocaine preferred by Carl Casians, suddenly it too would become a black drug, thus demanding stiffer prison sentences.

On the other hand, you can't ignore the pleas of many African-Americans who have complained that their neighborhoods have been ruined by drugs, and who have demanded stiffer jail sentences for those who indulge in buying and selling drugs. Therein lies the paradox.

The laws concerning so-called black drugs are unfair, biased, slanted, and prejudicial. But—and here's the catch—the law is the law. This makes it difficult to argue a passionate plea for someone who has willingly broken the law. "Yes, Your Honor, my client consciously committed the crime, but he deserves the same punishment as his Carl Casian counterpart," lacks a certain forcefulness to it, doesn't it? Any Brother sitting in prison because of a drug-related conviction knows that his knowledge of the unfairness of it all doesn't mean didley squat. Everyone—the President (and the President before him), the Vice President, Congress, the Supreme Court, federal judges, and local judges—knows the laws are unfair. So what? Nothing has changed. So in whose best interest is it not to run afoul of these laws? No, scratch that—In whose best interest is it to avoid anything that looks like cocaine or any other illicit drug?

The Making of a Crackhead

Contrary to popular belief, the first hit of cocaine, in any form, rarely hooks anyone. Good: Because there would be a thousand times more crackheads than there are already. Bad: Because many people are deceitfully lulled into trying cocaine again, thinking: "It doesn't faze me. I can handle it." Most people's first hit of cocaine is their last: mainly because an irregular heartbeat or a ten times faster than normal heartbeat, and, occasionally, because the first hit kills. Remember: Sudden death can happen anytime—the first hit or the millionth hit.

Amazingly, not everyone who continuously uses cocaine develops an addiction. No one fully understands why. But don't be fooled into thinking you are one in this crowd. A key distinction between quasi-crackheads and bona fide crackheads is that quasi-crackheads seldom buy cocaine or feel overwhelmingly compelled to go get some more. Which begs the question: Why do it at all, then?

Whether the first hit or the millionth hit, the moment the user hears bells or whistles, feels a tingling situation or any other earth-shattering physical sensation, feels one with the universe or anything else, experiences an epiphany or a revelation, he or she is hooked. This very first enlightening experience is what the crackhead will relentlessly seek to duplicate, at his own peril. This is akin to trying to relive losing your virginity. It cannot be done. But the powerful psychological addictive properties of cocaine tell the user he can relive the first experience again and again and again...And this is where it starts going downhill. The average cocaine high lasts an average of five to twenty minutes, sometimes more, most times less. However, the plunge downward is a lot more traumatic, long-lasting, and earth-shattering than the high. In street parlance, this is called "geeking," "Joneses," "beaming," and "fiending." In this stage the desire to do more cocaine takes on a life-or-death intensity. This is the stage that fuels desperate acts—baby selling, prostitution, theft, armed robbery, and murder.

In this stage of compulsive obsession, the crackhead's eyes are bucked wide, sweat drips down his face. His speech is slurred. He cannot sit still. His head swivels about, searching for something only he knows what.

This is what many mothers see after playing keep-money-for-me with a crackhead. At 3:00 in the morning, the crackhead shows up at his mother's house, where hours before, when he was sober, he told his mother to keep his money because he was afraid he might spend it. At this point, any doubts his mother may have been entertaining about him not being a crackhead are vanquished. There he stands...eyes bucked...pupils dilated...his head oscillating like a fan...sweating profusely...And he wants his money back. Now! The tone of his voice tells his mother that he will not accept "no" as an answer, so she—scared to death of her own son—quickly goes and gets the money.

Shortly after becoming hooked, the crackhead

undergoes a major physical and psychological transformation. His weight drops precipitously, his posterior the first to go, which is why you can easily detect most crackheads by their no-ass-at-all look.

If before crack he was gregarious and talkative, now he's taciturn and withdrawn. If before crack he was fastidious about his clothing, now he's sloppy and wrinkled. If before crack he worked hard and was punctual, now he's slothful and unreliable. If before crack he was honest to a fault, now he lies every time he opens his mouth. If before crack he refused assistance and never borrowed, now he begs relentlessly. If before crack he paid his bills diligently, now he shirks financial responsibility. Eventually he will either pawn or sell all that he has.

Not all crackheads steal; most do, but not all. This depends on a person's moral temperament before addiction, and it had to have been a strong one.

Depending on the quality of cocaine and how much he consumes, he may experience cocaine psychosis, a self-induced mental impairment that mimics paranoid schizophrenia. In short, he's flipped his lid. (To reverse cocaine psychosis, simply stop using cocaine.) When his wife or girlfriend sees him peeking out the window with a loaded gun in his hand, or searching under beds and couches for phantom guests, or combing the carpet for imaginary crack crumbs—with a sweaty I-just-saw-an-alien look on his face—she might leave him.

If she stays, she'll have to accept the fact that she has lost her man but has gained a baby, albeit a crack-smoking, "I-just-saw-an-alien" baby. She must assume the role of his guardian, and she will have to keep certain objects from within his reach, such as her purse, her friends' purses, money, TVs, VCRs, stereo sets, and anything else that can be sold on the street for less than a fifth its original price. Of course, when an item disappears, like a child with chocolate on his face, he knows nothing about it.

If she's smart she will insist he use a condom during sex (more on this later). If he has kids, he will practically forget they exist. And this is the saddest aspect of cocaine addiction: Family is the first to get overlooked and the first to get fucked over.

Cocaine demands attention. *Now!* Not tomorrow or next week, but *now!* Like a drill instructor, cocaine insists that action be conducted at breakneck speed. *Don't walk—run! Don't sleep—move! Forget the kids—go! Hurry up! Now! No time to eat! Go! Now! Now! Now!...*

Any argument, cocaine wins. Any moral conflict, cocaine wins. For example:

> "I can't do that. I can't go in there and take her money—she's planning to buy the kids Easter baskets. I—"
>
> COCAINE: "Now! Do it now!"
>
> "I can't do her like that...I just can't!"
>
> COCAINE: "Now!"
>
> "She'll be pissed."
>
> COCAINE: "Now!"
>
> "If I take some of it, I might as well take it all...same difference."
>
> COCAINE: "Now!"
>
> "Maybe she won't miss it. Maybe she won't miss it till next week sometime, and by then I'll replace it. Yeah..."
>
> COCAINE: "Now!"

Even when he is sober, cocaine hovers over him like a cloud, in the form of depression. Guilt hails down on him, resentment rains down on him, frustration sleets down on him, self-hatred strikes him, and suicidal thoughts envelop him in a gloomy, ominous fog. Still, cocaine thunders: *Now!*

At this point, whether or not he is employed or unemployed is insignificant: All his money, right down to the last nickel, goes to cocaine. Factually, he is homeless. This concept confuses most crackheads. Suffer no delusions about it: If you can physically work but refuse to do so, or if you do work but refuse to pay rent, buy groceries and personal effects, such as tissue, soap, or cigarettes, then you are homeless. You can easily tell how long a crackhead has been cracking by how big a celebration his family throws when he buys a pair of pants or a shirt, or when he actually chips in on his own living expenses.

Fact: Extracting a crackhead from a home is ten times harder than do-it-yourself hemorrhoid removal.

Below are the four cards that crackheads play to avoid joining the ranks of thousands of living-on-the-streets drunks and drug addicts.

The Mel Reynolds Card: Simply go ballistic. Go nuclear. Go spastic. This scares the hell out of most people, especially Momma. The key to this card is acting indignantly outraged so convincingly that the person who told you to "get your shit and get out" thinks that it will be safer to let you stay a few more days.

The Ken Griffey Jr. Card: By far this card is the favorite among drug addicts and drunks throughout. The key here: Make promises, but fail to deliver. "I'll be moving out next week." "I'll give you something on the water bill when I get paid Friday." "Next month I'm going into rehab."

Anna Nicole Smith Card: Feign preternatural affection. A family member isn't simply a family member, but he's your family member, and you love him or her to death and will gladly sacrifice your life for him or her.

This card looks similar to skinning and grinning; however, to the crackhead and drunk there is more at stake—heat in the winter, air in the summer, and all the free food he can eat.

The Slick Willie Card: Deny! Deny! Deny! Regardless of how overwhelmingly the evidence points to your wrongdoing, deny it. Of course, in the case of DNA evidence, photographs, and tapes, you immediately act contrite but deftly gloss over what you're acting contrite about. For example, your significant other finds a crack pipe with your initials on it in the washer and confronts you with it. Point your finger at her and vehemently and indignantly deny the accusation. Later, when she plays a videotape of you with crack pipe in mouth, show remorse, then blame the Coast Guard for allowing cocaine to enter country.

Enabling the crackhead kills the crackhead. Yes, it hurts to send him out on the streets, but it hurts even more to have him sitting around shitting his life away. On the streets his KISS probability rate will increase ten percent or more, but his chances of getting sick and tired of being sick and tired of the life he's living and finally doing something about it will increase twenty percent or more.

Coming Clean

Unlike many other drugs, including alcohol, cocaine does not impose a physical dependency. Yet cocaine's puissant psychological addictive nature does more than make up for that, which is why a cocaine habit is so hard to kick. Cocaine calls people by their first name and shouts: "Now!" So the key to quitting cocaine is tuning out the voice, or ignoring it altogether. Crackheads, like many drunks, cannot afford to simply admit they have a problem without doing anything about it. Many drunks, however, have disciplined themselves into being problem drinkers; but to anyone who has ever had a problem with cocaine addiction, reducing cocaine consumption is not an option but a deadly mind-fuck game. Another risk: cross-addiction. This happens when a crackhead simply trades one addiction for another, cocaine for alcohol, or cocaine for painkillers. This has the same effect as trading an aneurysm for lung cancer. Quitting cocaine is a twenty-four-hour war, so you must prepare to battle it as if your life depended on it, which it does. The following is a war plan that will work if assiduously followed.

1. **Assess your enemy.** He's stronger than you, more powerful than you, more cunning than you, and more manipulating than you will ever be. Admit it, he's beaten you down. But no more!

2. **Build your army.** You will need assistance to help defeat the enemy. Great allies: NA (Narcotic Anonymous); your preacher, clergy, or minister; outpatient or in-patient rehabilitation treatment centers. Don't take this lightly! You'll need a strong army.

3. **Determine where and when you are the most vulnerable—and avoid these situations like the plague.** Any place where drugs are used or sold, stay away. Paydays are extremely vulnerable times for attacks, so consider alternatives such as direct deposit accounts or allowing someone strong and trustworthy—not Momma or the old lady—to pick up your check.

4. **Get rid of spies**. Anyone, regardless if friend, family member, or lover, who uses cocaine or any other drugs should be considered a spy for the enemy. If you live with someone who uses cocaine, put''em out or move out yourself. You're battling for your life!—someone who isn't fighting with you is fighting against you.

5. **Fight one battle at a time.** You can't defeat this enemy with one fatal swoop. In an all-out war the enemy will easily defeat you. It's going to take time and many hard-fought skirmishes and battles.

6. **Never surrender.** At your weakest moments fight hardest. Make up your own battle cry—for example, "You can't beat me!" —and say it to yourself or out loud when you feel yourself starting to weaken. And even if you do lose a battle or two, never!—never!—surrender.

7. **Stay alert for landmines.** Finding cocaine and people offering free cocaine are landmines that you never encountered before going to war. Anticipate such events.

8. **Tend the wounded.** Make amends to those whom you have hurt. However, in some cases the wounds may be too painful or still festering to address, so it might be best to all concerned to let Father Time do the healing.

9. **Institute a Demilitarized Zone.** This is the place where you go to build up your strength. Participating in religious activities and volunteer activities are excellent places for a Demilitarized Zone.

Brothers who overcome drugs and alcohol problems tend to live much fuller lives. They have seen the worst of humanity from an inside view, so they are usually quick to forgive, slow to anger, and eager to help their fellow man. Throughout this book the term crackhead has been used loosely, though here the term incorporates all cocaine addicts. Yet no other word, save for the N-word, is as painful to hear. The word is ugly, nasty, demeaning. And like the N-word, crackhead is often used to inflict pain.

Which is exactly the intention here. Pain, like no other, forces people to look at their behavior. Drunks and drug addicts tend to mask pain with their addictions, but this causes more pain, which leads them to indulge even more. This deadly circle can go on and on, until one day their addiction either KISSes them or motivates them to quit.

So what do you call a Brother who has walked through hell, survived, turned his life around, and to this day serves as an inspiration to others? A man!

Chapter 7
Crime

"To a flea, a rat's ass is a good thing." H.H.

Though he is a fictitious character, this Brother's name is an epithet, a curse, an expletive, and an affront of the highest order to all African-Americans. You would think that this Brother committed some atrocious act to deserve being labeled the antithesis of anything remotely African-American. But you would be wrong. Here is what he did:

He loved his God and honored his God's word, the Bible. In the Bible, several edicts implore one to love thy neighbor *and* thy enemy, which he did. When this Brother was commanded to whip a fellow slave, a Sister, he steadfastly refused, and for doing so he was severely whipped. This one act alone puts this Brother on a higher moral plane than most people could even imagine. Later, when this Brother discovered a Sister hiding from the despotic master, he refused to tell, knowing he would be beaten to death for refusing to do so—which is exactly what happened.

Here is what this Brother didn't do: He didn't run tell Carl Casian anything, not once. He didn't skin and grin in Carl Casian's face, hoping to receive a pat on the head. He didn't sell his fellow African-Americans short for his own selfish gain.

So how in the world did this Brother's name become synonymous with an obsequious, ass-kissing, Carl-Casian-bootlicking sycophant? Who knows? Clearly the author, Harriet Beecher Stowe, intended for her character to expose the glaring inhumanities of slavery, and through this Brother, her lead character, she accomplishes her design. An ass-kissing Skinner and Grinner character would not have sparked a nation's conscious and attention to the evil practice called slavery, but an African-American martyr would and did.

Many African-Americans who have read the book see the conflict but refuse to acknowledge it; to defend this Brother's reputation one risks being called this Brother's name—and heaven forbid that!

The lie becomes the truth when the lie is more convenient and/or serves a greater purpose, and no one questions it.

A similar lie states that most, if not all, African-American males are crime-prone malcontents bursting with rage. As with the lie involving Harriet Beecher Stowe's benevolent character, this lie is readily believed because everyone says it is true, including many African-Americans. A distinguished reverend once stated to the effect that he would rather confront a group of Carl Casians than a group of young Brothers (either group, he would have run). His statement confirmed the age-old Carl Casian belief that young African-American males are predisposed to violence—*"Jeepers! If the good reverend can't trust em, his own people, what you think they'll do to us?"*

Many factors, including poverty, high unemployment, overpopulation, drugs and alcohol, predict a higher incidence of crime, but simply being young and an African-American male is not one of these factors. Yes, certain African-American neighborhoods have an extremely high crime rate, but believe it or not, not everyone in these neighborhoods is a criminal, or a budding criminal.

So how come every prison in the country is predominantly populated with African-American males? How come in almost every major city, one of every four African-American males is entwined in the judicial system—parole, prison, or probation? Excellent questions. In short, the answer: More African-American males are arrested, convicted, and sentenced to longer prison sentences than all other groups combined. This fact, combined with the media and Hollywood's stereotypical portrayals of African-American males as criminals, leads many, including many young African-American males, to believe that indeed the young African-American male is inherently prone to violent crime.

Thus the clarion for more police, tougher laws, longer prison sentences, and the death penalty. Another vicious circle. Therefore, the African-American male, the law-abiding and the criminal—especially the criminal—needs to know what he is up against.

The Police

When African-Americans are asked about the "Black Experience," the answers vary from being called the N-word by a Carl Casian to living in a bad neighborhood, to standing in line for commodity cheese, to being denied a loan at the bank. But none of these responses fully encapsulate one true encompassing experience that the majority of African-Americans have endured. Many African-Americans, especially Brothers like Cory Cockstrong, have never been called the N-word, and just as many have never stood in line for commodity cheese. So what can truly be called the "Black Experience"? Well, yes, receiving a nasty look from a Carl Casian could easily qualify as a true "Black Experience." After all, what African-American with eyesight hasn't experienced that. But that seems rather petty, doesn't it? Plus, many, if not all, African-Americans have received the same look from family members and other African-Americans. So what else? You guessed it! Dealing with the police. Whether you're a millionaire or a homeless drunk, if your ass is black, you will have not one encounter with the police but several. The average Carl Casian has never dealt with the police save for a traffic citation, so he views the police quite differently than someone who has been randomly stopped, jacked up, and treated disrespectfully. To an extent this explains the Rodney King verdict: *"Gee whiz! The police are out there risking their lives everyday!"*

One member of the jury who exonerated the policemen who delivered Rodney King a million-dollar ass whooping stated: "Rodney directed the action." Oh, yeah? With what? His nose, eyes, head? What film footage was she watching? Another mystery to that sad debacle: Did Rodney have speech problems before or after his million-dollar ass whooping? So many questions, so little answers. Yet most African-Americans know that but for the video, Rodney would have received a million-dollar ass-whooping without receiving one penny.

While politicians talk about racial profiling and unfair police practices within the African-American community, African-American males deal with these issues on a daily basis. Yes, this unfairness causes rage. However, rage does not truly exist in African-American males who are currently playing Cops-and-Robbers with the police. Rage exist in law-abiding African-American males, far more than African-American criminals, who are also caught in the nets of so-called police campaigns such as Zero Tolerance (also called Negro Intolerance) and denied their civil rights in the name of so-called wars on drugs and gangs.

Many police officials claim that though it is unfortunate that some African-Americans are unduly harassed, many African-Americans are arrested for the neighborhood's overall good. This is the same logic that justifies the killing of Iraq's children to get to Saddam Hussien.

In dealings with the police, remember one thing at all times: They have the power and the authority. The road to jail starts with the police, so what you do and say and what you don't do or say while encountering the police will play a large part in where you go and what shape you arrive in when you get there. This is of utmost importance because at any step of the way up the judicial system ladder, you may encounter a Carl Casian prosecutor, or a Carl Casian judge, or a Carl Casian parole officer who is suffering from a severe case of Negrophobia.

The following are do's and don't's in dealing with the police, starting with the don't's.

Don't:

Run. Running always creates more problems (a high risk for getting shot in the back).

Fight. You might win initially, but in the end you will certainly lose.

Volunteer information.

Sign anything without your lawyer present.

Admit guilt.

Act belligerent.

Do's:

Comply with the officer's orders, even if he or she is an A-Hole. (You can take his or her badge number and file a complaint later.)

Ask for legal counsel if arrested.

Respond courteously.

Remember the officer's name and badge number.

Do listen and follow all the guidelines to the Miranda Warnings.

The biggest mistake a Brother can make when dealing with the police is to fight or run, of course, but more often Brothers make the mistake of trying to outsmart the police by running off at the mouth. Oh, do police love when this happens! The Miranda Warnings are thrown out the window, the Brother starts blabbing, and—*Blab, Blab, Blab! Blam!*—he has talked himself into prison.

"Anything you say can and will be used against you"—now how simple is that? In other words: "Shut up!" Oddly, many Brothers interpret the explicit warning to mean blab on everyone, including family members. Such is the state of mind of the average criminal.

Let's face the facts: Many Brothers make the police's job so easy it is almost hard not to blame the police for taking advantage of easy pickings. Which is easier? Going door-to-door in Carl Casian's neighborhood and picking out the dealers, or lying in wait until the Brothers come out on the corner and deal their wares?

Cops and Robbers

Unless you have played Cops and Robbers, you cannot fully understand the dynamics of the game and the visceral thrill it affords the player. It's fun! It's exciting! It's exhilarating! And it can get you KISSed in a heartbeat! Here are the rules to the game. First, the player must develop a mindset that the police is an entity that perceives him as a unique individual whose criminal acumen is like no other they have ever seen. Second, commit a crime and get away with it. This reinforces criminal grandiosity and demonstrates the player's willingness to play the game. Third, do it again and again. Oh what fun you'll have, eluding the police, narrowly escaping, and basking in the joy of committing a crime to the best of your ability.

Sounds crazy, doesn't it? But many Brothers play this game everyday. Somehow the notion that the police see them as distinguished individuals has infected some Brother's thinking to a sickness—highly contagious in the field of drug dealing. This is the same self-importance that many gamblers attribute to themselves upon entering a casino. The casino becomes an entity that must be shown who Big Daddy is—this is not a game of chance but something personal. Well, the real news is, the casino and the police could give a damn about the individual.

Both organizations know that it is of little importance who plays the game, but of major importance how many play the game. Of course, some people win, which fosters the notion that everyone who plays can win. But far more people lose than win. And both organizations know that the more you play, the bigger the chance you will lose. In playing Cops and Robbers with the police, however, losing has more dire consequences than a week's pay.

The inveterate gambler who continuously loses all his money week after week will tell you of his gambling perspicuity, despite not having a dime in his pocket. The Cops and Robbers player will tell you of his criminal expertise from within a jail cell. Both defy logic.

The Cops and Robber game has higher odds than a rigged blackjack table. In part because Cops and Robbers usually entails an audience, and anyone in the audience can play a part in the game by simply picking up the phone and calling the police. Anyone who commits a crime implores everyone in observance to shut up and let him do his thing. In short: "Be my silent conspirator without benefit or reward." Even for petty crimes, that is a helluva lot to ask.

Plus, the Cops and Robbers game requires victims. Victims, as you know, often refuse to play silent conspirator; occasionally they demand retribution and justice. With drug dealers the victims are the entire neighborhood, the entire African-American race. Remember: You can't lose if you don't play.

Disappearing Acts

The last time you saw this Brother he was driving a new sports car with rims that exceeded the price of a certain pop star's nose job. His car had more accessories and gadgets than an electronics store. Of course, he stopped and showed you, a working stiff, his bankroll. Oh what a bankroll it was: big-head hundreds and a few big-head fifties in a knot so thick you wondered how he managed to pull it out his pocket.

This Brother was practically rolling in dough, and, as far as you know, he never worked a day in his life (unless you can consider illicit pharmaceutical sales work). Imagine, an industrious ergophobe! Though you might not admit it, you were somewhat awed by his immense success—actually, a little jealous. How could you not be? Unlike you, this Brother doesn't worry about unexpected bills, maintaining good credit, getting fired, asking the boss for a raise, and squeezing the price of a tune-up into an already over-squeezed budget. "No sir, I want be late again!" This Brother knows the secret to success.

Then he disappeared. *Poof!*—he was gone. A KISS

right smack on the lips. Whatshisface gave him up, sold state's evidence. Or whatshisface shot and killed him in a drug deal gone bad. Regardless, he's gone. In a short time his name will become a dim memory, like last year's hemorrhoid. In his wake some younger Brother, impressed by conspicuous consumption, will take his place, and the cycle will continue. This fact in itself makes it very difficult to even thinly defend drug dealers. Little do they seem to realize the impact of their actions on so many people. With the drug addict and drunk you can at least pinpoint a tangible object as the primary source of their insanity. The drug dealer, however, appears to be motivated by pure greed and self-aggrandizement, at the expense of others. Of course, it's not the drug dealer's fault that a crackhead breaks his kid's piggy bank to buy his product. It's not the drug dealer's fault that a spaced-out Sister who sells her body to buy his drugs has infected a battalion of men with the AIDS virus. Also, lest we forget, "If I didn't sell drugs, someone else would." This makes as much sense as, "If I didn't rape and kill, someone else surely would."

(The most obvious thing about all rationalization: It is structured so wobbly it cannot stand on its own; additional information, further explanation, and detailed justification must be added for support.)

Drug dealers rationalize their behavior more so than drug addicts, whom many drug dealers detest. The average drug dealer sees the drug addict as a low creature unworthy of a warm spit bath. Yet but for this creature, the drug dealer would be forced into the dreaded W-word—*work!* Other than the pre-civil-rights-era poor African-Americans who were routinely swindled and cheated by white merchants, no other customer than drug addicts have been mistreated so badly by the very people they make rich. Why? Because many drug dealers, like many of the white merchants whose customers were primarily poor African-Americans, realized at some point that "if all these creatures are in the same pool as me, then I must be one of them." This fact is too much to bear for most drug dealers, so they do what most people do when confronted with the fact that the people they despise are very much like themselves: They lash out.

The drug dealer lives in a fantasy world where he sits high above the muck; he's too smart and too clever to get himself dirty. *Those people,* the drug addicts, are not like him, they're nasty, disgraceful, and stupid. Still, though he cannot, or refuse to, see it, their world is his world. Like those whom he despises so much, the drug dealer's world grows smaller and smaller each day. Like the drug addict, the drug dealer is unwelcome in many social circles. Like the drug addict, the drug dealer maintains a constant vigil for the police. Like the drug addict, the drug dealer can be KISSed at any moment. Like the drug addict, the drug dealer cannot explain his activities on a job application. And just like the drug addict, the drug dealer has an addiction he cannot easily walk away from.

Oh yes, the drug dealer certainly has an addiction. What else would you call a self-destructive obsession? No doubt you know Brothers who have gone to jail for selling drugs only to come out and start up just where they left off. You know Brothers who have been shot or stabbed while selling drugs and are still selling. You may also know Brothers who sell drugs to their family. You may also know Brothers who enlist young children to sell drugs.

But you know that the entire business stinks!

So let's face the facts: The overwhelming majority of drug dealers are not young, bright, nascent entrepreneurs. First, illicit drugs sell intrinsically: no advertisement necessary, no sales pitch necessary, and no test-market studies necessary. Put an illicit drug vending machine out in the desert, and eventually it will attract a crowd all on its own. Second—cold but true—the majority of drug dealers are misguided Myrmidons who didn't consciously choose selling drugs over making minimum wage at Mickey D's but chose a fantasy-based endeavor simply because it looked like an easy way to make a lot of money.

The best and brightest of the African-American race do not sell poison to their own people, who are obviously sick. The best and the brightest of the African-American race see the drug business for what it is: a fool's game. Look at it...The police focus heavily on African-Americans in general, shining the spotlight brightly at all times on even innocent African-American activities—and the drug dealer, in his infinite wisdom, chooses to conduct illegal activities out in the open under this bright light. Ask yourself, how bright is that? Even in small towns across the good ole US of A, towns in which the population barely exceeds a high school game attendance, thousands of Brothers, too smart and bright for their own good, mimic the actions of their big-city cousins, forgetting the fact that the light might be smaller, but the willingness of the town folk to make a phone call is much greater. Again, how bright is that? Let's illuminate the situation even further by taking a closer look at the three types of individuals who sell drugs.

First-class A-Hole. He is one of every twenty drug dealers, and he is usually the one who moves up to the next level on the drug totem pole. The implicit rules regarding drug transactions are tailor-made to fit his personality. Arrears—injury or death. Late payment—injury or death. Snitching—injury or death. Fraud—injury or death. Attempts to defraud—injury or death. What more could a First-class A-Hole ask for?

Amazingly, for the First-class A-Hole's evil atrocities inflicted on others, he is admired and feared by other drug dealers and his drug addict customers.

Drug Addict: He is seven of every twenty drug dealers, and he is usually the one you read about in news articles describing a drug deal gone bad. These type dealers ignore a simple lifesaving caveat: Just because you don't think fat meat is greasy isn't a legitimate reason to go slide in it and bust your ass. The drug addict sells drugs to obtain his own drugs, but often during the excitement he confuses his personal stash with the For Sale stash, and that's when the drama occurs.

Wannabe KISSed: He is twelve of every twenty drug dealers, and he is the one most likely to misspell four-letter expletives. His motivation for selling drugs is to one day make a whole buncha money, then cut a few rap albums, then move next door to Dr. Dre on that island in the video where the good doctor has his yacht moored. In the meantime, though, he'll simply settle for a new pair of tennis shoes and a nice pair of FUBU slacks.

Of all three types of drug dealers only one in a hundred lives the drug dealer lifestyle as portrayed on television and in the movies. The drug dealers who do reach this level are highly distinguishable, not only in their toys but their intellect and budgeting skills. However, they, too, like their drug dealing cronies who can't spell GED, will eventually get KISSed. Considering the fact that most drug dealers would actually make the same amount of money working a minimum wage job, it is obvious that money is not the main attraction to becoming a drug dealer.

So what is? The need to be somebody. Everybody wants to be somebody, but only a nobody would attempt to be a somebody by hurting everybody—which is exactly what a drug dealer does. Some drug dealers actually believe the rainbow-in-the-sky lie. Name one drug dealer—one!—who has made it to the top by selling drugs? Don't mention some ex-dealer who is currently rapping; he doesn't count because the ability to sell drugs is not a criteria to becoming a rap star. And don't mention the guy you know who is currently living a millionaire's lifestyle. He, too—and you can write this down—will eventually get KISSed.

Now name the Brothers who you know are graveyard dead due to drug dealing? Name the Brothers who you know are currently serving long prison sentences due to drug dealing? Finally, name the Brothers whom you know are confined to wheelchairs, or who are paraplegics or quadriplegics due to selling drugs? Notice the difference? A big difference!

A street dealer is at the very bottom of the drug-dealing totem pole. Looking at this totem pole you can't help but notice that the faces near the top and the top face are something other than African-American. Theses are the Big Boys, the boys who bring the drugs over from Peru and Colombia and other countries, and the boys who garner less attention by the authorities. Very few African-Americans have gone to one of these countries and transacted a major drug deal, and very few African-Americans have flown or shipped a cargo of drugs from these countries' shores (Jamaicans are not African-Americans). Why? Because the true drug lords do not deal directly with African-Americans. Now, who is pimping who?

Drugs addicts and drugs dealers place a heavy burden on all African-Americans, and provide the police with a preposterous pretext to harass and treat all African-Americans as criminals. The fact that the majority of young African-American men do not use drugs or sell drugs apparently is of little importance. Still, we are our Brothers' keepers, aware of the fact that what affects one of us affects all of us. Therefore, the African-

American male who doesn't use or sell drugs cannot condone the practices of the African-American male who does. Ignoring, overlooking, and excusing are ways of condoning drug dealing.

Of course, as you're probably thinking, you can get KISSed poking your nose in some stranger's business. Yes, but what about your baby brother, your nephew, your friend, or the young Brother who used to look up to you before he got into the game? Would these Brothers think less of you if you frowned on their drug activities? You would be surprised how a simple "Brother, there's got to be another way" will cause some Brothers to take another look at what they are doing. Of course, many will pretend they don't hear you, or get angry, but they hear you—you better believe they hear you. Use caution. Never berate a Brother, and be sincere in what you're saying—which means if you're drunk or high your words are meaningless. Always wait till you and the Brother are alone before saying what you have to say. If need be, try other options to get the Brother's attention, such as a letter, or a postcard, but never go the indirect route by saying to others what you meant for someone else.

When an immediate family member is a drug dealer, your obligation to inform him of the error of his ways is tenfold. Comic tragedy occurs when family members ignore Junior's drug dealings but *ooh* and *aah* at his car, clothes, and expensive toys—and then act shocked when Junior is KISSed.

When they were borrowing tens and twenties from Junior, who they knew didn't have a job or any source of legitimate income to justify the means, not one of them thought: "Gee, Junior might get KISSed from doing this."

A young Brother in his teens and early twenties cannot contemplate time in centuries, which are what many

Brothers are being sentenced for dealing drugs these days. When the judge says, "Thirty to fourty years in the Department of Corrections," and bangs his gavel, its over. O-V-E-R! Freedom—Gone! Wife or girlfriend—Gone! Money—Gone! Car—Gone! Designer clothes and jewelry—Gone!

(It's a wonder why so many people facing a long prison stretch bend over backwards to avoid facing the camera; this is probably their last chance to be seen by family and friends for a very long time; so why not make the best of it and smile and say hello to as many people as possible.)

Sell drugs, and eventually you will be Killed, Incarcerated, Shot, or Stabbed—KISSed. It's only a matter of time. Think about it, 99.9 percent of the people you know who sold drugs were what? KISSed, with a capital K. So what was it that you told yourself that made you different than the majority? Your looks? Your smarts? Okay. Write your reasoning down on some paper and put it up somewhere. Then, when your next drug-related crisis occurs, take out the paper and read your reasons out loud. You be the judge.

Gangs

Before the movie Colors, gangs were primarily a big-city problem. Shortly after the movie, gangs were popping up in small towns such as Greenville, Mississippi, and Conway, Arkansas. According to the news media, gangs were a bigger problem than Saddam Hussein's chemical and biological weapons. Millions of young African-American men were reportedly in some gang or other. *Millions?* Gang hysteria spread across the country like wildfire. Gangs were reported to possess surface-to-air missiles and nuclear warheads. The American public bought it all, which prompted many police officials to institute various Negrophobic anti-gang campaigns.

During this time many law-abiding African-Americans realized that what they considered a gang contrasted dramatically to what their local police considered a gang. Oddly, law-abiding African-Americans considered Brothers who wore similar clothing and exchanged esoteric hand signals and openly admitted gang affiliation a gang. The police, however, had a much broader view: every young African-American male who could breathe in and out constituted a gang; two or more young African-American males together constituted a marauding mob.

Thus, every young African-American death, whether a fall out of a tree or a drive-by shooting, was labeled gang-related, or the old standby, drug-related—which implied that the police were not going to interrupt a good cup of coffee and a fresh donut to figure out who did it.

And as with so many other flagrant African-American propaganda ploys to promulgate African-American savagery and lawlessness, many young African-Americans, unaware of their contributions to such ploys, signed their names on the dotted line and became honorary gang members. A few older African-American men suddenly realized that they were OG's (original gangsters) despite never receiving so much as a jaywalking ticket. (One more thing about old geezers, er, original gangsters: Nothing besides copious consumption of dairy products causes diarrhea quicker than the sight of a Brother well past his forties emulating the dress and habits of young men in their early teens and twenties—in other words, if you're over forty, tuck your shorts inside your pants, buckle up, and get somewhere and sit down!)

To tell the truth, many who signed up to be gang members were assholes—not A-Holes but assholes. And that's putting it politely. What else can you call someone who would shoot a child simply because the color clothing the child wore conflicted gang colors. What else would you call someone who would shoot inside a house not caring who was shot or killed? Again, only a nobody would hurt everybody to become somebody.

Listen to their words: "My gang members show me more love than my real family." Lord O mercy! Who were their parents? Colin Ferguson and Susan Smith?

A small percentage of gang members, undoubtedly aware of the fatuity of gangs, implied that the only reason they were in gangs because they had no other choice, as if the gang dragged them kicking and screaming out of their house. To further this fallacy a news reporter sought and found the one Brother who was dragged screaming and kicking into gang membership. Think about it, what kind of a gang would tolerate a reluctant member standing alone in the corner moaning and groaning about wanting to go home?

And then the gang commotion fizzled, almost as quickly as it sparked. But contrary to what many politicians and police officials stated, gang affiliation didn't fizzle because of more police on the streets and tougher gang laws. The spark fizzled because many Brothers started to see what gang affiliation was all about: Bullshit.

The average organized or unorganized gang is run like an autocracy, meaning one individual, usually a First-class A-Hole, runs the whole show. What he says goes. The needs and the concerns of his charges are irrelevant, unless, of course, their needs and concerns coincide with his. Money problems, children problems, wife problems, girlfriend problems, and personal problems are never considered gang problems—even if you go to jail. Sure, you can always discuss them openly, at length if you desire, but the gang rarely feels obligated to assist you with your problems—in other words, "We love you, but your problems are not our problem."

To keep the gang intact and refocus the attention of those members who desire to lead, the gang leader must direct his charges to an enemy, real or imaginary. As long as his charges are hating so-and-so, usually a rival gang, they are not thinking: "What the hell am I doing here?" This is why the mentally impaired and the low self-esteemed make great gang members; they rarely ask questions and are easily emotionally charged to hate and hurt whomever a gang leader tell them to hate and hurt. The same dynamics apply to skinheads and other hate groups, of which the brain-dead, the ugly and facial-scarred, the coward and chicken-livered gravitate to.

Gangs blanketed all young African-Americans as thugs bent on destruction and mayhem, though the majority of young African-Americans never once considered joining a gang. If the two main gangs, the Crips and the Bloods, had not required that new entrants suffer a group ass-kicking to join up, perhaps the membership would have been greater. Another sticking point to those Brothers who could add two problems together and arrive at a quadruple prison sentence: mandatory participation in drive-bys (not to mention the tacky business of wearing the same colors day after day). Many Brothers who joined a gang and ultimately went to prison know how to add quite well now: "Time in prison plus the gang's apathy to my family while I'm in prison adds up to me standing on my two feet while I'm free."

Guns

To let many Carl Casians tell it, slavery had little to do with the Civil War. According to them, the Civil War was about tariffs, states' rights, and the price of eggs in Calcutta. You can only scratch your head and wonder how in the hell did they reach that conclusion? What they lack in fact they more than make up in passion. Let's set the record straight. In the numerous letters written by rebel soldiers and all of Robert E. Lee's correspondence to his family and Jefferson Davis, there are scant references about tariffs, states' rights, and the price of eggs in Calcutta, but a polyglot of references to slavery. Reading many of these missives, you cannot help but think that the rebel soldiers were being carpetbagged. Most were poor, unable to afford a single slave, but through their letters they expressed a dreaded fear to the end of slavery, and an even more dreaded fear that the Negro, as called then, if allowed freedom would ravish their white women in the manner in which a good number of them had ravished African-American women.

Now what demagogue planted that in their heads? Hmmm…What about those rich farmers who owned many slaves and had a vested interest in the continuation of slavery, or free labor?

Directive: If your forefathers were pimped, it's always a good idea to steer the subject to less painful subjects, such as the price of eggs in Calcutta.

A good percentage of those who believe that slavery had absolutely nothing to do with the Civil War actually believe that African-Americans with the assistance of the federal government will one day attempt to forcibly conscript the White man into slavery, or some other foolishness.

Yes, this does sound crazy, but it's true. Did you

really think Carl Casian was crying and sniveling about his second amendment rights because he feared losing his hunting license?

An even greater number of Carl Casians purchase guns in the hope and fear that a person of color will one day break into their home and give them the opportunity to use their high-powered rifle on something other than empty Coors cans. Let's set the record straight one more time: African-Americans are not fractionally as fanatical about guns and gun ownership as their Carl Casian counterparts. African-Americans disproportionately shoot other African-Americans, but African-Americans rarely stockpile guns; one is enough for most. And as far as a race war is concerned—forget it!—African-Americans understand the minority concept and know who has been planning and preparing for such an event for a very long time.

Perchance your state has a Right to Carry law—now what majority do you think garners the majority of licenses to benefit from such a law? In states with this law, Carl Casain can transfer his Negrophobic paranoia from his house to anywhere he goes. Why wait for a darkie to break into your home when you can walk the streets with your concealed gun and license to kill and increase your chances of shooting a darkie who just happens to be committing a felony?

Despite this madness, the fact that people kill people, not guns, is indisputable. As far as product reliability is concerned, guns almost always do what they are intended to—kill a living thing or inflict major injury on a living thing. A gun by itself is harmless. But the moment human hands touch it, it comes alive—power! Any person who has fired a gun is touched by this awesome power, the knowledge that this small object can be directed to kill or severely injure—life-and-death power! This power can corrupt the noblest of men. Put a gun in a man's hand and his entire perspective on life changes instantaneously. He becomes cocky. He becomes strong. He becomes omnipotent. Believe it or not, to many men a gun is intricately intertwined with their manhood—remove the gun and they are rendered impotent. Such is the power of a gun.

If you have ever listened to a group of men talk about guns, you know that mere dialogue about guns destroys brain cells. In their minds a gun that kills and leaves a bigger hole is preferable to a gun that kills and leaves a smaller hole; a gun that kills at a mile away is preferable to a gun that kills at a shorter distance; and a gun that kills in automatic rapid fire is preferable to a gun that kills in semi-rapid fire.

Keep in mind that an African-American male need simply to walk on his own two feet to be considered a threat to society. Therefore a gun in the hands of an African-American automatically becomes a threat on the scale of a nuclear meltdown. Because of this fact it is hard not to suggest avoiding guns altogether, unless for hunting purposes. But that isn't practical. However, it is wise to think long and hard when considering whether to purchase a gun or not. Why are you buying it? For protection? If so, protection from what, whom? What about applicable state and federal laws? Are there kids in the house? Can it be stored safely? How about your temperament? Your wife or girlfriend's temperament? Do you fully understand a gun's ability to change a person's perspective, personality?

Along with background checks, another requirement to purchase a gun should be passing of a stress management class or a personality test. Because, sadly, the majority of people who kill with guns kill their own family and friends. A greater number of people have pointed loaded guns at family and friends.

Here are ten safety precautions for African-American

gun ownership.

1. Never play with a gun or aim it at someone, unless intending to kill.

2. Never show a gun off to family or friends, or loan a gun out to anyone.

3. Never handle a gun while drinking or under the influence of any type of drug.

4. Never consider a gun a tool to end a disagreement.

5. Never, ever, consider using a gun in the commission of a crime.

6. Never carry a gun on your person or in your vehicle unless licensed to do so.

7. Never make threatening remarks about your gun or threaten someone with it.

8. Never allow children access to a gun.

9. Never hit a person with a gun.

10. Never assume a gun is not loaded.

You could follow all of the above and other gun-safety rules and still have someone break into your home and use your gun against you, which is what happens more often than a homeowner shooting an intruder.

One last thing to consider before purchasing a gun: your hair triggers, the buttons that makes you click. The majority of African-Americans possess two almost-inherent hair triggers; the first one, speaking ill of Momma; the second one, a non-African-American using the N-word. The first hair trigger most African-Americans learn and respect shortly after learning to walk and, amazingly, without someone having to tell them. The second one most non-African-Americans respect—unless when driving by in a speeding car or safely hidden behind a CB mike or on-line on the Internet. But some Brothers have an unlimited number of hair triggers, and are just waiting for someone to touch one, then—*Pow!*

Many factors contribute to hair triggers: self-esteem, PMS (Penitentiary Mentality Syndrome), urban areas, unemployment, depression, alcohol, drugs, gangs, and many more. One particular example of having an incredibly sensitive but also irrational hair trigger was the Brother who grabbed a tire iron and chased a Sister to her death into a river after she accidentally bumped her car into his. No doubt if he had had a gun he would have shot her. His hair trigger: "Touch my car, and you're dead!"

These type of incidents are senseless and heartbreaking, and the individual who lets himself get enraged to the point of murder usually has trouble explaining his actions: "Hey, I lost it!" Well, that doesn't cut it.

Long after the senseless crime has been committed, a devastated family is still struggling to cope with the loss of a family member: a mother, father, brother, sister, child, lost forever—and why? Meanwhile, not too far away, another family is dealing with the loss of a family member to prison. Yes, he deserves to be where he is, but his family will pay the price as well. Can you imagine…twenty years in prison with another twenty years in front of you for a few seconds of infantile, uncontrolled rage? A gun for protection? Protection from what, whom?

KISS—"My ass!"

The African-American male is not an endangered species. In fact, regardless of what catastrophe strikes this country—nuclear war, major earthquake, disease, famine, or a direct hit from a meteorite—if one or two Carl Casians survive to talk about it, one or two African-Americans will survive to preach about it.

But the fact that African-Americans kill other African-Americans at an alarming rate cannot be overlooked. In a sense, a young African-American male between the ages of sixteen and thirty-five is a target for the police and the very people he calls family, friends, and associates. Granted this, it would be wise to present yourself as small a target as possible.

Let's take a quick look at the Brothers whose targets on their chests are very small, so small, in fact, you'll have to come fairly close to see it. These Brothers go to work during the week, spend time with their families, participate in volunteer activities, and go to the church of their choice on Sunday. This lifestyle looks boring to some people, but you can't deny that these Brothers have a particularly small target sign on their chests and have an extremely low KISS probability ratio. These Brothers possess a surfeit of self-confidence and self-esteem; their perception of themselves is not clouded by other people's perception of them but rooted deeply in their religious beliefs and planted firmly in their commitment to family and community.

Hollywood and the media have no use for these Brothers. And many Brothers have no use for these Brothers. But these Brothers are the best and the brightest of the African-American race. Some are college educated, some are high school educated, and some have little or no education—but all are men, strong, proud African-American men.

Now let's take a longer look at the Brothers with the big, neon targets on their chests. These Brothers are more interesting to watch because they incite more drama. Which is why Hollywood patterns their scripts after them. "Action!"—Gunfire, screams, bloodletting. This, as you've guessed, influences more real-life gunfire, screams, and bloodletting. Another vicious and deadly circle.

Many Brothers with big, neon targets on their chests do not realize they are following a movie script; they play the part with the aplomb of Academy Award-winning actor—and they get KISSed. If you have watched two or more action movies, you may have detected the classic Hollywood formula plot. The protagonist, the good guy, is basically minding his own business, then this A-Hole, the antagonist, comes along and does something so mean-spirited and evil to the good guy that he has no other choice but to pick up his automatic weaponry and brush up on his oriental ass-kicking skills and seek revenge. Alerting the authorities, obviously, is not an option. Uh-uh. Some sumbitch has to pay and has to pay dearly! Notice also that when the bad guy stoops to the lowest, such as cutting off body parts of the good guy's girlfriend, this gives the good guy justification to stoop even lower, such as sticking ignited dynamite in the bad guy's throat.

Yes, indeedy, Americans love it when an A-Hole finally gets his comeuppance.

In real life if a guy came along and burned your dog to death, brutally raped and murdered your significant other, burned your house down, crippled your best friend, terrorized your aging parents, and sent you letters saying *There's more to come,* chances are more likely that you would have a nervous breakdown than go get your automatic weapons and take a crash karate course. Even if you did seek revenge, you would still go to prison, a place not conducive to mourning.

If you can see the pattern of BS in movies, you can see the same pattern of BS in real life. Brothers with big, neon targets on their chests rarely look for patterns.

Their awareness is low because their thoughts are on something else, usually their image.

Believe it or not, but the majority of Brothers with big, neon targets on their chests who were injured or killed by other African-Americans were warned in some shape, form, or fashion, but did not heed the warning. In many cases the warnings were verbally explicit, such as the following:

- "Stop playing with me!"
- "Don't come up here with that bullshit!"
- "I'm not going to tell you again to pay me my money!"
- "I don't play the dozens!"
- "You need to stop fucking with me!"
- "Do it again!"
- "I told you to leave me alone!"
- "Don't come round here no mo'!"
- "If I see you again, you'll be sorry!"
- "Don't have my money by tomorrow, and see what happens!"

(A good rule of thumb whereas money is concerned: never borrow more than you can pay back. If you have doubts about your ability to pay back, don't borrow. If you for some reason cannot pay back, then it's a good idea to keep a low profile if possible. Brothers have strict rules about loans, and these rules totally differ from rules held by banks and other lending institutions. The biggest mistake many Brothers make is to giggle in the face of a Brother to whom they owe money—and risk the possibility of being KISSed. No one giggles in his landlord's face when the rent is past due. So if you owe a Brother money, treat him the same way and don't be in his face if you can't honor your agreement.)

Another characteristic of Brothers with big, neon targets on their chests is their penchant for arguing. If you have ever heard two idiots arguing, you know that the objective of both parties isn't to convince the other of the salient points of their argument. Instead, the objective is to determine who can argue the loudest and the longest. The best method to ensure that your point of view will not be considered is to argue that point of view. Arguments escalate in part because one or both arguing parties realize that their point of view isn't even being considered, then anger seeps in, which often leads to name calling, which often leads to drama, which often leads to one or both parties getting KISSed.

This is why petty, trivial, childish disagreements can result in someone getting killed. You can disarm anyone who loves to argue by simply refusing to play his or her game: "I've said all I've had to say about it."

Remember this: Arguing is a tool for the emotionally desperate and the shallow-minded to reinforce their own belief in their argument.

Remember, many A-Holes love to argue and ridicule at home but refrain from doing so in public. This is the mark of a coward, who falsely believes his chance of being hurt by a friend or family member is extremely low. Two facts: Most violent incidents happen within the home; and only a fool thinks that he can constantly berate, criticize, and demean his family and friends and never encounter consequences.

Finally, Brothers with big, neon targets on their chests choose friends with big, neon targets on their chests—and increases their chances of being KISSed even more. Again you are responsible for your friends' actions, therefore you should always know who you're dealing with. Observe. Watch. Listen.

Bad Credit

Bad credit hurts almost as much as racial discrimination. Once the bad credit report spits out of the machine, the guy who only moments before was smiling in your face, inquiring with great interest as to what you do for a living, now wants you off his showroom floor, out of his building and out of his face. Even if now you can pay the monthly note, even if you have changed your prodigal ways, and even if you put on your best suit and your friendliest smile, a bad credit report makes you persona non grata.

As far as credit is concerned, it's not what you gonna do, it's what you have done.

And this is exactly how you should judge the people whom you call friends, lovers, acquaintances, homeboys, buddies, girlfriends, fiancées, or whatever. A person's crime history can be considered a credit report. Some crimes constitute serious breaches of fiduciary and moral responsibility while others constitute minor oversights in the form of late payments. To assist you in determining who has bad credit and should be considered persona non grata, the following crimes are assigned a credit number from 1 through 10. A low number, of course, is a good ranking; a high number is a bad ranking, with 10 as the worst possible score.

Murder Credit number: 7 through 10. The number varies because, believe it or not, most murderers commit murder only once. A serial murderer rates a 10, but who in their right mind considers a serial murderer a friend.

Rape Credit number: 10. Most rapists rape more than once, and most rape people they know. Why have someone like this near your wife, girlfriend, mother, or sisters. If the victim was a child, the rapist is almost a hundred percent likely to do it again.

Assault Credit number: 7 through 10. Leave it to the criminologist and the psychiatrist to figure out why some people routinely hurt others, but your concern is what he or she did, not why he or she did it. Assault is a blanket term, ranging from a barroom fight to a brutal attack on a defenseless person.

Armed Robbery Credit number: 10. Armed robbers are very dangerous, ranging from crackheads to First-class A-Holes. Imagine going to a store with someone who suddenly pulls out a gun and robs the place. In order to avoid being charged with the same crime as he, you must somehow distance yourself from him without being shot.

Forgery Credit number: 6. Nine times out of ten, forgery is the mark of a drug addict. The forger who doesn't have a drug impetus is usually a First-class A-Hole.

Burglary Credit number: 7 through 10. A daytime burglar is usually a drug addict, but a nighttime burglar is something totally different. He knows someone is probably inside the house, which means he's there for something other than stealing.

Arson Credit number: 10. Firebugs almost always have underlying problems. In some cases they are in the early stage of NUTS, and if so, remember this: your house or place of residence can burn just as quickly as someone else's.

It's your decision, of course, with whom you turn corners. Though surely you agree, someone who has injured a child isn't someone to truck with. You may also have reservations about other negative tendencies as well, criminal or not. That's your decision, your choice! For example, adultery is not necessarily a crime by most people's standards, but if you feel uncomfortable with someone who commits adultery, that's your choice. Even though family and friends may not agree with your viewpoint, no one but you should decide what behaviors you condone or what behaviors you do not condone. Remember this: Silence, overlooking, and ignoring are all forms of condoning negative behavior.

The Free World

Many people point toward the Internet as the greatest invention in their lifetime. But for today's African-American male, the greatest invention in his time is DNA testing. Thanks to DNA testing, a good number of African-American men (and men of all races) have been exonerated of committing heinous crimes. Also thanks to DNA testing the old saying "Momma's baby, Daddy's maybe" has been replaced with "In doubt go find out."

What more terrible miscarriage of justice than for an innocent man to languish in prison. Witnesses misidentify suspects (especially in cross-racial identifications); incompetent or undedicated public defenders and judges sleep during trials; paid professionals slant their testimony for big bucks; police and prosecutors overlook exonerating evidence; jailhouse snitches weave self-serving yarns; and innocent men go to prison—a sad fact of life.

Another sad fact: The overwhelming majority of men in prison belong there.

Even for the innocent, membership into prison requires a process. No one can simply go up to a prison wall and request admittance. A crime has to come first—either one you committed or someone thinks you committed—then an arrest, then a trial, then a conviction, and then admittance into prison.

Prison is another world, with different codes, rules, and regulations. So different is this world, inmates label everything outside the prison, including clothing and cigarettes, "The Free World."

Many prisons in the South still require that inmates perform field labor, picking cotton, picking pecans, and digging ditches, etc. Most prisons in the North do not require such labor, but the one thing prisons the world over have in common: loss of freedom. A funny word, *freedom*—like air, one rarely considers it till it is compromised.

An inmate cannot go here and there on his own accord. An inmate has no privacy. An inmate considers the terms *convict* and *inmate* expletives. An inmate must be watchful of other inmates at all times. An inmate cannot have sex with his wife or girlfriend—though some prisons allow conjugal visits, most do not. An inmate is alienated from his family and friends. An inmate can be detained, strip-searched, and denied certain rights because of his behavior or the whim of his keepers. In short, being an inmate is a bitch!

If your name is Carl Casian and you are timid, soft, maladroit, and weigh less than two hundred pounds, then being an inmate is a bigger bitch. The backlash to inordinately sentencing African-American and Latino men to prison longer and more often is that when a young Carl Casian enters prison nine times out of ten he is treated like a—you get the picture.

Prison life is the epitome of human tragedy—and it has a way of recycling human tragedy.

To many people in the free world it is incomprehensible that someone would go to prison, get released, then commit another crime and go back to prison, also called recidivism. Most people in the free world believe this happens because of two reasons: the individual is either institutionalized or criminally deviant, or, in the words of one old man, "He left something down there he couldn't do without."

Those two reasons sound valid, and may be true in a percentage of cases, but to the majority of recidivists a bosom buddy and three meals and a cot are not the reasons for a return visit. So what is? Another good question. A short answer would suffice here, but by now you know that this book prefers going to LA from Chicago by way of New York. Another thing, even though you are a fine, upstanding, law-abiding citizen, the explanation will be told in the second person—meaning you.

Being sentenced to prison is a punishment—not a correction; not rehabilitation; and not an accommodation. The judge may throw "society" about here and there, as in *"A menace to society..." "For the best interest of society..."* and *"To protect society..."*—but make no bones about it, you are being punished. Unless your sentence means that you will be spending the rest of your life inside prison, your accepting the fact that you are being punished is the first step to not putting yourself in a position to be punished again.

Thus, the following is not why you are being punished:

- "I took the fall for my homeboy."
- "Whatshisface snitched me out."
- "The man had it out for me."
- "I plea-bargained and got a good deal."
- "I got too big."
- "Haters!"

But, you say, *a few pages ago, remember, something about African-American males being disproportionately sentenced to prison?* Applaud yourself for your astute observation. However, whereas freedom is concerned: Knowing that the game is rigged doesn't excuse the fact *you* got caught cheating. Okay.

Once you've accepted the fact that you are being

punished, you can turn your attention to what you are being punished for. Although this sounds relatively simple, this is the one hurdle many inmates, for whatever reasons, cannot clear. Go to any prison, talk to any group of inmates, and ninety percent or more will deny committing the crime that placed them there. Denial is always self-destructive—moving in a backward direction.

Denial is also the antithesis of rational thinking. For example, most prisons allow AA (Alcoholic Anonymous) and NA (Narcotic Anonymous) groups to meet, but few inmates—though many have alcohol- and drug-related issues—take advantage of such groups. (Not only with AA and NA, an inmate would be smart to commit himself or herself to all self-improvements activities available, including GED and college courses.)

Denial, like guilt, can be deadly. And denial hovers like cigarette smoke inside a prison, permeating everything it comes in contact with. Which is why "Bullshit Endorsement" is the game of choice in most prisons. The rules of this game are simple; first, ignore the facts that put you in prison, then find a partner, preferably someone you knew from the streets, then spend countless but wasteful hours embellishing past criminal exploits and planning future criminal exploits. To add even more excitement to the game, adopt a hardcore image and break prison rules; whoever winds up doing more time than originally sentenced wins.

Another exciting game to play while serving time is the "Blame Game." Simply blame anything you can imagine as the reason why you were sentenced to prison. To add further excitement to play, focus your attention on those who committed the same crime as you but received a lesser sentence.

"I've found Jesus!" is another game played by many inmates. This game is more complicated than the others, in part because the player can only be declared a winner if he comes back to prison.

Whatever the game, if you are in prison and you are not focusing on what brought you there—your behavior—you will fall back on the same behavior shortly after being released. Remember this: In order to successfully change negative behavior, first recognize the behavior, then accept responsibility for the behavior, then imagine yourself behaving differently, and finally, practice, practice, practice behaving differently. Of course, in prison you may not be able to practice confronting certain negative behaviors, but you certainly should not spend time endorsing and embellishing bullshit behavior. For example, you have a problem stealing. In prison you will be confronted with the opportunity to steal, but since you are practicing behaving differently, every opportunity to steal is an excellent time to practice not stealing—which will make not stealing in the free world that much easier. Face the facts: If you don't make the decision to change your behavior, it will not change on its own, no matter how true your intentions.

Finally, recognize the anger and resentment. Denial intensifies anger and resentment. Prison life in itself promotes anger and resentment. The look—a hard downward glare at the floor—that many inmates have in prison is the same look many former inmates have on the street. Admittedly there is a difficult transition going from free world to prison, but even a more difficult transition going from prison to free world. In the free world you have more opportunities but you also have more responsibilities. Your food, your living quarters, and your not going back to prison are your responsibility.

If you are angry and resentful about your prison stay, and you have spent the last X number of months or years in denial, you will almost certainly fall back to the activities that put you in prison in the first place. Think about it, how logical is doing the same thing that put you in prison the first time? You got smarter criminally while in prison? Or, your anger and resentment about going to prison justifies your doing something stupid that might send you back to the place you are so angry and resentful about? Believe it or not, the more you go back to prison, the bigger chance you will spend the majority of your life there. Do you really want that? Of course not.

Everyone knows the one Brother who has spent the better part of his life in prison. Often he gets out for a short period of time, then he does something stupid and goes right back. To his family and friends he has become similar to Ralph Ellison's invisible man: He is there but they cannot see him. In time his children will not mention his name. And, usually in a shorter period of time, his significant other will replace him with another.

More reasons why the first trip to prison should be the last trip to prison: Many Brothers have gone to prison, done their time, and then gotten out and become fine, law-abiding, productive citizens. In other words, they stopped playing the game. When asked, these men say the same thing: "Prison is no place for an Black man to be."

(Author's note: Regardless or color, many First-class A-Holes belong in prison, especially those who abuse children and commit violent, heinous, insensible crimes. As in the case of the Little Rock Brother who, when told by his ex-girlfriend that his coat couldn't be found in her house, came back with his Second-class A-Hole buddy and tossed a gallon of lighted gasoline on her three small children. Upon seeing the picture of these three young African-American children tragically burned for life, bandaged from head-to-toe, unable to raise from their hospital beds, you cannot help but feel outraged, and you cannot help but feel that prison is too good for this

First-class A-Hole Brother and his Second-class A-Hole buddy.

At the least, the Second-class A-hole buddy could have said while giving the First-class A-Hole a ride back to the house, "Yo, Holmes, I know you're mad, but throwing fire on her kids is not the way to go." These three children's livelihood was partially predicated on one Brother standing up to a First-class A-Hole. And that Brother, a coward at heart, failed them.)

Chapter 8
Bungee Jumping

"If sex equaled love and love equaled sex, prostitution would be a respectable profession." H.H.

Stereotypes put people in boxes and attempt to classify an individual as a group. This is why stereotypes hurt. You're shaking your head again—why? Oh! Well, what's going on here is not exactly stereotyping; this is a form of satirical superciliousness, which would take another book to explain but should only be attempted by professionals. You are still shaking your head? Well, while you are shaking your head, let's at least agree that some activities cannot be considered African-American activities. No doubt a few African-Americans have participated in these activities, but their number is so small it is safe to label the activity un-African-American.

The following is a brief list of un-African-American activities:

Bungee Jumping: This activity places life and death on the elastic strength of a rubber. If the rubber breaks, that's your ass, which is why you rarely if ever see an African-American standing in line at a bungee jump.

Turkey Hunting: Many African-Americans living in the South occasionally hunt turkey, but rarely if ever do they don camouflaged clothing, hide in bushes, and make turkey noises while other hunters, mostly Carl

Casians, are also out hunting for turkey.

UFO Searching: Interesting enough, not one single African-American has ever reported an alien abduction. In part because the overwhelming majority of African-Americans know that when a vehicle, regardless of shape or size, suddenly appears out of nowhere with lights off, or emitting a strange light, it is time to go inside and lay on the floor and be as quiet and still as possible.

Whale Fishing: The African-American rule of thumb to all fishing: If it cannot be retrieved by a regular hand-held rod-and-reel or a stout cane pole, then leave it the hell alone.

Big Foot Hunting: Big Foot and his kind have all but said, "DFW me!" What else can be inferred when he shuns the camera and runs back into the woods? You don't have to tell the average African-American that when a seven-foot or taller, hairy, beast-looking man says, "DFW me!" you do just that.

Alligator Wrestling: Supposedly there is a spot on an alligator's underbelly that if pressed will cause the animal to go into a trance-like stupor. However, no definitive instructions exist on how to get the animal to roll over to accommodate such a maneuver.

Russian Roulette: The handful of African-Americans who have played this deadly game are no longer able to explain why they did so.

Human Cannonballing: No explanation needed.

Poisonous Snake Handling and Charming: There is a widespread belief that African-Americans in general have an inherent fear of snakes—it's true!

Mountain Climbing: African-Americans do climb mountains, but only mountains that are not snow covered nor require nailing spikes and dangling from ropes to reach the top.

Skiing: Only on small hills that aren't surrounded by

trees.

Sky Diving: Wesley Snipes and many African-Americans in the military sky dive, but most African-Americans shy away from the sport. As one Brother put it: "It's not that I have a fear of heights, I have a fear of landing real hard."

Make-'em-yourself Explosives: Firecrackers, many African-Americans claim, are the loudest bang they wish to hear. Therefore, any explosive device that one has to break his neck running from or has a high risk of exploding on its own and causing loss of life, limbs, or eyesight is avoided.

Car Surfing: This activity involves riding on the hood of a moving car. However, the few African-Americans who have car surfed claim that doing so was not by choice.

Tornado Chasing: Thousands of African-Americans have gone outside or peeked out the window to see the big whirly thing across the way, but not one African-American has jumped in his car to go chase the whirly thing.

Rappelling: Involves rope.

Scuba Diving, Surfing, and Rafting: The African-American rule of thumb to all water activities: Multiply the number of surrounding people who know CPR by the estimated time it will take them to get to you, then divide this number by the approximate gallons you think your lungs can hold. If quotient ends in an odd or even number, then leave it the hell alone.

Fire Eating and Fire Breathing: Never intentionally.

Cliff Diving: Occasionally, but only if ten or more people go first.

Big Game Hunting: African-American rule of thumb: If the hunted animal's droppings match or exceed your own, then leave it the hell alone.

Grave Robbing: A Brother may have taken said item

at the morgue, or possibly during funeral procession, but if said item disappeared while underground—a Brother didn't take it.

This list would not be complete without mentioning two vocations that African-Americans simply do not do—wild animal tagging and homesteading with wild animals.

Apparently the Carl Casian rule of thumb to animals is: If you cannot shoot it or bring it into your house as a pet, you can always devise elaborate methods to catch it and attach a tracking device. Would not it be easier to surmise: "No one has seen Cool Breeze the polar bear in a long time, so maybe it's dead." Of course, African-Americans sympathize with wild animals, but as far as losing sleep or becoming misty-eyed over the death of a smelly wild animal—forget it!

Even more baffling to many African-Americans are the misanthropes who spend the majority of their lives living with wild animals, ostensibly for scientific research. A gutter load of ugly thoughts come to mind when considering a woman who has lived twenty or more years with primates and fondly refers to them by names such as "Boo-Boo," "Cuddles," and "Mister Big."

To the African-American certain jobs and activities pose an unusually high DEF (Dying Extremely Fast) risk. For instance, skiing: Even before Sonny Bono attempted to slow his downward plunge with the assistance of a large pine, African-Americans assigned skiing with a 10—the highest number—on the DEF risk scale. No doubt this type of danger assessment saves lives, but, unfortunately, the primary focus is on the immediacy of death instead of the likelihood of death.

Which segues to a cataclysmic tragedy.

African-Americans in startling numbers are partaking in a lethal cocktail. This particular cocktail has no age limit. This cocktail is tempting. This cocktail is alluring, This cocktail makes one feel good. Inexpensive, sometimes free. Looks good, feels good.

To make: Add an instinctive desire to procreate to a large dose of unawareness of sexually transmitted diseases, then pour in a heavy dose of sexually suggestive themes from music and other entertainment mediums, then add a heaping of unwillingness by leaders to tell African-Americans that they are being clobbered by STDs, which includes AIDS. Shake vigorously. Serve cold.

No one likes to talk about STDs. The subject makes many people uncomfortable, especially those who have practiced or are currently practicing a lifestyle conducive to contracting a sexually transmitted disease. When was the last time you and your friends talked seriously about STDs? When was the last time you talked to your significant other about STDs? When was the last time you talked to your child or children about STDs? Once? Occasionally? Never?

Why the reluctance to broach the subject? Fear. Which is also one of the reasons why so many people never seek testing for STDs, and why so many people who know or suspect they are infected with an STD never reveal it. The latter group includes people who fear that telling their partner might result in losing their partner. Another group is those who really do not know they are infected and unknowingly infect others.

Fact: Each group comprises millions of people.

In short, this is not your granddaddy's sexual climate. Today's sexual climate, if you do not prepare to confront it, can kill you. You do not have the luxury of basking in it and hoping that the rays will not affect you. And, as you will read later, a condom cannot always protect you from getting burned. Fact: As in Bungee jumping, it is unwise to place your life in the elastic strength of a rubber. A condom, though a wise precautionary measure, is not a panacea against the contracting of STDs. Condoms offer little or no protection against genital warts if warts form outside of condom-protected areas.

Abstinence is the answer. Abstinence is a strange word for many who are already sexually active, but it is the most effective way of inoculating oneself from STDs. And yes, you can do it. More on this later, but now let's take a closer look at seven different STDs that pose serious health risks: AIDS/HIV, genital herpes, chlamydia, gonorrhea, genital warts, syphilis, and hepatitis B. Note: Some of the words here you will almost never hear in real conversations, such as Neisseria gonorrhoeae, but the more you know about STDs (and not just the information provided here), the better equipped you are to protect yourself and others.

AIDS/HIV

On October 21, 2001, the U.S Senate approved a $700 million increase in proposed spending over the next two years to combat AIDS in poor countries, particularly sub-Saharan Africa, which, reportedly—sources vary—has more than seventy percent of the world's AIDS cases. A portion of this aid will help finance the cost of expensive drug cocktails that have dramatically reduced AIDS deaths in the USA. This is a first. Also not until recently did several pharmaceutical companies offer to reduce the price of these life-saving drugs as much as ninety percent to accommodate the majority of Africans suffering from HIV or AIDS who couldn't even dream of paying such prices.

Yes, both actions are laudable and most certainly a

godsend. But why did it take so long? Why is it that until millions of Africans die no one—including the majority of African-Americans—seems to care? Yet let someone like Britney Spears lose a navel ring—the world stops. It is as if the African as an individual doesn't count; his pain, suffering, and ultimate death is of little consequence. But millions of Africans as a group, well that large number of human suffering and death cannot be easily overlooked. This is madness, utter madness!

In Thailand and Uganda the government has helped reduce the spread of HIV through education and other public health measures while in many sub-Saharan African countries such preventive efforts have been stymied by political, economic, and cultural issues. These problems, combined with abject apathy from the outside world, will ensure that many more Africans contract HIV, and many more will die.

Which makes you wonder what would happen if African-Americans, though bedraggled with their own problems, voiced a collective concern about those Africans—whose namesake they proudly declare—who are suffering and dying in large numbers, leaving armies of orphaned children in their wake.

Unlike in Africa, here in America the sick and the dying do not roam the streets, begging, dropping dead on the spot—in part because Americans prefer not to see the sick and dying other than in institutions. To see such conditions would reduce the luxury of living during but ignoring an epidemic that will eventually surpass the influenza epidemic of 1918 that killed twenty million people. Oh the luxury of being an American!

In America, unless the mass media shines the spotlight on the sick and dying, somehow the notion prevails that the sick and dying are or no longer sick and dying. *Poof!* It's gone.

When AIDS first hit the scene, it was considered

endemic to gay men, Haitians, and intravenous drug users; and the media coverage was relentless. With each passing year more information was learned about the disease, including the fact that heterosexuals were also at risk. Then the paradigm shifted. The HIV infection rate with gay men declined, primarily because of safer sex practices, while the HIV infection rates with minorities, particularly African-Americans and Latinos, shot up. Near or about the same time, the media focus on HIV/AIDS declined. Coincidence? Maybe, maybe not.

Nevertheless, it's your responsibility to know and learn as much as you can about HIV/AIDS—not only for yourself but for your family, social relationships, and your community.

The following questions and answers offer additional information about HIV/AIDS.

What is HIV infection? A chronic disease that undermines the body's immune system, or ability to ward off a variety of infections and disorders. Normally, when a virus or other pathogen enters the body, it is attacked and destroyed by the immune system. HIV or human immunodeficiency virus, however, attacks the immune system itself. HIV attacks CD4 T cells, monocytes, and macrophages, each essential elements of the body's defense system. In short the HIV virus takes over the CD4 cells, forces the cell to produce new copies of HIV cells, and renders the cell defenseless to protect itself. Once infected, billions of HIV particles are produced each day. The immune system produces billions of new cells to compete, but cannot produce new cells indefinitely. The virus, however, can.

What's the difference between HIV and AIDS? AIDS is diagnosed when the number of CD4 cells in the blood drops below a certain level (200/ul), or the onset of a condition that is defined as an AIDS marker. During the asymptomatic phase of HIV—before the onset of symptoms—the immune system is at war with HIV; cells are infected and destroyed. A key point to remember: During this phase, which can last from two to twenty years, the virus can be passed on to others—even though no symptoms are evident—and during the early weeks of infection, tests to determine the presence of the virus can prove negative. This is a chilling aspect of HIV infection: people unaware of their condition, feeling fine but unknowingly spreading the virus to others.

How can you contract HIV? HIV cannot survive outside of cells and body fluids, so there is no need to worry about contracting HIV from eating utensils, toilet seats, mosquito bites, or any other object. Nor should you worry about hugging or being in contact with someone who is HIV infected. Primarily, HIV is passed by three modes of transmission: (1) sexual contact; (2) direct contact to infected blood; (3) an infected mother to child during pregnancy, childbirth, or breastfeeding.

Transmission during sexual contact is more likely during unprotected anal or vaginal intercourse. Unprotected oral sex also carries risks but not as high as the aforementioned—still it is hardly worth the risk. Poor oral hygiene or the brushing or flossing of teeth before or after oral sex increases risk. The mouth, anus, vagina, cervix, and penis all have fragile linings and can have tiny tears present, which can facilitate the transmission of HIV, which makes rough sex risky even when protected. And the presence of other STDs in any of the aforementioned areas makes it two to five times easier to contract HIV. Male-to-female transmission is more likely than female-to-male transmission. Remember: All body fluids can carry traces of HIV, even in preejaculatory fluid—but tears, sweat, and minimal amounts of saliva are not believed to carry enough of the virus to infect someone else.

Direct contact to infected blood can transmit HIV through needles, tattooing, and piercing of any part of the body, including ears. The sharing of needles is the second leading avenue of HIV transmission. Especially true in the African-American community, where half of all new HIV cases are related or indirectly related to the sharing of needles. Though providing addicts with needles is controversial, logic would deem it necessary to hamper HIV transmission. (Honestly, who starts an addiction because drug paraphernalia is free?) Addicts can greatly reduce their risk of transmission by not sharing needles and cleaning needles with bleach and warm water—though not a guarantee.

Mother-to-child transmission, also called vertical transmission, occurs during pregnancy, childbirth, or breastfeeding. Unlike in many undeveloped countries, the risk of mother-to-child HIV transmissions here in the United States has been greatly reduced, thanks to early detection and antiviral drugs which reduce the chance of the mother passing the virus onto the child.

What are symptoms of HIV infections? During the first few days or weeks of initial infection, many people experience rashes, headaches, fever, fatigue, swollen lymph nodes, body aches, night sweats, diarrhea, sore throat, and diarrhea. These symptoms resemble other common illnesses, so often they are misdiagnosed as something other than HIV infection. Later, as the immune system weakens, the infected person may experience lumps, sores, rashes, swollen lymph nodes, or growths under the skin or on the mucous membranes of the eyes, mouth, anus, or nasal passages. Also: dry cough, fever and drenching night sweats, persistent yeast infections, unexplained weight loss, persistent diarrhea, shortness of breath, easy bruising, inexplicable bleeding, profound fatigue, persistent or recurring pain, changes in senses—taste, hearing, smelling, seeing—and tremors or seizures. Plus: memory loss, difficulty in swallowing, and changes in mood and other psychological symptoms.

Of course, these symptoms can be the results of other illnesses. And remember: It's natural to feel uncomfortable when reading or hearing about symptoms to any disease. On the other hand, if such symptoms exist, or you have reasons to suspect possible infection, then it is wise to get tested as soon as possible. Doing so may help preserve immune function, slow the progress of the disease, and reduce transmission to others.

Is there a cure? Not yet. But again, early diagnosis is important. And this is an area in which many African-Americans fall short. This may in part be due to the fact that HIV in the African-American community carries a greater stigma, which in part makes many African-Americans reluctant to get tested. Who wants to be ostracized by family and friends? This terrible disease calls for insight and compassion, not fear and alienation.

Remember: Regardless of the route of infection, a Brother, or anyone, is still human, still in need of human touch, still in need of love and concern.

Genital Herpes

Genital Herpes is more common than you may have imagined. Herpes simplex one, or HSV-1, usually causes cold sores and is estimated in fifty to eighty percent of U.S. adults. Herpes simplex 2, or HSV-2, usually causes genital herpes and is present in twenty percent of U.S. adults. Both HSV-1 and HSV-2 can cause either cold sores or genital herpes. HSV-2, however, is almost always sexually transmitted. Unlike the AIDS virus, HSV-2 can, though rare, be transmitted by contaminated clothing or other objects. And of course, when active sores are present, transmission during unprotected sex is almost automatic. Since HSV-2 is often asymptomatic in the majority of people infected, many people are unaware they are infected, which makes HSV-2 very easy to contract and very difficult to contain.

If you have ever had a genital herpes outbreak, you should always consider yourself contagious—and inform your partners. On occasion, a newborn can be infected during passage through the birth canal if the mother is infected with HSV during the third trimester of pregnancy. Sadly, without treatment more than half the babies with HSV will die, and many who survive will suffer some degree of brain damage. These are more reasons to discuss sexual history with your partner and an imperative for expecting mothers to inform their doctors of any STDS.

The first outbreak of genital herpes causes flu-like symptoms in addition to genital lesions (again: the overwhelming majority infected never exhibit symptoms). Usually, the lesions last about three weeks, but the virus lives, hiding within nerve cells. People newly infected with HSV-2 average five to eight outbreaks a year. In time the outbreaks are less frequent and less severe. Fatigue, illness, stress, sexual intercourse, menstruation, and sun exposure can trigger outbreaks.

Unfortunately, no cure for herpes exists, and the virus lasts a lifetime. Acylovir and other antiviral drugs can alleviate the severity and duration of the symptoms.

Chlamydia

Chlamydia is caused by a bacteria, chlamydia trachomatis. Chlamydia is prevalent in the sexually active age group between eighteen- to twenty-four-year-olds. A good percentage of those diagnosed with gonorrhea also have chlamydia. Though males and females can contract chlamydia, women—as with most STDs—suffer a greater burden. Chlamydia increases a woman's risks of tubal pregnancy and can lead to pelvic inflammatory disease, also known as PID. (PID is a serious health problem to women, resulting from untreated chlamydia and/or gonorrhea moving upward, past the cervix into the uterus, oviducts, ovaries and pelvic cavity, which can cause tubal pregnancy and infertility.)

Chlamydia can also cause infertility in men, though not as often as in women. Males under thirty-five can also suffer epididymis, an inflammation of the sperm-carrying ducts, and urethritis, an inflammation of the uretha. Symptoms in both sexes are rare, but some men can experience painful urination, watery discharge, or pain around testicles, while some women can experience burning with urination, painful intercourse, or lower back pain. A newborn passing through the birth canal of an infected mother can suffer eye infection and pneumonia. Laboratory tests can detect this infection, and prescribed antibiotics can cure it in one dose—which can negate the pain and suffering associated with infertility, damaged reproductive organs, and a sick newborn.

Gonorrhea

Gonorrhea is caused by a bacteria, Neisseria gonorrheoeae. This infection can also cause PID in women. During delivery, an infected mother can expose her newborn to gonococcal conjunctivitis, an infection that can cause blindness. Gonorrhea can cause arthritis and rashes and, on occasion, affect internal organs. Though most males associate this infection with burning and painful urination and a colorful discharge—caused by urethritis—up to one third exhibit no symptoms at all. Still, even with the absence of symptoms, the infection can be passed on to others. (By now you've noticed this recurring theme: The infection, though void of any noticeable symptoms, can still be passed on to others.)

In women, the presence of symptoms is even rarer. Those who do can experience painful urination, increased vaginal discharge, and severe menstrual cramps; almost half the women infected will develop PID. Tests can determine infection, and antibiotics can usually cure, so there is no reason to suffer needlessly or expose others to infection.

Genital Warts

Genital warts, a.k.a condyloma, is caused by human papillomavirus, or HPV. The Centers for Disease Control (CDC) estimates that 24 million people in the USA are currently infected and another 5 million will be infected each year. Genital warts has about eighty different strains. Of that eighty, over twenty cause genital infections—and five of this twenty have connections to cervical cancer. Genital warts is very contagious.

Genital warts can occur in areas where a condom cannot protect, such as the base of the penis and around the anus in both men and women. Many people infected with genital warts exhibit no symptoms but are still capable of passing the infection on to others. Of course, those with existing warts pose a higher risk of transmitting the infection.

At first, the warts look like common warts; and they can resemble bumps. Often the warts clump together. In males who experience symptoms the wart appears first on the opening on the penis—and then spreads inside. This may cause irritation, bleeding, painful urination, and a discharge. In females, the warts can appear on the labia or vulva and may spread between the area of the vagina and the rectum. Newborns can also be infected during delivery.

Treatment to this infection focuses primarily on the warts themselves, but the infection itself is rather unpredictable and incurable. Genital warts often runs it course after a number of months (warts may recur), but even in cases where the warts have come and gone, the individual can still infect others.

Syphilis

Once a carrier of death and heartbreak for millions, syphilis can now be treated with antibiotics. This disease has a way of rebounding: A few years ago, syphilis was limited to patches of geography across the country; and though easy to treat, it is difficult to detect. Usually syphilis is transmitted by sexual contact—vaginal or anal intercourse and oral-genital contact. Also, an infected mother can transmit it to her fetus.

Syphilis moves through three stages. First, the primary stage, in which a chancre appears, usually on the genitals but also on other body parts. A chancre is highly contagious, containing large numbers of bacteria, but it is often painless and disappears in a few weeks. Untreated, the disease moves on to the second stage, secondary syphilis, where a rash may appear on parts of the body or the entire body, including the palms and soles of the feet.

Untreated, the disease moves into the third stage, tertiary syphilis, which can damage many organs and cause dementia and incurable paresis, blindness, and death. Remember: All stages of syphilis can be treated with antibiotics, but damage caused by tertiary or late syphilis is often permanent.

Hepatitis B

Hepatitis B or HBV is similar to AIDS, in that the virus can be detected in all body fluids. HBV, however, is far more contagious. This virus can be transmitted by any type of sexual contact, and by drug-injecting paraphernalia, body-piercing needles, eating utensils, toothbrushes, and razors; it can even be transmitted by close contact with an infected person. Multiple sex partners and drug-injecting paraphernalia pose the highest risk of transmission.

Once again, many people infected with HBV never exhibit symptoms. Symptoms of a mild case of hepatitis can include chills, fever, loss of appetite, and body aches. A progression of the illness can cause vomiting, nausea, dark urine, jaundice—a yellowing of the eyes and skin—and abdominal pain. Acute hepatitis can cause prolonged illness and death. Some people recover completely from the virus but can still infect others. Some develop chronic liver disease or cirrhosis of the liver. There is no cure for HBV and no treatment plan for acute infections; however, hepatitis B immunoglobulin can protect those who are exposed to the virus.

More STDs

Yes, unfortunately, there are more, including

trichomoniasis, pubic lice, and scabies (and there are more than listed here). These are not as serious as the others, but all are related to sexual activity. Trichomoniasis, also called trich, flourishes in warm, moist conditions. In men, symptoms are rare. In women, the discharge can cause severe itching of the vagina and vulva, causing redness and pain. The drug metronidazole (Flagyl) is often prescribed after diagnosis, but if both partners are not treated at the same time, they will only pass the infection back and forth.

Scabies is an infection caused by mites, Sarcoptes scabiei, that deposit eggs beneath the skin. The eggs hatch in a few days, and the babies congregate around hair follicles. This activity causes severe itching, especially at night. A prescription, permethrin cream, can treat condition. Clothing or bedding should be treated to prevent re-infestation.

Pubic lice, commonly called crabs, are highly contagious, sexually and nonsexually. Often difficult to see, the lice feed on human blood, preferring the pubic area but also attaching themselves to hair on other body parts. They can also be transmitted by infested clothing, bedding, and yes, toilets. They causes intense itching but can be easily treated with nonprescription medications. Again: Remember to treat clothing and bedding area as well to prevent re-infestation.

Protection

Look toward Africa...widespread famine, civil wars, mass poverty, and the world's highest population of AIDS-related deaths and HIV infection. Africa needed another epidemic like a terminally ill lung cancer patient needs a lobotomy. Yet you will rarely hear an African express shock or dismay in regard to his country's current problems, nor will you see Africans in the throes of widespread panic, sudden religious fervor, or mass hysteria.

These characteristics are where the African differs from the African-American. In the face of population decimation, the African views death and imminent death as a part of life. Of course, this is admirable in some regards, but this is not the African-American way. If African-Americans were placed in the same set of circumstances as the Africans, you can bet the whole world would know about it.

Yes, we are truly African-Americans, but heavy on the American side. Because, while we may not look like our neighbors of European descent, we certainly think and act like they do—and we, like they, do not take death lightly. Death and its little brother Terminal Illness are subjects Americans would rather not even think about, let alone discuss.

Yet, whether you are in shanty in Johannesburg, Africa, dying from an incurable disease, or residing in a Palm Beach, Florida, in the best of health, waiting for your butler to bring your limousine around front, you are affected or will be affected by an STD. For as comparison goes, you can compare your bank account, but you cannot compare a pandemic. The loss of one man or woman can bring down an entire neighborhood, an entire village. Now think…millions…millions! …How can you not be affected?

One single person can intentionally or unintentionally infect hundreds of people with an STD. That hundred has a thousand or more in family and friends; each suffers. Therefore your responsibility is not only to protect yourself against STDs, but also to protect your family, your neighborhood, your town, your country, and your planet from STDs. What kind of man or woman would not inform someone that he or she has an STD? Never is the answer to a problem to multiply the problem?

This all leads back to abstinence—yes, abstinence, that vile and ugly word. But, mind you, abstinence does not mean forever; abstinence means "using wise judgment." Even if you haven't practiced abstinence before, it's never too late to start. Practicing abstinence is not relinquishing control but keeping control. You decide what, when, and who. Think about it: To a degree, you've been doing that all alone. Of course, you have your standards: There are some people who you wouldn't dream of touching with a ten-foot pole. Abstinence simply expands that list.

Unless you are in a long-term, monogamous relationship and you and your partner are STD free and committed to each other, abstinence is your only guarantee to avoid an STD. Genital warts certainly stamps that fact. Abstinence offers many benefits: A peace of mind—those who practice abstinence need not worry about the latest STD or the slightest itch; self-confidence—those who practice abstinence are independent thinkers, unfazed by peer pressure and negative viewpoints; and respect—though most people will not admit it, they are awed by a man who controls his sexual impulses.

Another plus is that you decide who bears your child. An accident does not decide, a woman with whom you have no plans to spend your life does not decide, but you decide. Control! Why would you have it any other way? Relinquish that control, and you allow others to dictate your future, your health.

Fact: Whatever the goal or endeavor, if you can imagine yourself doing it, then you can do it.

So don't dare say you cannot practice abstinence, because you most certainly can. It is your choice. Yes, this is an extremely difficult choice for a young African-American male because stereotypical images such as "The Player" and other mass entertainment mediums practically demand that he go out and prove his manhood by having sex.

Plus, a Brother practicing abstinence is often bombarded with ridicule and jeers by friends and sometimes by family members. They cannot understand him. Something is wrong. Perhaps he is sexually confused…and on and on and on…

Therefore a Brother who practices abstinence is one strong, self-confident, independent-thinking Black man; he does not follow the crowd, he makes his own footprints, he knows what he wants, he does not let others define who he is, and he is at peace with himself. Misery loves company, so his peers constantly make it their business to try to get him to do what they do—sleep with sexual strangers.

Suffer no illusions: A sexual stranger is someone you may know but know not of their sexual history. This interpretation covers anyone whom you have not taken the opportunity to get to know and trust over an extended period of time—at least six months (and still that's not a guarantee).

As you very well know, people lie. The Centers for Disease Control can fairly estimate an STD's transmission rates, but no way can they estimate the number of people who lie about not having or suspecting STDs. Nor can you tell who is lying. Now combine those facts with the millions of people whose infections are in latent stages.

Sex with a sexual stranger is a complicated form of mutual masturbation, in that the only goal is to get off. This explains in part why the majority of sexual relations with strangers involve alcohol and/or drugs. (Drugs and alcohol and sex are always a dangerous mix: It promotes risky sexual behavior; and those who have drug and/or alcohol problems have an inordinately high rate of STDs.) Drugs and alcohol silence the little birdie that says, "Who is this person?" *A stranger!* Here is typical dialogue between two sexual strangers.

"You got something?"
"No. Do you have something?"
"No."

And that's it. Many people don't even exchange that scant dialogue before jumping into an activity that could possibly alter their entire life. This is the universal "Don't Ask, Don't Tell" policy. This avoidance is based on fear. Imagine a more truthful dialogue: "You got something?"

"Uh, yes. Trichomoniasis. Last year I had an ugly bout of gonorrhea, but that's cleared up now."

Yes, imagine. Because you will almost never hear it in the real world. Someone who is this candid about his or her sexual history—and whose IQ is higher than room temperature—isn't too quick to jump into a sexual-stranger relationship, because this is often the reason why his or her sexual malady occurred in the first place.

Avoiding questions about STDs also assuages the ego, because there is always the chance that the magical charm thought to have enticed someone out of his or her clothes isn't the true reason—he or she jumps out of her clothes at the drop of a hat for almost anyone, which is information no one wants to hear.

Abstinence nullifies lies, half truths, and obfuscation. The most beautiful aspect of abstinence: It is the best foundation for a relationship. Look at it this way: Who do you know that builds a house from the roof down? No one does, right? It isn't feasible. So why attempt to build a relationship from the highest point and then work down? Now how asshole backwards is that? The ultimate gift exchanged, the highest peak reached—"So now let us go further." Where the hell might that be?

A relationship built on sex seldom survives the first mild storm. Abstinence says, "I would like to get to know you. I respect you. I respect myself."

Let's take a quick look at two couples in the early stages of their relationships. Couple #1, Moe Smegma and Vanessa Del Rio, who consummated their relationship in the back of Moe's Ford Expedition after meeting at KFC; and Couple #2, Harold Smith and Sasha Hughes, who are currently practicing abstinence.

On a typical day, Moe and Venessa get together, watch television, go to a restaurant, and have sex. On a typical day, Harold and Sasha discuss their ideas and goals, talk to their families, go to the park or museum, take walks together, and participate in religious functions.

Venessa is already complaining that Moe doesn't do anything with her, and Moe is already complaining that Venessa wants too much of his time. Predictably, Moe and Venessa's relationship will not last two months. Harold and Sasha, meanwhile, are just getting started. They enjoy doing things with each other and are surprised at how much they have in common. Supported by family and friends, the two are considering marriage.

Well, you say, Harold and Sasha's relationship sounds boring (apparently Hollywood and television think the same). Moe and Venessa's moribund relationship offers more entertainment value. From the start they were suspicious of the other, and, amazingly, doubted the other's true intentions. A fight here and there also livens things up, and both Moe's and Venessa's exes have a habit of popping up—which leads to more suspicion of true intentions. Though boring by appearance, Harold and Sasha state that their relationship is growing, trust is forming, and, they never get tired of the other.

One script works, the other seldom works. You make the choice. *But what about those Brothers who would rather donate a testicle than consider abstinence?* This group of Brothers, by far the majority, should always use a condom if they are not in a long-term, monogamous relationship. Remember the key word here: *always!* The backyard remedies and suggestions do not work, and they range from the bizarre to the basically bullshit. Gargling with mouthwash before or after oral sex actually promotes the likelihood of STD infection. STDs do not react to ear wax—yours or anyone else's. Urinating before or after sex offers little protection against STDs. Remember this: Rarely can you tell if someone has an STD simply by sight. STDs are transmitted by sexual contact or contact with body fluids, including shared drug-injecting paraphernalia, so how clean or unclean a person is or isn't has very little to do with STDs.

The condom, if used properly and regularly, can offer reasonable protection against most STDS, but cannot offer guaranteed protection, nor can it offer much protection against Hepatitis B and genital warts that form outside of the condom-protected areas.

Condoms lull many people into a false sense of sexual confidence. Two people, say, Bull Baughs and Carrie Raybees meet, like each other, and have sex using a condom. For three months the two continue to use condoms, then one night Bull is out of condoms and the stores are closed. So in he goes, he and Carrie thinking: "Hey, we've been together for the last three months and nothing has happened." This happens every day. The fact that the condom in all likelihood is the reason why "nothing has happened" is flushed down the toilet.

Prudently, condom use should be practiced religiously until both you and your partner are tested for all

STDs, and then, several months later, return for more tests to ensure that no false-negatives resulted from early testing—*and* you and your partner are committed to each other. Then and only then should the condom come off—and still there's no guarantee. Yes, this is easier said than done, especially if you bounce back and forth from one relationship to the other. And yes, very few people do it this way.

Occasionally condoms do break, but not because of the reason that many Brothers claim or imply. Improper application of a condom is usually why condoms break—not because "I have a big dick." The illustrations below show the proper way to apply a condom.

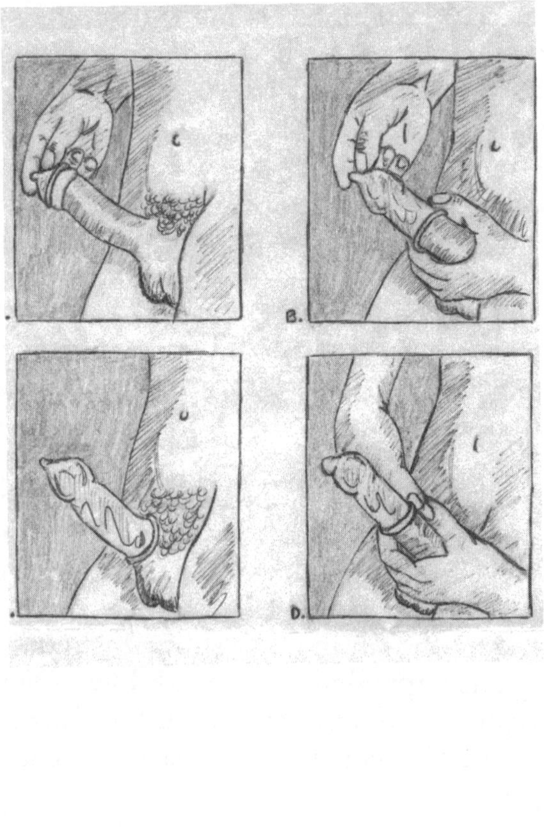

Place the rolled up condom over the head of the penis. Hold the top half-inch of the condom (with air squeezed out) to leave room for semen. (B) While holding the tip, unroll the condom onto the penis. Gently smooth out any air bubbles. (C) Unroll the condom down to the base of the penis. (D) To avoid spilling semen after ejaculation, hold the condom around the base of the penis as the penis is withdrawn. Remove the condom away from your partner, being careful not to spill. Flush material in toilet. Wash hands thoroughly with soap and water. (Never apply oils, ointments or Vaseline, to condom; this can diminish condom's effectiveness.)

Also remember that a condom is only a small part of the safe sex picture (actually the term "safe sex" is a misnomer, but "less risky than other sexual activities" is a tad too wordy). Discussing sexual history and STDs are equally important components of safe sex.

Sadly, tragically, and unbelievably in this day and age, there exist Brothers who are sexually promiscuous but steadfastly refuse to even consider using a condom, citing such inane reasons as " being uncomfortable" and "diminishing the feel." If this were the early '60s or before, and if their actions only harmed themselves, it would be easy to overlook such foolish, self-destructive behavior. STDs are far more uncomfortable and painful than a condom, and STDs can diminish feelings terminally.

There are four types of males who bungee jump without a safety device.

Superman: He is the man of steel. Virus or bacteria cannot penetrate his armor—at least he thinks. He can leap from one sexual tryst to the other with the grace of a gazelle. By day he's a mild-mannered wallflower, by night he's a sexual dynamo. When he finally succumbs to an infection (only a matter of time), he'll blame it on Kryptonite or anything else besides his own behavior.

The Boy Wonder: His body is of that of a man and his chronological age is of that of a man, but his mind is that of a boy, a very young boy. Everything in life to him is a wonder, including sex. He cannot imagine that something that feels so good can have negative consequences, so he consciously dismisses all the fact about STDs. When he finally succumbs to an infection, he'll run home and tell his mother. Unfortunately for him, her kissing his boo-boo will not help matters.

The Joker: "Life is such a joke, so why worry about anything," the Joker says. "You gon' die anyway, so drink, be merry, and get all the poontang you can get." The Joker is infected with an STD, and he knows it but refuses to acknowledge it. His ludicrous rationalization compromises his own treatment and put others at risk.

The Riddler: He does not have a clue, though he does ask questions—but to the wrong people. Ironically he avoids people with symptoms not related to STDs and engages in sexual contact with those who are at higher risk for STDs. When confronted with factual information about STDs that contradicts his friend's falsehoods about STDs, he sides with his friends.

As you may have noticed, abstinence is strongly recommended here but no suggestions of alternative sexual activities such as masturbation, sexual fantasizing, pornography, and rubbing, also known as dry humping. Although these activities are undoubtedly safer alternatives to the exchanging of body fluids, each has inherent potential for problems. Rubbing or dry humping can easily lead to the real thing. Sexual gurus, many of whose last sexual escapade occurred during the Roaring Twenties, claim that sexual fantasizing and pornography are harmless. Perhaps, but when is it dangerous? When an offense occurs? Ask yourself, does this activity benefit me, does it benefit those around me, and does it increase or decrease my self-respect, my respect of others? To avid pornography collectors, what is the distinguishable difference between one naked woman and the next?

It is always a good idea to leave the subject of masturbation in the hands of people who know, the people who have a better grasp on the subject, but what they promulgate is contrary to what millions of men have been taught since childhood—masturbation is not necessarily a good thing. Of course many men have no qualms with this activity and consider it healthy. On the other hand, many men masturbate and feel…well, embarrassed, ashamed. To those the gurus say there is no need to feel that way. First, to each his own. But remember this: Just because someone says something is right for you, but you feel it is wrong, then to you it is wrong—even if the world disagrees. Remember, at one time half the country thought slavery was to the African-American's benefit.

These newfangled precepts tend to suggest that a man has no control of his sex drive. To let the septuagenarian sex gurus tell it: A man has to do something! Yet no man has ever fallen ill or died from lack of sex, and millions of people have enjoyed a life of celibacy. In short, the decision is yours. If you are young and healthy now and want to remain so, abstinence is something you will strongly consider.

Chapter 9
Joy Riding

"She who claims that all men are dogs should select her companions from somewhere other than a kennel."
H.H.

If you have ever traveled via this country's interstate highways you've probably noticed that very few African-Americans hitchhike. Why? Because the objective to hitchhiking is to catch a ride. The Brother you see walking the highway on your way out of town is the same Brother you see walking the highway on your way back to town, regardless of how long you've been away.

The African-American rule to traveling: If you don't have a car, plane fare, Greyhound fare, then it's best to keep your ass at home.

In the African-American community, a car says it all. It speaks of your status, your prestige, your position, and your personal drive. Of course, this is a shallow way to judge someone, but this is the way it is. And yes, women of all colors judge a man by his car. Again, this is somewhat shallow, but a man's car provides a woman with tons of information to what type of man he is…

Women know that crackheads and drunks prefer walking to driving. Women know that a man who has chicken bones, rib bones, Coke cans, and other trash scattered in his car is a man who has the same scattered at his home. Women know that a man who painted his car with latex paint is a man who receives a monthly check. Women know that a man who scrolls his name or dumb phrases on the back window is a nobody seeking attention. Women know that a man who drives an expensive car but lives in the projects is a man whose priorities are mixed up. Women know that a man who permits everyone to drive his car is a man who will be walking soon. Women know that a man with numerous holes in his car seat smokes marijuana. Women know that a man who puts miniature toys on his dashboard is a man not far away from potty training. Women know that a man who has yet to get his tags can barely pay his car note. Women know that a man who drives an expensive car but doesn't work is either a drug dealer or an insurance beneficiary. Women know that a man who walks one day, then rides the next, is borrowing someone else's car. Women know that a man whose radio or rims cost two times more than his car is a man who throws money away. Women know that a man who drives on steady Eddie (almost empty tank) doesn't budget his money. Women know that a man who washes his car daily, refers to it by name, and buys it gifts, is a man who should consider dating his car. Women know that a child's car seat in the back means the man has children. And finally women know that regardless of what kind of a car man drives, a buckboard or a Bentley, he can still be an A-Hole of the highest order.

Men, on the other hand, rarely judge a woman by the car she drives. In fact, to many men a woman's look isn't the most important thing but the only thing. Remember the Barbie Doll Syndrome. Believe it or not, character and good looks are two totally different entities. Of course it is a great find if a woman possesses both, but to overlook negative qualities simply because of good looks is foolhardy. Therefore in this chapter you will learn to read signs of character, from the overt to the covert, from the implicit to the explicit, from the poorly lit to the highly illuminated.

To save time let's go get a car…uh, by the way, in your name. Before embarking you understand that to buy a decent car you must either have good credit or a reasonable down payment—sometimes both. Since you're buying, you can decide what car you prefer to buy. Naturally. You also decide where you prefer to buy. Car lots that have only five or six cars on the lot and car lots that double as barbecue shacks don't even register on your attention meter. Of course you're picky—this is a major financial and emotional investment. At the preferred lot, you also ignore the loquacious dealer; you know from experience that what he wants you to buy seldom coincides with what you want to buy.

You also know from experience that everything that looks good isn't always good. So even if the car looks like a million dollars on the outside, the inside, the car's heart and brain—motor and transmission—might not be worth a plum nickel. So you look past the glossy paint job, the recently cleaned interior, and start the engine and pop the hood…You're looking for oil leaks or cracked hoses or belts or anything that looks out of place, and you're listening for ticking or knocking or grinding or anything that sounds abnormal.

Everything looks good, sounds good, smells good, but you're still not satisfied. You take the car to a reputable mechanic and ask him to give it the once-over. He does, and gives it a green light. Now you're ready to negotiate—not buy, but negotiate. You negotiate the total price. You negotiate the monthly payments. You negotiate the warranty. Then you spend time by yourself and ponder. Then and only then do you decide to sign your name on the dotted line.

Okay. Now that you have wheels, let's ride over to one of the top ten places to meet women.

Church or other Religious institutions: No doubt, as the old saying goes, "You can find a devil in church," but your chance of finding a true soulmate, someone you can reasonably trust and someone you can share a lifetime with, is better here than anywhere else. Most women who are spiritually anchored honor their commitments, specifically their marriage vows, and are less inclined to jump ship at the first sign of stormy waters.

Voluntary Organizations: Whether at a hospital, a drug and/or alcohol treatment center, a school, wherever—a woman who spends her free time assisting others is a good woman to have. These women love people and they possess the ability to see the good through the bad—an admirable trait. Another big plus: They view life through a big lens; therefore trivial matters about money and toys are of no major concern to them.

Library: Women who frequent libraries are either in school or book lovers—a plus either way you look at it. These women are not only improving their education but are also opening the doors to new places, new worlds, and new people. Often these women will hold your hand and take you along with them to places you never dreamed of.

Museum and Art Centers: As with libraries, women who favor museums and art centers are broadening their horizons, peering into worlds outside their own. These women appreciate the work of others and understand that there are various ways of self-expression. Remember: To love art is to love life.

Health Club: A good rule of thumb: Never date a woman whose muscles are bigger than your own. However, most women who regularly attend health clubs are health-conscious, more concerned about their overall health than looking like Chyna on WWF—a disturbing sight. After reading the previous chapter, you know that being health-conscious is a big plus.

Car Wash: Unlike men, women almost never wash a car that doesn't belong to them. Also unlike men, women seldom wash a car that is worth less than the car wash itself. A safe bet, a woman who washes her car is single, most definitely independent, or has a couch potato at home whose days are numbered.

The Theater: Plays and theatrical performances, like churches, have female-dominant audiences. Even if you do not meet the woman of your dreams, you can still enjoy the performance.

At Work: Opinions vary on the subject of met-at-work relationships. Think long and hard about embarking on a relationship with a subordinate, and it is also a good idea to let the woman initiate the relationship. The pluses to these relationships: usually manifested over a long period of time; friendship resulted before anything else; ability to work together proven; and, most importantly, you never have to worry about a ride to work. However, one big minus: If relationship ends on a sour note, you'll still have to work together.

At the Lake: A woman who baits her own hook without screwing her face up in disgust, casts her line, and waits patiently and silently for a bite, without once asking for the time or scratching mosquito bites as if she were in a malaria-infested country, is a woman definitely worth foregoing the bass boat and buying a diamond ring for.

Laundromat: Yes, the Laundromat. If she neatly folds her clothes and puts them in a basket, she may very well be a woman worth pursuing. Yes, she may not have the accommodations at her house, but at least she makes a determined effort to keep that which she does have clean. However, if she throws all her belongings into a plastic garbage bag straight from the dryer…well, a safe bet, she's homeless.

You may not have noticed it, but you also drove by ten of the worst places to meet a woman. No, no, no! No need to back up. Let's just go over them.

The Crackhouse: This would be mildly funny but for the fact that many men go to the crackhouse ostensibly to meet women. Again, regardless of what the drug of choice is, someone, male or female, who uses drugs has a higher incidence—a lot higher!—of STDs. Yes, she may bathe more frequently than everyone else inside the house but her likelihood of a STDs is the same—extremely high!

Men's Club: Let's set the record straight here: A man who falls for a woman who dances nude or semi-nude for a group of strangers isn't a Sugar Daddy but a Sugar Fool.

Casino: Thankfully, what prevents many relationships from alighting and then exploding is that most women at the casino are so preoccupied with their slot machines and gaming tables they forget a man—boyfriend, husband, or the guy behind them trying to get their attention—exists.

Night Clubs: Of course, there's nothing wrong with going to a club or a bar to have a good time, but going with intentions to make a love connection is the wrong reason—and the reason why most men go. The ingredients are all wrong: alcohol, sweat, pheromones, loud music, women baring flesh, and a man's overwhelming desire to screw something. The dance floor says it all: Men, most of whom have never tapped their feet to a beat while sober, in various stages of inebriation, bouncing up and down like…like drunks with hard-ons.

Rehab: Liz Taylor learned this the hard way. Yes, it's noteworthy for someone to seek recovery from drug and alcohol problems, but while doing so the last thing he or she needs is a new relationship.

Family Planning Clinic: No three words are more oxymoronic than "family planning clinic." A safe bet: No couple has ever sought the services of a family planning clinic to plan for a family—reducing a family is not planning for a family. (What has this got to do with the ten worst places to meet a woman? Absolutely nothing.)

Friend's House: An age-old mystery revolves around the fact that a friend's significant other looks more an exciting prospect than the millions of other women in the world. This is a dangerous game—and a selfish game as well. Isn't it better to have one friend than one risky new love and a bitter enemy? Don't forget the old cliché: What goes around comes around.

Family Reunion: Uh...well...most people in attendance at family reunions are, you know, sort of related, by blood and that kind of thing. Okay? Which means it's rather disgusting and despicable to look upon cousin Bobbi Joe as anything other than cousin Bobbi Joe.

Jail: Unlike women, men do not easily fall for someone who has been convicted of a felony. However, many men have no qualms about misdemeanors. Still, jail is jail, and a woman who goes to jail repeatedly is a woman capable of busting a man's head wide open.

Truck Stop: Unless she is working in some capacity at the truck stop—truck driver, waitress, cook, manager, etc.—then five will get you twenty she's a...well, the W-word is too strong, and trollop and courtesan doesn't fully cover the bill, so here the word is WASP, which stands for: *Whore? A Strong Possibility.*

Seeing Is Believing

Before you say one word, check her out. Look for things that don't match. For example:

Coat—summertime
Short pants—wintertime
Sandals—crusty toenails
Halter—underarm hair
Nose ring—snotty nose
Tattoo(s)—ashy skin
Bifocals—cockeyed
Navel ring—belly button lint
Open shirt—chest hair
Toothpick—gap teeth
Corn on the cob—toothless
Lip gloss—cold sore
Fan or air conditioner—BO (body odor)
Striped shirt—checkered pants
Sagging pants—no underwear
No bra—sagging breast
Coughing—halitosis

Pay particular attention to WASP indicators such as wigs, tattoos, and body rings. The wearing of these items doesn't necessarily suggest promiscuous behavior, but on the same token the items do suggest promiscuous behavior. That doesn't make sense, does it? A better explanation: Body rings and tattoos in and on visible body parts, arms and legs, are usually faddish in nature. Body rings and tattoos in or on personal parts, specifically parts with hair or an aureole, says much more about the individual. After all, the main object in getting a tattoo or a body ring is to show it off, right? Which means if it's in or on a private part somebody besides you has seen it—hey, she didn't do it herself.

For the most part, wigs are innocuous, and often are an added plus to many women's appearance. The line is crossed when the wig wearing is inconsistent or bizarre. In other words, the damn thing should at least fit properly on one's head—everyday, not every other day—and it never hurts to comb it once in a while. A federal law should mandate that no one can possess more than four wigs at any given time, and the colors green, red, and orange be banned—and with the exception of Halle Berry, Sisters would be denied access to blond wigs. (Any Sister who can stare lovingly into a White man's eyes, as Halle did with Warren Beatty in the movie Bulworth, and declare, "You my nigga!" deserves a blond wig.) An addendum to such a law: Lying about hair color, hair length, and hair authenticity should be a misdemeanor. Beautiful women like Jill Scott, Erica Badu, and Tracy Chapman demonstrate that their beauty lies in their abilities and their hearts, not their hair.

The applies to men as well. Be honest, though you may love to see Sisqo, Prince, Michael Jackson, or Dennis Rodman perform, would you really want to ride through the neighborhood with one of these guys? Doesn't Rodman look like the kind of guy who would set his opened can next to yours just to see what would happen? Apparently one of the perks to being rich and famous is that you can look and act weird and be praised for doing so. Besides Prince, who has the slightest idea what "Purple Rain" means? Besides Dennis Rodman, what Brother do you know who would even consider putting more than one ring in a nostril? And could you imagine what would happen to a Brother in your neighborhood who suddenly changed from dark-skinned to pale white?

Fact: Being yourself requires less effort, less holes, less painful tattoos, and less money.

Being yourself also attracts people who like you for yourself. Face the facts: Everyone you meet will not like you. For some people this axiom is too hard to digest. Think about it, you don't like everyone you meet. Flip the script. Actually you can put people in three groups:

those who don't give a damn about you (the majority); those who lie about giving a damn about you; and those who truly care about you (the small minority, family and friends). So why waste time and energy trying to be something you are not? Simply be yourself.

Chitty Chitty Bang Bang

Isn't it amazing how a used car that hummed, purred, and cooed on the dealers' lot, farts, poots, and burps the moment you pull into your driveway? If it had made all that racket while at the lot, you would not have bought it. Then when you take it in and request your money back, the dealers points to the little sign on the back window that says: SOLD AS IS. NO WARRANTY.

Often the same thing happens during the middle stage of many relationships: Everything is running smoothly, an emotional investment is committed, then *fart, poot, burp,* all hell breaks loose. But unlike a car, people usually let you know early on that something is out of whack with their master cylinder. If you are not listening, for whatever reason—Barbie Doll Syndrome, infatuation, or temporary insanity—you will miss the noise. And yes, you will pay later.

For example, a Toni Braxton lookalike tells you: "I'm crazy about you. You're the man of my dreams…and, by the way, could you refill my prescription for Thorazin?"

If you hear the noise, Thorazin stands out in your mind more than anything else; it signals that something is not right here and something will not be right here in the future. However, if you are mesmerized by her beautiful brown eyes, her lovely breast, and her curvaceous figure, Thorazin, the noise, doesn't register in your mind. Then, not too far in the future, when you're in knee-deep emotionally and all hell breaks loose, you will say: "I didn't know she was crazy!"

This phenomenon is called NOSE, the acronym for Neglecting Obvious Signs of Eccentricities—also referred to as "Having your nose wide open," and being "Led by the nose." This condition occurs in men and women, but is more prevalent in men who suffer from low self-esteem and/or occasional inexplicable hearing loss.

Listening for noise is a key to avoiding lemon relationships. Some noises are extremely loud, while others are barely detectable to the human ear. To enhance your hearing abilities, here is a list of noises that signal potential problems.

A Whining Noise: This noise is made by women who believe the Cinderella story. One day, they hope, their prince will arrive and sweep them off their feet, and they will live in a castle with maids and servants. Until that day they'll whine incessantly about the vicissitudes of life. Whining gets old fast. Notice that whining almost always starts with I, as in: *"I got to go to work," "I got to clean the house,"* and *"I got to do everything myself."* Of course everyone makes these statements from time to time, but only a whiner can draw out a six-word sentence into a paragraph. Boo-hoo, sniffle, whine! Initially, she who whines about everything will avoid doing so, because she knows it is a turnoff. You can detect most whiners by sight, though; their posture is usually poor, shoulders slumped, eyes on the ground, and their countenance a perpetual when-is-the-earthquake-coming look.

A Smacking Noise: This noise is made by women who have a love/hate relationship with food. They love to eat, but hate to be told to slow down, or to save some for someone else. These women can practically eat you out of house and home. Often men make the mistake of thinking a big woman a voracious eater, but many are not, and many an Olive Oyl can out-eat a women three times her size. During the early stage of the relationship, she who can eat her weight and yours in one sitting will eat sensibly, nibbling on small bites, and, though painfully, leaving food on her plate. So pay close attention to her conversation, and notice if her eyes light up when you mention a double cheeseburger with fries. Other early warning signs: biting tongue or finger while eating; picking up morsels of food from floor; requesting a doggie bag after selecting the buffet; and groaning when passing fast food restaurants.

A Squealing Noise: In cars this sound usually indicates failing brakes; in women this sound usually indicates childishness. These women are usually attractive and have grown accustomed to having things their way. To get their way these women will pout, play the silent game, and throw temper tantrums. And, sadly, they usually succeed. Yes, some men enjoy playing the Big Daddy role, but they run the risk of a bigger Daddy, with a bigger wallet, usurping their authority.

A Slurping Noise: This noise is made by women who demand oral sex. Many women will beat around the bush on the subject, but you know what they're getting at. Let's set the record straight on this: Oral sex, like rape, is about power and control. Pure and simple. Women's magazines and pop songs extol the pleasures of cunnilingus and fellatio, but the writers of both cannot swallow the fact that oral sex puts someone in a demeaning, demoralizing position. Of course, the critics say: "What goes on in private between two consenting adults is no one's business." Yes, this is true. But even if the act is private, between two consenting adults, does not mean that it is not also a demeaning and demoralizing act. In the name of pleasuring someone does it really take all that?

No, it does not. Better yet, ask yourself the following questions:

Is this something I can honestly say I am proud of doing?

Is this something that I'm ashamed of?

Is this something I would not mind being requested to do?

Is this something I would suggest others do?

Is this something I would rather do in the dark?

Is this something where eye contact is best avoided?

Fact: Oral sex almost always hurt a relationship.

What sad and foolish a man who believes that performing cunnilingus is a sure-fire way to pleasure a woman. And for Pete's sake, if a woman is particularly skilled in fellatio, where do you think she developed the skill? *In art class*? Guess again. Control is what it is about. Once you give over control, especially in areas regarding your self-respect, you cannot easily gain it back.

Backfire: A raucous cacophony made by five or more children. It is not necessarily bad to date a woman with five or more children, but many women complicate the matter by not mentioning their children or the exact number of their children till later in the relationship. Whereas there were once two, five months later a few more pop up. Not good. (More on the subject of children in the next chapter.) Another noise to suddenly become alarmed to is a woman who has a child or children but does not have custody.

A Banging Noise: Many unscrupulous dealers will not tell you that a car has been wrecked. Therefore it is always a good idea to find out the car's history—several Internet sites provide such information. To discover a woman's history of emotional wrecks the simplest way is to listen. For egotistical reasons, many men prefer not to hear tales of a woman's ex or exes—especially if the number of exes goes into double digits. But what better way to delve off into someone's personality? Look for the pattern.

Contrary to what many people think, a series of bad relationships is not bad luck, but bad choices. Think about it: If the penultimate guy she dated was on anti-depressant and tried to kill her in her sleep, why in the world would she date another guy who was on the same prescription? The same logic applies to drunks, ergo-phobes, drug addicts, and emotional and physical abusers. Thus: Who she dated says a lot to who she is.

Many men make the mistake of trying to be her knight in shining armor, or trying to best the last guy she was with. Usually this backfires, and the man mysteriously finds himself doing exactly what the last guy did. This phenomenon is called A-Hole Imprinting. Remember this: The last thing a woman who has been emotionally wrecked needs is a new relationship. If you honestly care about her, suggest counseling or therapy or some avenue in which she can focus on getting herself back together.

A Growling Noise: This is noise an aggressive woman makes before acting out, which can range from busting your head wide open to breaking your favorite fishing rod. Though men are far more aggressive and violent than women, more and more women are joining the ranks of ass-kicking harridans. Why? Xena and the World Wrestling Federation, possibly. But no one knows for sure. Regardless of which sex is the aggressor, physical and emotional abuse is wrong. Admittedly, no one deserves to be abused, but there is more a comic tragedy when a woman whoops a man's ass. Which is probably the main reason why many men who have been abused will not call the police or seek a protection order.

The dynamics to an abusive relation are always the same: The abuser leads with an emotional outburst, insults, then simple assault, a slap, a push, then irresolute remorse, and then more violence, remorse, violence, remorse, escalated violence. One discernible difference with abusive women, however, is that they tend to broadcast their deeds—usually to family and friends—while abusive men seldom if ever tell anyone.

Initially, the abuser comes off as charming, sensitive, and patient. In time the potential for emotional outburst will rear its ugly head. Pay close attention to how she treats others, especially when she is driving. If you suspect an abusive nature, try tossing a less-than-complimentary comment on the table and see how she reacts to it. Make sure the table is in public.

Similar growling noises to be attuned to are name-calling and putdowns. In this day and age you would think that most people know that name-calling and putdowns have the same damaging psychological effects as physical abuse. Not so. A woman who calls her family and friends—especially her children—"stupid," "dumb," "ignorant," or anything similar is a woman not worth speaking to, much less dating. Don't fool yourself, if she does and says bad things to the people she supposedly loves, what makes you so unworthy of the same treatment?

A Clicking Noise: It's funny how a car stops making that strange clicking noise the moment you arrive at the mechanic. This makes you wonder if you are losing your mind. The same thought runs through your mind when you deal with a woman who clicks; one moment she's laughing and having a good time, then the next, she's mad as hell—for what? You haven't the slightest idea. Often men make the mistake of trying to figure out what was the impetus to the sudden change in mood. A waste of time. Not only will she not tell you what the problem is, but she will be upset that you cannot read her mind and discover the problem without her having to tell you.

The key to these type women: Immaturity, Impulsiveness, and Irrationality. So listen closely to what she says about old accidents, emotional and physical, that left her or someone else "traumatized for life."

A Boiling Noise: This sound usually indicates a car is running hot. In women this is the sound of a Sugar Baby, a Hoochie Mama, a Gold Digger, and other names for women who use their body as a tool to get in a man's wallet. If you don't mind being a Sugar Daddy and enjoy paying for superficial affection, then ignore the noise. If not, keep in mind that a woman who exposes more cleavage as she asks for more money is not a woman worth having. Remember: Women read men better than men read women. The moment a Sugar Baby catches you watching her butt with that I-see-it-but-can't-believe-it look, she knows she's got you where she wants you, her hands in your pants, and not on what you are thinking about, either.

There are many more noises to listen for, but there's no need to list them all here. If you are not comfortable with the noise, then eliminate it. It's just that simple. Notice how many parents who apparently have a low threshold for noise often make the mistake of buying their children a toy that makes a tremendous racket. Eventually they wind up breaking the toy or hiding it. Then, within a few weeks, they forget and buy another toy that makes more racket than the one before. The same results: frustration, followed by termination.

Noisy relationships that end in termination leave emotional scars. The more scars you have, the less attractive you are. Just like a woman who has five or more children is less-than-attractive relationship prospect, so is a man who has five or more children. Believe it or not, the more relationships one has, the further away one gets away from the mystical and elusive "True Love," and the closer to "Going Through The Motions."

Oil Leaks

By now you would think it would be time to move away from the used car lot on to bigger and better things, right? Well, hold on a for a moment more. It would be shameful to leave without checking for oil leaks. To do that, you must look underneath, on the ground, in the spot where the car was last parked. In other words, you must go beyond looking at what is in front of you and search for potential problems. Rude, yes, but so practical and cost-saving.

Yes, as you expected, the same search-for-potential-problems campaign can be used in deciding to start or continue a relationship. For example, your lady friend says that she owns a dog. No problem. But you do more than ask what kind of dog it is; the first time you go to her house, you go around back to take a look at the dog. You are looking to see if the dog has adequate food, water, and space. If the dog is skins and bones and has cornbread and grits in its supper bowl, that tells you a lot about your lady friend's personality. Then again, if she has the dog inside the house, ensconced in its own room, wearing a miniature smoking jacket with an ascot, that tells you a lot about her personality as well.

A word of caution: Observe casually, nonchalantly. In other words, don't speak about what you see, just look. "Hey, I'm going round back to see if your dog is starving" is a crude insult, even if it is starving.

This especially applies to speaking ill of a woman's children. Regardless of what the child or children look like, it is best to keep it to yourself. Many a men have been injured as a result of an offhanded comment about a child. Still, pay close attention to the dress and upkeep of her child or children. If she is dressed to the nines with an expensive coif, then her child or children should be dressed to the nines as well. If not, this says a lot about what kind of woman she is and what kind of mother she is—and none of it speaks favorably. Also keep count of the number of children she introduces you to, and keep in mind that some children resemble each other, so make sure you get an accurate count.

Note the child or children's demeanor. Withdrawn? Diffident? Relaxed? Ebullient? "Are you my daddy?" signals confusion. Don't grin and bear it if your lady friend says, "Yes, he is."

Keep in mind that children are generally the world's greatest judges of character. If your intentions are to toss their mother around in the sack and then split, they know it before you sit down, before you offer them a few dollars, and before you start talking nonsense. Think about it: If you perceive her child or children as road bumps on your way to her bedroom, why not save yourself and everyone concerned the trouble—and rent a motel room. Would you want someone skinning and grinning in your face, faking and shaking, with the sole intent of getting your mother into the bedroom? Of course you wouldn't. And you probably don't care much for the suggestion, either. So why treat someone in a manner in which you would not like to be treated? However, even if those were not your intentions, think long and hard about starting a relationship with a woman who has children. If you cannot handle the responsibility, or would rather not handle the responsibility, then by all means say so.

While you are in the house or apartment take a look around...Is it clean? Filthy? Then politely ask to use the bathroom. Bathrooms tell people secrets. Often people who clean up moments before expected company neglect to hit the bathroom. A clean bathroom is the mark of someone who is hygiene-conscious. Pay close attention to the bathtub and/or shower and the commode. (The absence of both says...well, you know what it says.)

Thick crusty rings in the tub and/or shower suggest infrequent use. Calling cards in the commode suggest you should flush it, even if it isn't yours. Now turn your attention to the medicine cabinet; open it gently, quietly...Vaseline, rubbing alcohol, CamphoPhenique, calamine lotion, hair grease, and other accoutrements are not your primary concern. You are looking for prescriptions.

You are shaking your head again. Oh, well, yes, this is rude and an invasion of someone's privacy, no doubt—not to mention sneaky and inconsiderate. Justification for doing so: none whatsoever. Meanwhile, note the wording on the prescription containers, especially the containers with the color tabs warning not to eat or drink alcohol or operate a vehicle. Those which are unfamiliar to you write down on the little pad you brought with you, to be checked on later.

This should be the extent of your deceit. Anywhere else is off limit. A word of caution: You can get your head busted wide open for rummaging through someone's effects.

Another treasure chest of information is her family and friends. Her girlfriends or lack thereof says a mouthful about her personality. As with men, women tend to mimic the behavior of their friends. Therefore, if her friends talk about "bumping some man's head"—dumping a Sugar Daddy—then you should wonder if your head is in line for a knot. If her friends drink cheap whiskey or wine, your lady friend probably does too. If her friends sprinkle a little nose candy on marijuana joints, your lady friend probably does too. Also observe what role she plays with her friends. Is she the weak one? The strong one? Any Grover Getover tendencies?

No girlfriend whatsoever strongly suggests that she thinks other women—all of 'em!—are jealous of her. This is almost always the case. What these type women lack in girlfriends they more than make up in men friends. Most men have a problem with a woman having an affectionate male cousin, much less a man friend. With these type women your memory acuity should always be at its peak. One day he's her friend, then a month later he's her cousin, then later, an uncle, even later, a nephew, then a third cousin, and finally back to a friend. If you don't keep up with the constant changes, don't be surprised if you start calling him Daddy.

When around her immediate family, look for dysfunctional family members. The brother or sister who talks and responds to himself or herself. The brother or sister who wears his or her underwear on the outside of clothes. This behavior is often hereditary. Also be exceptionally curious about the family member who takes his or her meals in the attic or basement. Yes, you most definitely want to take a look at him or her. Pay close attention to the relationship she has with her mother and father. A poor mother/daughter relationship reeks of pettiness, selfishness, and intransigence—though both sides can be equally guilty. A poor father/daughter relation for any reason—father absent, father abusive, whatever—often predicts future problems, specifically: she'll expect her man to fill the void. Another potential problem: If Daddy spoiled her, she'll expect the same treatment.

Also be exceptionally wary if she backbites or speaks ill of her family members—unless, of course, she is related to the Black Avenger.

Most families try to keep family business within the family. But there is usually one family member who makes it his or her business to tell all family secrets that do not shine a bad light on him and her. This is the person you want to remain in earshot of. With a little practice you can learn how to listen intently to a conversation without staring into the talker's mouth—a tremendous benefit when conversing with someone who is edentulous or has horrendous halitosis.

One area in which many families unintentionally reveal family secrets: nicknames. Nicknames often originate from behavior or resemblance. And this is another area in which African-Americans differ from other races. African-Americans generally accept nicknames and rarely resort to mass murder after being called such. A word of caution: While African-Americans generally acquiesce to nicknames, they usually condone the use by friends and family members only. In other words, your saying "Bigun" can lead to you getting your head busted wide open.

The following is a brief list of nicknames. Keep in mind that some nicknames have double meanings, so the definition given here should not be used as a guide to judge character.

Pork Chop, Pork Rinds, Pork Skin, Pork Salad, Pork n Beans, Salt Pork, Sausage, Chitterlings, Ham, Ham Hocks, Fat Back, Ribs, Bacon, Souse, Pig, Piglet, Piggy, and Pig Feet, suggest obesity, or the potential for obesity—or a penchant for swine.

Low-cal, Cottage Cheese, Oprah, Jenny Craig, WW(Weight Watchers), and SlimFast usually suggest an ongoing struggle to lose weight.

Popeyes, KFC, Taco Bell, Red Lobsters, Church's, and Wendy's indicates a passion for fast food, or a phobia of cooking.

Shaky, VA, Mental, Cuckoo, Dingy, Head Case, Schizzy, Special K, and others suggest mental illnesses.

MD20/20, Tough Wille, White Port, Gin and Juice, Scotch, Tequila, Thunderbird, Forty, Hot Forty, Double Deuce, Rum, 151, 80 Proof, and the name of any cocktail drink suggest a fondness for alcoholic beverages.

Candy, Lollipop, Sucker, Blow Pop, M&M, Snicker, Juicy Fruit, Now and Later, Goodbar, Lemon Drop, suggest WASP (Whore? A Strong Possibility) tendencies—and so do bodies of water: Atlantic, Deep Sea, Blue Hole, Pacific, and Lake-Anything.

Cricket, Lice, Tick, Flea, Ant, Roach, Chigger, Mite, Spider, Worm, Bee, Bug, June Bug, Mosquito, Gnat, suggest irksome and annoying social tendencies.

Hawk, Buzzard, Chicken, Turkey, Wild Turkey, Owl, suggest Sugar Baby tendencies; and so do: Rat, Squirrel, Beaver, Hood Rat, Vamp, Hoochie Mama, Lizard, Lot Lizard, Snake, Python, Moccasin, Thang, Hot Thing or Hot Thang, Gold Digger, and Trick (unless on birth certificate—Starla, Trixe, Darlene, and Spanky also fall under this category)

Lexus, Mercedes, BMW, Bentley, Jag or Jaguar, Camry, Roll Royce or RR or Double R, Cadillac, Infiniti, SUV, suggest pretentiousness, unless, of course, she owns one. Also: Paris, NY or New York, Cali or California, Chicago, Windy, Chi Town, Norleans, Hotlanta. (This especially applies to women who have traveled to these destinations and within a matter of days adopted the dialect.)

Spike, Fix, T's and Blues, Horse, Smack, Blunt, Powder, Black Molly, Lucille, D-Pills, B-52, Wet Daddy, Mushroom, Hearts, Ludes, Mary J, Blunt, Thai Stick, Misses Jane, Star, Rockstar, Head, Toons, Shooter, and many more, suggest drug addiction.

Ortho, Bucky, Beaver, Rabbit, Camel, Butter, Yellow, Oleo, Margarine, usually suggest poor dental hygiene.

Penny, Fifty, G, Paper, Dollar, Bo Dollar, Hundred, Ends, Cheese, Ducky, Skins, Ice, Onion, Susie B, Change, Gold, Sapphire, Ruby (occasionally), suggest an inordinate passion for money.

Peaches, Banana or Nana, Berry, Strawberry and other fruity nicknames suggest a sweet disposition.

Fox, Cat, Cheetah, Tiger, Panther, Weasel, Bat, Moon, and Ferret suggest sneakiness.

> **Blossom,** Bubbles, Buttercup, Sheba, Tinkie, Winkie, La-La, Po, Cat Woman, Wonder Woman, Minnie, and Isis, suggest childishness and/or a furtive imagination.

Some nicknames are very common, so it is unwise to apply meaning to them. For example, Red, a nickname often given to light-skinned African-American men and women. Southerners utilize nicknames far more than Northerners. Old Southern favorites: Mae, Joe, B, Ann, which often double as nicknames and middle names. Thus: Joyce Mae, Ula Mae, Fanny Mae, Annie Mae, Bobbi Mae, Bobbi Joe, Linda Joe, Wanda Joe, Annie B, Sheila B, Linda B, Joy Ann, Debra Ann, Joe Ann, and on and on.

By now you are probably thinking: With all this checking under the hood, listening for strange noises, and interpreting sobriquets, a Brother might never find a mate.

Yes, this does entail a degree of nit-picking, and it definitely slows the process of picking and choosing a mate to a snail's pace. Yet there are a plethora of advantages to moving in the slow lane. First and foremost: You make the decision to date or to continue dating after weighing the pro and cons. You are thinking and analyzing—not simply looking and reacting. Yes, she looks good—damn good!—and she can probably make a man feel good—damn good!—in bed...but...is she worth it? A big question, which begs other questions, such as: Her health, mental and physical? Her personality? Trustworthiness? Compatibility?

If the question of her expertise in bed is answered before any other question, every other question, the important questions, takes a second seat. Her lying every time she opens her mouth is overlooked because of the other thing she does with her mouth. Then a situation arises, one in which her ability to tell the truth is crucial—and *spit, gargle, cough!*—she lets you down. Think about it, even a man who is in the best of health can have sex for only so long. The average sex act from beginning to end lasts about ten minutes. A day has 1,440 minutes in it. So even if you used up 440 minutes in a day having sex (a Wilt Chamberlin-like feat), what do you do with the other thousand minutes? And don't say bask in the afterglow.

Believe or not, sex is actually better when two people have taken the time to get to know each other first; much better, and much safer.

Another plus among many to moving in the slow lane: Women will come to you.

Notice the desperate Brother in the club...He is in a hurry...The club closes in fifteen minutes, and he wants to take someone home with him, badly...so he asks everybody. Notice the desperation written on his face. Read the lips of the women he asks: "I'm not interested," "Keep steppin'!" "Get lost!"

Now notice the Brother sitting in the corner, chilling, relaxed...And notice the women moving toward his table. Now read his lips: "I'm not interested."

Control is what it is all about. You control when, where, and with whom. A popular misguided notion says a man will be a man, which attempts to rationalize a man's sexual indiscretions. Under such logic, a disease is a disease, a divorce is a divorce, an unexpected child is an unexpected child, a terrible relationship is a terrible relationship, and a death is a death. But notice the difference when it is *your* disease, *your* divorce, *your* unexpected child, *your* terrible relationship, and *your* death.

Four More Lemons

Lets take a look at four lemons—The Married Woman, The Lush, The Druggie, and The RRHOID (Reckless Remorseless Hedonistic Obnoxious Devil) — all of whom should be avoided at all cost.

The Married Woman: Have you ever watched a pet for someone for a period of time and then became attached to the thing? If so, you probably said after whoever came and retrieved it: "I will not do that again." If you are honest about it, you almost shed a few tears. You and the thing made a connection, and you—you believed—were the only one person in the world who could treat the thing like it was supposed to be treated. Unfortunately, the owner did not think the same.

This is exactly what happens, though with a higher degree of emotional commitment, when a man falls for a married woman. Eventually the rightful owner returns for his property—though far less gleefully than someone retrieving a pet. "Less gleefully" is putting it mildly; the rightful owner might try to put a couple of pop knots on the borrower's head. Or the borrower might try to put a couple of pop knots on the owner's head. Either way, one or both parties could get KISSed.

Unlike women, men seldom initiate contact with a married person with the intent of a long-term relationship. Men go in with a hit-it-and-quit-it attitude and then discover that the quit-it part is more difficult, a lot more difficult, than the hit-it part. Admittedly it's thrilling diving behind bushes, hiding behind trees, sneaking into cheap hotels, having someone make your phone calls, and devising codes and secret forms of communications—and all this is before anyone takes their clothes off. You would think with this much fun before sex, why bother with sex at all?

Though very few libertines in adulterous liaisons will admit it, the main reason why so much energy and excitement is put into pre-sex activity is because sex is all there is to the relationship. Any other activity—a walk in the park, dining out, shopping, a movie—is usually out the question, unless, of course, there is long-term planning beforehand. Why? Because somebody—her husband, her husband's family, her husband's friend or associate—might be out and about.

Other areas of concern: gifts and holidays, including birthdays. Of course, she cannot take whatever you buy her home. And you cannot reasonably expect a turkey leg, eggnog, firecrackers, expensive Christmas presents, or an invite to a barbecue. Yet you can expect lonely nights, ambivalent feelings, and frustration. Word of warning: Very few people sympathize with someone who bemoans an adulterous relationship.

Men take up with a mistress for a wide range of reasons, including boredom and a fear of growing old. Women, however, usually take up with a Mister Mistress for emotional reasons: revenge (hubby did it, so she will, too); lack of communication (hubby doesn't talk much); and loneliness (hubby is often away from home). Still, the dynamics are the same: Both genders expect the outside love interest to remain true. And this is part of the insanity. "You stay at home, alone, while I go home to my spouse." Women tend to follow this edict more so than men. Yet the rationalization is always the same: "I'm in love."

Think about it, while she is not with you, she is at home with her husband doing husband and wife things, which includes bouncing together naked (how someone can rationalize this fact is beyond comprehension). Another ugly thought: If her hubby gives her something, particularly a STD, she will give it to you. So, in effect, you are sleeping with her and her husband and all the people he is sleeping with. When the time comes for her to make a final decision—and eventually it will—she will choose her hubby, even though she told you a hundred times he was such a dud in bed.

Okay, for the sake of argument, say, she chooses you. Now you are the main man, the alpha male, and she is...well, uh...she is, you know, sorta, well, she is someone you cannot trust. After all, she cheated on him with you, so what makes you think—and you will be thinking about it a lot—that she will not cheat on you? This one is a no-brainer.

The Lush: Yes, it is unfair. A man who chases women is considered a stud while a woman who chases men is considered a WASP. A man who drinks to excess is considered a piss-poe drunk; a woman who does the same is considered a piss-poe drunk and a WASP. Unfair, yes, but you must admit, it is more disturbing to see an intoxicated woman mistake a flowerpot for a commode.

A woman's body does not metabolize alcohol as quickly as a man's. Thus smaller amounts of alcohol can cause a woman to become intoxicated. Another fact, though sadder and most disturbing: Women, unlike men, are always at risk for being sexually assaulted while intoxicated.

Again, alcohol provides a built-in excuse for men and women to say and do things they don't have the guts to say or do sober. Emotional creatures by nature, women tend to run the full gamut of emotions while intoxicated, at the same time calling you every name in the book. Any deficiencies on your part—erectile dysfunction, premature ejaculation, a fondness for leather, whatever—an intoxicated woman will make public.

For the most part, piss-poe drunk women pick piss-poe drunk men, and vice versa. But remember, at one time—a week or two—a piss-poe drunk woman was a vivacious, decent-looking woman. Then, a sip here, a swallow there, and a chug over yonder, and *hic!*—a full-fledged pathetic piss-poe drunk. For a woman, the journey to Piss-poe Drunkville almost always involves a sexual assault or two along the way. The probability of her becoming a victim, as in being found murdered, is ten times higher than other women, but slightly lower than women drug addicts and/or prostitutes.

Thus, if you are not a piss-poe drunk or a drunk, why consider this woman at all? Frankly, she's not worth the trouble. And remember, good sex has never rehabilitated anyone.

Piss-poe drunk women are relatively easy to detect. Staggering, vomiting, and falling facedown are good indicators. When those signs are not apparent, notice her skin, her eyes, and clothing. Alcohol causes wrinkles and rubbery skin. Bloodshot eyes and/or eye bags are also good indicators of being a piss-poe drunk. All drunks and piss-poe drunks are notorious for passing right by the Goodwill Thrift Store and going to the liquor store, which is why the same dress she wore last year is the same dress she has on now.

Pay close attention to what she drinks. If she prefers Wild Irish Rose or Charter Eight rather than chardonnay, that should tell you something. Also pay attention to how she drinks. If she favors drinking from a paper bag and wrapping her lips around the bottle rather than a cup or a glass, this should also tell you something. Even more revealing: She passes the bottle to you and says, "Here...alcohol kills all germs."

The same goes for beer. Only a drunk or a piss-poe drunk would upend a beer bottle and make sucking noises in an attempt to get the last drop.

More facts: Married and widowed women tend to have fewer problems with alcohol than divorced and single women; women who shack tend to have more problems with alcohol than any other group—perhaps because the wedding is constantly postponed.

If her parents—especially her mother—were/are drunks or piss-poe drunks, then her chance of becoming the same is high. And while drunks of either gender share the same behavior traits—excessive drinking, morning drinking, denial of drinking problems—women often take bigger steps to conceal drinking problems than men (yes, the stigma is greater). Many men and women often rationalize a loved one's negative behavior simply because the misconduct is committed at the house. Thus: "I would rather have so-and-so get drunk, talk shit, and try to kill me at home than to do it out on the streets."

Rationalizing someone's behavior generally precedes becoming a victim of someone's behavior. In other words, you can become a drunk or a piss-poe drunk without ever taking one sip of alcohol.

The Druggie: Three type of women fall under this category: Linda Script, Felicia Festiva, and Chrissy Crackhead. As you may have guessed, Linda Script is addicted to prescription drugs, ranging from Antabuse to Xanex. Always remember that a drug addiction, regardless of what the drug of choice is, leads to one of four things: prison, death, insanity, or rehabilitation. And always remember that drug addicts are basically sick people, incapable of starting or maintaining a loving relationship. So, why bother?

You will need time to spot Linda's problem because she doesn't believe she has an addiction and will never admit to one. Yet she is always at some doctor's office or at the hospital—to obtain a prescription. She spends an inordinate time in bed, dead asleep, in part because of the side effects of the drugs she is taking and in part because of depression, which always goes hand-in-hand with any addiction. Her mood fluctuates by the minute, though mostly stuck on dolorous. No, you cannot cheer her up. No, you cannot love her into rehabilitation. The best you can do: acknowledge her problem and suggest that she seek help—and the rest is up to her.

Of the three types of women drug addicts, Felica Festiva has the best chance for simply dropping drugs and never returning to them. Basically Felicia is a party girl. She's young, late teens through early twenties. She's cocky, because she has yet to meet a situation she could not handle—that will soon change. Bless her heart, Felica enjoys the attention of men; and she thinks that a group of men, alcohol, a little blow, a little smoke, and herself the center of attention as the recipe for a grand party. On occasion this mixture of ingredients combines without incident, but without a doubt, this is a recipe for rape or a gang rape. The morning Felicia wakes up dimly remembering the night before, when she passed out and some guy pulled her clothes down and got on top of her, then four or more other guys followed, or the night the guy, who she thought was the coolest G in the world, less-than-subtly demands sexual reciprocation for the freebies he has been giving her, she will do one of two things—quit drugs and the crowd she was running with altogether, or change her name to…

Chrissy Crackhead, a veteran of sexual assaults and a hardcore drug user, including cocaine and heroin—not to mention a more-than-likely candidate for sexually transmitted diseases. Make no mistake about it, Chrissy is also a prostitute; whether she walks the streets or occasionally provides services at her home, she is still a prostitute. Therefore, she, more so than the other two, is not capable of embarking on a loving relationship. In fact, she considers most men as johns—sex customers.

Unless you utilize the services of a seeing-eye dog, or your name is Chris Crackhead, no way should you make the mistake of beginning a relationship with a Chrissy Crackhead. Men who make this mistake—and it's always a mistake!—are either super Sugar Daddies or totally void of self-esteem. Believe it or not, but usually it is the man who insists on attempting a relationship with a Chrissy Crackhead. She's only in it for the drug money. And often a Chrissy Crackhead will state the facts up front: "Hey, I get high—pay me, or I'm out of here." Now how explicit is that?

A man void of self-esteem has a way of twisting, bending, and contorting what a woman says into what he wants to hear. Thus, "Pay me, or I'm out of here" becomes "If you give me enough money, I will love you." This bizarre phenomenon also occurs when women leave men. "I don't want you no more!" inexplicably becomes "If you will raise enough hell, I will love you as before."

Chrissy does not want your love; she wants your money. But she needs rehabilitation. Sex does not have rehabilitation properties, never has, never will. Apparently many men think the opposite. Think about it, if sex could rehabilitate, surely Chrissy would have stumbled onto one guy who would have rehabilitated her a long time ago.

If you remotely care about someone like Chrissy, the best you can offer her is a local listing of the rehabilitation programs and drug treatment centers.

The RRHOID (Reckless, Remorseless, Hedonistic, Obnoxious Devil): Yes, you guessed it again, Rhonda Rrhoid is the female version of the First-class A-Hole—a sociopath, no conscience whatsoever. Various studies say these type women make up three percent of the female population; so by way of guesstimation...over two hundred million people...over half women...times this and divide that...which roughly figures to about three million women, plus or minus a few hundred thousand.

Whatever the correct number, a woman like Rhonda

Rrhoid is a woman you do not want to tangle with. She burns men, in more ways than one, including the one that first comes to mind. Rhonda and women like her are usually attractive, and when they are not, they know how to use their attributes—big butt, big knockers, whatever—to their advantage. These type women can write volumes of books on the topic How to Get a Man To Do What You Want—Even if It Kills Him.

Picking Rhonda's hold card early in the game is extremely difficult; she knows the game better than you. She comes off so sincere, so genuine, so concerned about you and what you do. It's all an act. Greater-Later is her middle name. Her goal is to get you hooked first, then reel you in, and then, when you are no longer of use to her, throw you on the bank and watch you gasp for air.

To avoid this, pay attention to what she says. Rhonda and women like her are pathological liars, lying when the truth would suffice. For example, someone asks her if her hair is real, and she says, "Of course it is," though you recall seeing the same scalp underneath the bathroom sink that morning. Also pay close attention to her fondness of personal property—clothes, bric-a-brac, cars, furniture. While there is nothing inherently wrong with someone cherishing their property, there is certainly something wrong with someone crying or throwing a hissy fit over nicks, scratches, cracks, and hard-to-see dents—which is often what Rhonda and women like her do. They certainly love what they own, and usually what they own, someone else paid for. She may or may not tell you who paid for what, but if she does, definitely write that down in your notepad. Think about it: If four or more people, regardless of gender, furnished her apartment, what did they get out of the deal?

When she stops blowing fake flattery into your ear, she will venture onto her favorite topic: money. Money drives her, so she is definitely interested in where you work and how much money you make. Of course she will never directly ask you for money, but she will indirectly convey the message loud and clear.

Watch for signs of paranoia. She may pull you through a financial and emotional ringer, but the mere thought of you, or anyone else, doing the same to her is her worst nightmare, and her biggest fear. She has no girlfriends (a red flag in itself), but she claims that other women think she is after their man—ninety-nine times out of a hundred these women are correct in this assumption.

You can avoid this type of woman by simply listening to your conscience: *"Something isn't right!"* No matter how sweet and charming she comes off, it is a façade, one which takes a tremendous amount of energy to maintain, so it will not last long.

Many men make the mistake of intentionally summing up the good over the bad. "Yes, she is selfish, somewhat ridiculous at times, but man! What a body! What breasts! What fun in bed!" This foolish rationalization is what a Rhonda Rrhoid thrives on.

A word of caution: Don't naturally assume a woman is a Rhonda Rrhoid simply because she cleans you out in divorce settlement case or moves out and takes everything with her while you are at work. One single act of outright greed and selfishness does not a Rhonda Rrhoid make. A true Rhonda Rrhoid is an advanced opportunist—someone who takes advantage of every opportunity, and devises advantageous opportunities.

The business of selecting and choosing a mate is very complex and difficult, and the onus is definitely on the man. The man usually initiates contact, which in itself is a risky proposition. The woman may reject his advances. Even to highly confident men, rejection hurts to some degree. After a few rejections, many men develop a fear of rejection, which often results in them taking the first thing that comes along. Not a good idea. And a fear of rejection is why many men stay in a bad relationship. "Hey, it took forever and a day to get this one."

One can easily avoid rejections and at the same time increase confidence by simply becoming an OWL—Observing, Watching, and Listening. Notice that an owl, the bird, does very little talking, if any, and spends most of its time watching, intently. A man can go one step better. He can think, analyze, and predict to a certain degree. If prudent thought precedes a man's actions—and his lips—and he does not let his emotions contaminate his thinking, then he is already at the top of the game. For example, a frowning woman says what? (a) Please come talk to me; (b) I find you rather attractive; (c) Stop staring at me!

Yes, *C* is the correct answer. If you chose *A* or *B*, then you are probably accustomed to having your face slapped. Some men have no problem with being rejected, time after time. Notice how they proposition any woman, any time, any where. Family reunions, wakes, funerals, and the VD clinic, in their minds, are excellent pick-up spots.

And usually they stick to the same pick-up lines, such as "Do fries come with that shake?" Quite original, huh? Amazingly, lame introductions occasionally work. But how many long-term relationships you know resulted from "Baby, if I were that halter top you got on I'd be the happiest man in the world"?

By observing, watching, and listening, the situation will manufacture its own introduction. Good social skills will actually invite others to talk to you. Think about it: How often do you implore someone who you know will go on and on for days when asked a simple yes-or-no question? How often do you implore someone who you know is not concerned with what you have to say?

So flip the script. If you can tell by so-and-so's perfunctory nods and *"uh-huh"*s that he or she could give a damn about what you have to say, then people can tell when you do the same. Honestly, this is not an endearing trait. To be a good listener, simply listen with soul, mind, and body. This allows you to hear and feel. Listening is the key to starting and maintaining a good relationship, any relationship. If you are truly listening, you are not planning what you have to say in response, you are not getting angry, because you understand that people have opinions different than your own, and you are not concentrating on something other than what is being said. Listening with soul, mind, and body is undoubtedly the highest respect one can pay to another. Try it, and you will be surprised at the results.

Chapter 10
Quack Quack

"Those whose wombs are the most desiccated should not bethe most vociferous for choice." H.H.

The female emperor penguin drops her egg shortly before Antarctica's winter season, when temperatures often drop below minus sixty degrees Fahrenheit, and immediately passes the egg to the male emperor penguin. Then she says, "See ya, don't wanna be ya," and heads off to warmer climates. Amazingly, not one male emperor penguin has said, "The hell with this," and eased off with the females. No, not one. The moment the male gets the egg, his soul and being is centered on keeping the egg alive and warm, in a furry pouch between his webbed feet.

The male doesn't eat, sleep, or worry about what his old lady is doing while he's taking care of an egg. To survive the fierce cold, the males shuttle about in one large group, generating heat in the middle, with each penguin getting a fair share of warmth time. During the incubation period the male often loses a third to a half of his body weight. But the sacrifice doesn't stop there. When the chick hatches, the male produces a curd-like substance to feed it. By this time he's certainly worrying where the hell Momma is because he can only produce so much baby food, not to mention he's hungry as hell. When the mother shows up, the male goes out to sea to feed but returns to assist with care of the chick.

As you know, this is pure instinct. Otherwise the emperor penguin would be extinct. Notice that all species have natural instincts toward procreation, including asexual reproduction, but not all have the natural instinct toward care of offspring—including man.

Imagine if you will that man did have a fatherly instinct—wait a minute, what's up with the head shaking? A non-believer, huh? Okay. If men had a smidgen of fatherly instinct, do you think any man would prod his wife or girlfriend or whatever to eliminate his offspring? If men had a smidgen of fatherly instinct, wouldn't you think that all men would at least make an effort to be in their offspring's life during the first five years? More importantly, if men had a smidgen of fatherly instinct, would they allow more than 1.6 million viable human beings to die each year under the guise of "a woman's right to choose," also known as "The Omega Contraceptive."

No, man does not have it, never has, never will.

Still not sold? No doubt you're thinking about the men—the majority—who truly love their children and willingly make sacrifices for them. If you take a closer look, you will notice that the majority of these men have one thing in common—they were there from the beginning. In other words, when the baby or babies arrived home from the hospital, the home where was the natural father lived. This is an important point to remember. Men who love their children live or have lived with their children.

What's the average man's reaction after being told he is a father-to-be? Is he mad, sad, or glad? Try confused. Listen to what he says: *"How in the hell did that happen?"*; *"By whom?"*; and *"What makes you think I'm the father?"* Of course, this drives women crazy.

To add diarrhea to a shortage of Huggies, many women, the educated and the uneducated, actually think that a baby will pop a fatherly-instinct switch in a man and thereby animate him to reform his behavior—and he and she and baby will live happily ever after. This almost always backfires when the man and the woman are not married or do not live together—and even then there's no guarantee. An abject lack of fatherly instinct is also why so many women shake their head in disgust while watching the father of their children living across the street with a woman with five children, not one of 'em his.

There is no more poignant sight than a young mother at a hospital or a bus stop with two or more small children, holding one in her arms and trying to keep the others close by. You cannot help but wonder: Where's the father? Wherever he is, it's a safe bet he wasn't around when the baby or babies arrived home from the hospital. So who's to blame? Both, actually. But the woman and children suffer the most. While the woman is struggling to raise his and her children all on her own, the man is doing his thang, whatever that may be—and the thought of his children, and the mother, seldom crosses his mind. Cold but true.

Many men who are absentee fathers were themselves fatherless and can remember, as boys, longing for a father, playing imaginary father-and-son games and envying peers whose fathers were there. Yet the cycle continues.

Another sad fact: Child-support payment and an occasional visit are to fatherhood what lip-syncing is to singing—a very poor comparison.

First, child support rarely covers a tenth of the financial burden to raise a child. Think about it, if your child were living with you, certainly you would allot more than a small percentage of your earnings to him. Second, a periodic visit is simply that, a periodic visit. Call it "bonding" and "quality time" if you like, but at least admit that a few hours a month is scarcely enough time to get to know anyone, regardless of activity.

Many men think that the entire child-support check—usually court-ordered—should go exclusively to the child. A rather ridiculous assumption considering all the expenses involved in raising a child, including rent, utilities, and the new boyfriend's bus fare back and forth to work. Hey, in order to control it, you need to abode in it. On the other hand, many women do abuse the funds—drugs, alcohol, anything but their children's needs. If you were observing, listening and watching, you would have probably seen it coming.

This all leads back to the ugly A-word—abstinence. Abstinence, remember, controls the who, when, what, and where. Abstinence is never a mistake. Abstinence could care less if the pill is lost, stolen, forgotten, or overlooked. Abstinence always works. Abstinence doesn't break, pop, or fail. Abstinence eliminates regret. Abstinence ensures that, after the state and federal take theirs, you get your full check. And, like most NA meetings, abstinence accepts anyone at anytime, free of charge.

Think about the one woman you would rather lose a testicle than have a baby by…Now imagine her with your child…and imagine the next eighteen years you will deal with her directly or indirectly…A nightmare, isn't it? But this is the risk many men take when sleeping with a stranger.

Once the sperm leaves and the shouting subsides, you have no control over what happens next. If a sperm cell fertilizes an egg, there is nothing you can do about it. If she decides to eliminate the baby, there's nothing you can do about that, either (thirty-eight states allow her to do that without even consulting you). But you can control pulling your pants down.

By now you may be growing somewhat weary of the

advocating of abstinence, but no other plan works so effectively, and doing so most definitely eliminates the pain and suffering caused by poor and regrettable choices.

Turn to any daytime talk show and you will see a parade of people who have made horrendous choices in their lives. Not to veer too far from the subject, but how in the hell do you get intimate with someone without discovering his or her true gender? This oddity and others like it pale in interest to "Paternity Confusion," which is probably the all-time favorite subject of daytime talk shows. If you have watched one of these shows, you know that for every three Second-class A-Holes who have foolishly and vehemently claimed that the toddler in the playpen who looks exactly like them isn't theirs, only to be proven wrong via DNA testing, there is a RRHOID crying and sniveling and blowing snot and claiming that the baby is most definitely her boyfriend's, only to be proven not his by DNA testing.

More often than not, men do not request proof of paternity. Yes, it's rather impertinent to ask, "Is the baby mine?" But if you do not know a person as well as you should have before tossing the sheets back, you really need to check it out.

To add warts to swollen testicles, many of today's judges are adopting a "finish what you started" policy in paternity cases. Specifically, the defendant should have determined whether or not the child was biologically his before buying the first case of Similac; therefore and henceforth the defendant shall continue buying Similac and anything else the child needs, because, according to these judges, a child's needs are far more important than a man's desire not to take care of someone else's child.

While laying a child at the wrong man's feet is odious and duplicitous, you can easily see the logic in some cases. For instance, a woman has intimate relations with two men—Henry, an aluminum can collector, and Tyrone, a restaurant owner—and she becomes pregnant. Now who do you think she will name as the father? Yes, Tyrone will soon be adding baby food onto his menu.

This occurs quite often, but is easily preventable. Take the well-documented case involving an African-American celebrity—yes, you know his name, but here…well, let's just call him Bill. During his salad days, Bill encountered a young woman. Actually he did more than encounter the woman, but Bill, a champion of African-American causes and a generous contributor to such causes, deserves deference. Unbeknownst to Bill, this woman was sexually engaging another man while she was encountering him. When she became pregnant she had a tough decision on her hands. Name the true father, whose job appeared to be taste-testing cheap liquor, or place the responsibility on Bill, an actor with a promising future. Of course she chose Bill, and he, being a man predisposed to doing the right thing, agreed to assume financial responsibility for the child and insure the child's college education—higher education has always been high on Bill's list.

This went on fine and dandy until the child, a girl, grew up. Possessing her mother's spirit, the girl decided that a lot wasn't enough; in fact, she wanted millions—and she wanted them yesterday. To make a long story short, Bill was not about being blackmailed, especially by someone with a question mark behind her name. The girl was arrested. The mother decided that she didn't need a paternity test to clear the issue up—all she wanted was her little baby girl to come home. Boo hoo! If she had told the truth a long time ago, when she was grinning and cashing all those checks and lying to little Miss Greedy Too about who her father was, then she could have avoided the pain and embarrassment.

Bill's case is by no means an example. Very few

women, after years of ill-gotten gains through deceit and cunning, suffer consequences. And many men do not voluntarily pay child support, whether the child is theirs or not. Current laws, however, dictate that you will pay one way or the other. Yes, in some cases this is a good thing, especially for those who simply do not pay because of stinginess or spite. But in some cases, a man simply cannot pay; he's out of work, or he's underpaid, or he has too many children to support. Whatever, if he cannot pay—just like the man who refuses to pay—he risks jail.

While in jail, child support arrears continue to accumulate. The hole becomes deeper and deeper. Thousands of dollars behind in child-support payments is pretty deep. Often this state of affairs can be avoided. Of course, if you are not working, paying child support is almost an impossibility. Still, the judge may not see it that way. Therefore the judge should be the first person you go see after a few weeks of unemployment. If at all possible, go the payroll deduction route. This ensures that payments are made and curtails confusion and bitter confrontations. There is no greater hell on earth than a woman who is short a couple child-support checks.

Another good idea: Don't get angry about paying child support. Oddly, a good number of men who pay child support express animosity about doing so, mostly because many men think that the money should go exclusively to the child. Yes, she may be riding around in a new car, and your child-support payments may have or may have not contributed to it, but your child also benefits from her having a car. And yes, some mothers do spend the money unwisely and selfishly, but your getting angry will not help matters. Keep this in mind when consulting a lawyer. Angry clients have netted lawyers millions if not billions of dollars. Unless custody, back payments, big bucks, or other complicated issues are at stake, why seek a lawyer? Most states determine child-support payments by earning guidelines that are etched in stone. Therefore there's no need to play If She Gets a Lawyer, I Will Too.

In matters of custody battles and child-support cases, once should always be enough. These type issues are almost always extremely bitter and acrimonious. So why put yourself through such an ordeal more than once? A woman who has three or more children in today's climate is not an attractive mate. But guess what, a man who has three or more children and is paying child support is also not an attractive mate—unless of course he's rich.

Women know that a man who has six children by six different women is a man who takes home a very little check. They also know that at least one of these women is a termagant, the type of woman who drops her child off without notification and raises hell at the drop of hat.

Women, ten times more than men, buy off into BBB—Brady Bunch Bullshit, the fallacy that stepfamilies can live in peaceful harmony without ever incurring a major malfunction. But note, women in general rarely suffer BBB with the man's children; it's usually expected of the man with their children. Men rarely say, "If you love me, then you gotta love my kids," because they know this is a pipe dream, totally unrealistic. The best hoped for, the woman treats his kids with respect. With many women he will not get even that. Selfishness, childishness, and pure jealousy are why many women have such a hard time taking to man's children, though fully expecting a man to take to her children as his very own. Whereas your children are concerned, always think safety. No woman in her right mind would leave her children in custody of someone she's dating. This applies to men as well. Men are more inclined to do so because women are generally considered safer. This is true, but in matters of your children and the new woman in your life the dynamics are different, so even if she looks good, smiles, and has a wonderful time with children, your children still should not be left in her care (at least till you get to know her).

What usually happens in these type situations, man with outside children meets woman with inside children, is this: The man compromises his relationship with his own children. If his relationship with his children is already poor, that is he never lived with them or took the time to know them, nothing really changes. In other words: "Daddy, who never calls or visits, has a new girlfriend." However, if the relationship with his children was fair to middling, and he suddenly breaks or compromises contact, then he and his children suffer tremendously. The harsh resentments caused by this mistake can last a lifetime.

Loving and caring for a child other than your own is not a bad thing, quite admirable really; with most men this occurs naturally with a child living with them year after year. But loving and caring for a child other than your own is a bad thing when you neglect your own child or children, not to mention the fact that everyone suffers. A man in this type situation often feels guilty for not spending more time with his biological child or children, which causes him to occasionally feel resentment toward those children living with him. They, the children living with him, in turn occasionally feel cheated because of his periodic bouts of resentments. His biological child or children could write books about ill feelings and resentments.

Two ways this can be avoided. First, the moment a new child or children come into the picture is the moment to start or strengthen the relationship with biological child or children. Second, raise your own children. Which leads to…

When to Say When

In matters of sex, very few people consult a book before acting. Flipping to the chapter on "Satisfying Your Partner's Emotional and Physical Needs While Getting Your Rocks Off" would probably kill the moment. People tend to do what comes natural. Therefore it is a stretch to tell someone when or when not to consider having a baby. Yet clearly there are times when the arrival of a baby might cause frustration and hardship to all concerned. For example, someone other than your wife having your baby can be a major source of frustration and dread.

Remember this: A baby is never a mistake—even if the contraceptive used fails.

Again, the donation of sperm is the only factor in pregnancy a man can control. Everything else, the natural process of childbirth, is out the man's hands. Also remember, that of all the various contraceptives on the market, not one offers one hundred percent prevention of pregnancy. Abstinence never fails.

Okay, let's say you want a baby. You want to experience the joy of looking into a pair of little eyes that says your genes will live on far into the future. You want to be a father. Okay, not a problem. But first it would be wise to consider AAA, or triple A, which stands for Age, Assets, and Attitude.

Age: Many people say, "Age is nothing but a number." But try telling that to a young boy trying to play catch with an aged father leaning on a walker. Or try telling that to a child whose father hogs the PlayStation. Geezers and whippersnappers—males under eighteen years old—make for poor fathers. Proving one's masculinity is a particularly poor reason to enter into parenthood. Notice that the overwhelming majority of young men under eighteen of age do not raise their children. In effect these guys say, "Hey, look who else I brought home for you to take care of." Often the responsibility of raising the child is placed solely on the mother and her mother.

Another important factor to consider: your true mental age? This is a tough call to make. Very few men will admit, or even think for that matter, that their chronological age is substantially higher than their mental age. A good indicator of a significant disparity is the number of times someone says, "When are you going to grow up?" Another good indicator: impulsive and infantile anger. What more childish a sight than a man over seventeen years of age with his mouth poked out like a little kid? The same applies to a man who hits someone or breaks someone's property simply because he's angry.

Young fathers in their late teens through mid-twenties pose a higher risk of Shaken Baby Syndrome, which can cause an infant to suffer brain damage or death. This form of physical abuse occurs much more than reported—one third of the infants die, one third suffer brain damage, and one third survive without symptoms. Only a mental idiot would shake an infant. Remember this: An infant's crying is his or her way of expressing needs—hunger, thirst, sleep—and feelings—lonely, bored, anxious—and a lot more. The demands of caring for an infant can be both rewarding and frustrating, thus it's a good idea to have a strong support system, family and friends to assist in times of need. When you are at your wits' end, do the wise thing: Call someone, and ask for help.

If you use drugs and/or abuse alcohol, you can determine your mental age by dividing your chronological age by two, then dividing the results by two again, and finally dividing the number by two again—this will give you your true mental age. For example, say, forty-years old would equate…uh, divide by two, then divide again…and one more time…uh…Five! Now who in their right mind would leave a five-year-old in care of a child? If you abuse drugs or alcohol, at least be man enough to avoid contact with children, yours or anyone else's, until you pull it together.

Assets: This is not a tough decision. If you cannot afford a snow cone, you definitely cannot afford a pack of Ultra Huggies. On average it takes almost nine-thousand dollars a year to raise a child. That's not a tremendous amount of money, but, as you know, a quarter is a lot of money if you don't have it. Some jobs offer health insurance that covers delivery and mother and child aftercare, while others do not; but not one form of hustling offers health insurance. In other words it's a good idea to have a job before you consider a baby. As stated earlier, if you truly want to raise your child, your first step would be to raise the child in your home. Which means, of course, the mother of the child should be living with you. Marriage, as old-fashioned as it sounds, is the ideal way to go. Though no relationship is a guarantee, marriage offers a stronger family bond than cohabitating, shacking, and semi-shacking (moving out when the rent is due, then moving back after it's paid). Also, marriage motivates men toward responsible fatherhood more so than any other type of relationship.

Another factor to consider: your significant other. Is she an asset or a liability? Particularly, do you and she get along well enough to consider having children? If you and she are having problems now, then, when the baby comes, the problems will multiply exponentially. A few men, like so many women, actually think that a baby will strengthen a rocky relationship. Wrong! This almost always backfires.

Ideally, you and the mother-to-be should be on the same page in certain areas, such as child-rearing, moral values, and religion. In the beginning, differences may not seem a major issue. But say, for example, your religion does not exclude pork as a food source, while your significant other's religion shuns pork. No problem when you were stuffing yourself with pork rinds while she was nibbling on tofu, but when the baby dives into his first can of Beanie Weenies this may be a major problem. If you believe in spanking, while she believes in time-outs and psychiatric counseling, this too can be a major problem. Vast parenting differences confuse a child because of inconsistency, which, as you will see, is a detriment to raising a child in a healthy environment.

Attitude: Questions to ask yourself: Do I really want a baby? Do I like children? Do I fully appreciate the fact that infants cry, toddlers keep up a bunch of racket and break things, and small children sometimes say the darnedest things—sometimes things that pisses me off? Am I willing to make the tremendous sacrifices necessary to raise a child?

Tough questions. But if you cannot answer yes to each one, then you seriously need to think long and hard before deciding to have a baby. Honestly, if your heart is not in it, do not do it. Otherwise you will open the door to a tremendous amount of pain and frustration to everyone involved. The ultimate whiner is someone who has several children and complains about it. "I can't do nothing—all these damn children!" Duh, gee, George, why didn't that thought occur after the second child, or the fifth, or the sixth?

Think about it, if you are focused on a college education or a career, a baby, more than likely, will be a stumbling block in your path, and this can serve as a source of anger and resentment. Your attitude will determine whether you will be there for the child, whether you will make the tremendous effort to raise the child to the best of your ability, and whether you and your child will experience the love that exists between a father and child.

R.I.P.

During slavery, and a long time afterwards, it was prudent for African-Americans to practically beat the dog shit out of their children for certain transgressions, including reading, stealing, back-talking, and fighting. If they didn't do so, they risked the chance of the massa, or the law, or the Klan, doing so in a manner that would risk the child's life. Today's good news: You no longer have to beat your child bloody for the massa's benefit. Unfortunately, no one has expressed this fact to a good number of African-Americans, many of whom say: "My mamma and daddy beat the snot out of me, and look what it did for me!"

Before going further, let's agree on one thing: Beating is the antithesis of disciplining, and no matter how unruly, unmanageable, disobedient, and smart-mouthed a child may behave, a good ass-whooping will not change his or her behavior. Actually it will make the child's behavior worse. Let's go even further, and agree that slapping, kicking, punching, shaking, snatching, and vicious name-calling have nothing to do with disciplining either.

Disciplining children is a touchy subject for many African-Americans, in part because of passionate viewpoints—very passionate viewpoints! Notice that you rarely see an African-American child throwing a temper tantrum in a public place. This suggests that African-Americans lean to physical punishment with their children more so than any other group. But keep in mind that African-Americans were subject to more punishment than any other group. This fact makes it somewhat difficult to tell an African-American to consider alternative forms of disciplining rather than spanking, such as time-outs or eliminating certain activities or toys. So here the emphasis will not be placed on whether to spank or not to spank, but on responses to behavior that does more harm than good, specifically R.I.P, the acronym for Rage, Inconsistency, and Permissiveness.

Rage: While being enraged is the worst time to physically discipline a child, it is most often the time when children are physically disciplined. The main problem with this is, rage or anger increases adrenaline, which increases strength, which usually results in more punishment inflicted than necessary or intended. This is almost always the case when you hear of someone who has injured or killed a child. The child commits an offense, crying usually, then the parent, frustrated and emotionally immature, shakes or strikes the child, again, and again…The child cries in pain…whimpers…and becomes quiet, realizing this is the way to end the abuse. Hell, if someone much bigger than you were to shake or hit you hard and long enough, chances are you too would shut up. Then when the rage subsides, and guilt kicks in, the parent goes to check on the child. "Oh God!" The child is not moving. "Oh God!" The child is black and blue. "Oh God!" The child is dead.

Another catalyst to rage: personification, attributing adult characteristics to a child. Regardless of what a child says, keep in mind that he or she is still a child (especially in matters concerning stepchildren). It's easy to forget this fact when a child is running off at the mouth, yet while the words may be adult and scathing, the person saying them is mentally and emotionally immature. Yes, children will test you; they will say and do things that will rub your last nerve, but this is a part of parenting—a big part and, believe it or not, part of the bonding process. Honestly, have you ever loved someone who didn't occasionally make you angry, aggravate you, piss you off? There's a thin line between love and getting on somebody's last damn nerve.

Absence of nerve rubbing is why it's difficult to bond with a child outside the home. During brief periods together, both parties, the man and the child, are on their best behavior. Where's the dealing with frustration? The overcoming problems? The loving reunion during resolution? You cannot get this at a ball game, a movie, a trip to the circus. You can only get it during day-to-day interaction, at home, where a child lets his hair down so to speak. If you have a child or children, you know the behavior at home is often different than the behavior outside the home. This is in part because a child feels safe at home; this is where he or she lives, where he or she feels protected and secure.

To ensure that security, you cannot let emotions get the better of you. It's amazing how much a child will forgive a parent, but memories of verbal and physical abuse can last a lifetime. Verbal and physical abuse destroy self-confidence and motivation, two ingredients that an African-American child will need in abundance.

Think about this the next time Junior doodles on the back seat of your leather upholstery, the next time he breaks your favorite pool stick, and the next time he pours water down the back of the television. Is it worth yelling and cursing over? Is it worth getting physical over? Remember, as an adult, a man, you control the situation—and you can do so without getting bent out of shape.

If you recognize that you have a problem with overreacting, becoming unnecessarily upset, or resorting to physical or verbal abuse, then practice doing something different. Actually you do this more than you think. At work, no matter how strongly you want to go upside your supervisor's head, you squelch the impulse. Well, you can do the same at home. The moment—the very first moment—you sense the tell-tale sensations that you are getting angry, such as heavy breathing, burning sensation, nose twitching, whatever, is the moment you should tell yourself: "I'm getting angry here." If need be, remove yourself from the situation. A walk. A trip to the bathroom. Anywhere, as long as you take the time to cool off. But if you use the time away to refuel your anger, you have wasted your time.

Also avoid stockpiling anger. Doing this invites the tiniest sparks to set off a nuclear explosion. Simply express what made you angry. "Junior, you upset me when you put a match to my toes while I was sleeping!" Okay, maybe that's a stretch. But expressing your anger does work, and it avoids stockpiling. For the most part, children try to avoid disappointing their parents, so a little constructive guilt can be just as effective as any other form of discipline.

Inconsistency: A father tells his son during visitation that he will take him to the park next Saturday. The intended day, the son wakes up early, gets ready, and sits on the front step to wait for his father. A few hours later, his mother tells him to come in the house, "Your daddy isn't coming. If he was he would be here by now." The father rationalizes his failure to appear: "Next week I'll take him," or "He won't mind," or "I'll make it up to him." Regardless, the son is crushed, and if the same thing continues to happen, the father and son's relationship will be damaged. There's a simple way to avoid this: Don't make promises you don't intend to keep. It's also not a bad idea to call.

Inconsistency is a tumor to parenting; it causes utter confusion. This is especially obvious with parents who are drunks or drug addicts or A-Holes. For example, Junior writes on the wall, and, daddy, drunk, laughs at the artwork. Later, when daddy is sober, Junior does the same, and gets his butt spanked. Mixed messages, double messages, and confusing messages promote negative behavior, or inertia, in children because they can not discern what exactly they are supposed to do. Think about it: If Junior is spending an inordinate amount of time trying to figure what makes Daddy tick, what makes Daddy upset, then he's not concentrating on other matters, such as schoolwork—and his self-esteem and self-confidence take a nose dive. Junior, because of his skin color, will take a tremendous beating to his self-esteem and self-confidence as he progresses through life, so wouldn't it be wise to build him up in preparation for this, at home? Of course it would, and the sooner the better.

Being consistent is not as hard as it sounds, and it doesn't necessarily mean change. The key word to remember: *unequivocal,* which simply means no misunderstanding. There's no misunderstanding with a man who says what he is going to do and does it. His words and actions are quite clear. Usually with this type of man, his words are short and his deeds are long. Thus he need not make petty threats to a child (threats promote negotiation, not action). This guy sounds like a saint, doesn't he? Well, he, like everyone else, makes mistakes, but he admits to making them.

Always keep in mind how much children look up to their parents. Yes, Junior very much wants to grow up and be just like his daddy, regardless of who his daddy is or what his daddy does. Unfortunately, this includes bad habits. If Junior sees his daddy go upside Momma's head, then, more than likely, Junior will do the same as an adult. If Junior sees his daddy passed out drunk in the front yard, then chances are good he will do the same in the future. Speaking of alcohol, one of the dumbest things a drunk can do is to let a child take a sip of alcohol. Some drunks actually think this is funny. It's not. Actually it's an introduction into alcoholism.

Children are not stupid. *"Do what I say, not what I do"* doesn't work with them. They may or may not can spell *hypocrite* but they clearly understand the concept. If you desire your children to be honest, hardworking, independent adults, then you must exemplify the same. Any other way you are dreaming. Take for example, Earl Woods, Tiger Woods' father, who introduced his son to golf at a very young age. Undoubtedly Earl loved golf and wanted his son to love the game as well. Chances are Earl did not imagine his son going on to become inarguably the world's greatest golfer, but he did. Certainly there were occasions when Tiger did not want to go out in the heat and chase golf balls, and occasions when Earl wanted to chase Momma around the bed rather than wait in the heat while Tiger chased golf balls, but the two stuck with it, consistently.

Of course every child cannot grow up to be the next Tiger Woods, but there are other areas for greatness, all of which can be achieved by a father planting a seed. In any field or endeavor you desire your child to excel in, the key is to introduce them as early as possible, shortly after arriving from the hospital. Serious. You will be surprised at the results. Spend a few minutes reading to a baby each day, and watch what happens. He or she will be reading long before peers start doing so. The same goes to teaching moral values and moral conduct; the sooner the better. Young children crave information and new learning experiences and are very receptive to learning. If Junior, at the tender age of three, can recite three or four hip hop songs verbatim, surely he can master the alphabet and a few simple addition problems. And if Junior can twist and bend his small fingers into gang signs, he can learn the sign alphabet and how to write his name.

Permissiveness: One of the saddest spectacles of permissiveness is parents who wheelbarrow their two-hundred-pounds-plus two-years-olds out on a talk show stage. Honestly, these parents need their ass whooped. They shouldn't even be called parents; "immature idiots" is more appropriate. Unless a child has a medical condition, no way should a parent allow a child to eat until he or she blows up to five times their normal weight. What's wrong with "No, Tubby, you can't have a second hog for lunch!"?

One young woman, who couldn't even lift her three-year-old two tons of fun, said, "If he's hungry, I'm going to let him eat." Goodness, the kid could survive two years off body fat alone. Then, Maury Povich, that paragon of human dignity, directed the camera to a buffet table covered with enough food to feed an army. The mother unashamedly said, "This is what he eats for breakfast." Goodness! Imagine the droppings this kid produces. Then, without invitation or preamble, the kid starts stuffing his mouth ravenously.

Watching Tubby devour a turkey leg the cartoon way—putting the entire piece in mouth and then removing only the bone—you couldn't help but wonder what his mother will say when he has heart problems, or when she needs a forklift to get him out of bed. Permissiveness is child abuse, pure and simple, no doubt about it. Perhaps if Tubby were of adult mind, he would choose not to eat large animals in one sitting, but Tubby is a child, who has not the experience of making adult decisions; nor should he be expected to make adult decisions.

The nickname for children raised by permissive parents: Bebe's Kids—named after the unruly kids portrayed in the cartoon movie *Bebe's Kids*. If you've seen the movie, you might agree that Bebe, the mother, needs her cartoon ass whooped too. She drops her three children, one of whom a toddler with a penchant for declaring his bowel movements, off with a friend, with no money, no diapers, no food to speak of. Sadly, many real-life mothers make Bebe look like Mother Teresa. Let's set the record straight: Whether you are a man or a woman raising your children alone, with very little financial support, there is no reason to let your children run wild. Yeah, yeah, yeah, raising children alone is a difficult job, but still that is no excuse to treat your children like refugees.

If Junior is at home at a reasonable time, then no way is he out on the street doing you-don't-know-what with you-don't-know-who. "B-but I can't control him!" many parents whine. Yes, this is true, because they waited till Junior's first stint with the law to try to curb his wayward behavior. Perhaps, you think, if Junior had been directed to rules and regulations at a very young age—when he was still wetting his diaper—then rules and regulations wouldn't be such an alien concept to him now.

If you don't assume the responsibility of being the parent, which includes not only being a friend but also being a teacher, a counselor, an instructor, and a provider, then someone else will. Let the schools do it, and they will label your child, drug him, and pass him on from one grade to the next with a substandard education. Let the government do it, and they will label your child and provide a small cell—for life on some occasions. Let the streets do it, and they will ensure that your child gets KISSed. If you love your child, you raise him or her!

Teaching your child values, self-discipline, and confidence—the goal of parenting, right?—is not the world's greatest challenge, and it doesn't require tons of money, or screaming and shouting, or beating your child unconscious. All it takes is time, patience, consistency, and lots of love. And yes, you can achieve all three and still be your child's friend, but by simply being your child's friend, you negate your role as parent. It's rather amazing the steps some parents make to avoid hurting their child's feelings. To these parents, guess what? If you never aggravate or anger your child, then you really have parenting asshole backward.

The apex of asshole backwardness is a young child sitting with his parent(s), watching adult-type situations on television. The response from these parents when asked why Junior is sitting there watching two adults get it on—"He's seen it all before." Hell, why stop there? Why not give him a subscription to Playboy or Hustler magazine? Then, when Junior goes to school and wags his wing-wing at a schoolmate, watch the utter shock spread on his parent(s)' face. Usually, the shock is ephemeral, quickly replaced with indignation: "Not my son!"

Ask yourself, what does television offer the African-American child? Absolutely nothing! Yes, no doubt, the television keeps Junior quiet for a few hours, but, at the same time, it tells Junior that he and his family do not compare to the family on the sitcom who can solve their problems in thirty minutes. Plus, whoever told television producers that the average African-American family has three or more potential stand-up comics was telling a blatant lie.

So why not turn the television off, or at least limit your child's television watching. Doing so will promote family interaction and encourage your child to explore and experience life on his or her own terms. Plus the more you and your child interact, the more you and your child get to know each other, enjoy each other, love each other.

Once you've limited, or done away with, television watching, you will need a list of things to do to prevent boredom. The following list is suggestive, of course; you can follow it or write one of your own.

Family outings, such as the park, library, or zoo

Scheduled family talks

Behavior charts, which work great with smaller children—again, consistency.

Curfews—child's age the determining factor, but a child under fifteen years old shouldn't set his or her own curfew

Chores—while it's a good idea for children to have chores, they shouldn't assume the role of house servant

Religious activities

Reading

Cardinals Rules—each family member can contribute in naming Cardinal Rules: unacceptable behavior, such as fighting, shouting, lying, etc.

Games—board games that involve entire family

Volunteer Activities—children who along with their parent(s) volunteer their time and energy to help others will do so as adults

Above everything else, *praise your children* and let them know you love them, verbally and physically. Often the emphasis is placed on disobedience, but rarely does a child behave badly twenty-four seven. So when your child is trying his or her hardest, struggling to overcome a difficult task, let him or her know: "You can do it!" Your child has the potential to do anything, has the potential to be whatever, so tell him or her. You planted the seed, so love and nurture, and behold a miracle.

Keep on Stepping

Many children living with a stepparent wish that the step had kept on stepping, right out of their life. These children know that the Brady Bunch Show was bullshit with a capital B. Face the facts: Being a stepparent is much different than being a parent. Therefore think long and hard before taking the job. If your heart is not in it—even if your new love says, "If you love me, you gotta love my children!"—then don't do it. This cannot be emphasized enough.

Fact: Very few men are prepared for the job of being a stepparent.

This flies in the face of current family trends, where a growing number of families consist of stepfathers and live-in father figures—also called Mama's boyfriend. Why, you ask, is the job so hard? Good question. The answer boils down to one word: *resentment.* The stepfather resents Junior because he's not his child, and Junior resents the stepfather because he's not his true father. This is as natural as the changing of seasons. This explains why so many children refer to their stepfather by first name and why so many stepfathers seldom speak to their stepchildren. Not speaking to someone you live with is rather tacky, but it's ten times better than trying to kill each other on a regular basis.

A small minority of men can put on a stepfather suit and actually look good wearing it. A very small minority! These type men are exceptionally patient; they do not expect too much too soon. They know that relationships take time. They see children as individuals who may have different ideas, opinions, and beliefs than their own. Above all, these type men are self-confident, drug-free, moderate drinkers or teetotalers, non-whiners, and highly motivated. A well-known example is Phillip Harrison, Shaquille O'Neal's stepfather. Mr. Harrison could have done what so many stepfathers do: ignored his stepson; whined and bitched about having to feed and house his stepson; shaken his head and complained to Shaq's mother when Shaq made a meaningless mistake; beat his stepson (considering Shaq's size, that would have lasted but so long); or simply run off. But Mr. Harrison did none of that. He raised his stepson, motivated him, and loved him. This is apparent in how often Shaq refers to his stepfather in his songs and interviews, always referring to Mr. Harrison as "my father."

Ironically, Shaq's biological father, experiencing a strong urge of fatherhood upon hearing of his son's success, attempted to connect—Uh-uh! Shaq was having none of it. This is the price many men pay when they abandon their children. That has to be a queasy feeling, watching the child you abandoned and his stepfather living large while waiting for the mailman to arrive with your social security check.

Okay, all of that does not pertain to you, because you're in love, and you agree to accept her children as yours. Not a problem. Best of luck. But before you attempt to put the suit on, you might need to consider three factors that might choke you.

The first factor to consider: the child's or children's age. The ideal age to insinuate yourself into a child's life is from birth to five years old. At this age, you and the child are more likely to bond. From six to nine years old is the second best time for introduction, but attempting to don the suit now will take greater effort. At this age the child probably knows his true father—even if not, the child probably knows you are not his father. Still, a bond can form if both you and the child are receptive to forming one.

From nine to fifteen years old is third best, but keep in mind that this is the time most children enter puberty, a difficult and trying time. From sixteen years old and beyond…well, at best you can hope to achieve a respectful relationship, but the prospect of bonding is very slim at this point.

The second factor to consider: the child's environment. Factually, single mothers tend to lean to too strict or too permissive (most often too permissive) with their children. Too strict, while more convenient to the incoming stepfather, stifles a child's confidence and motivation. Too permissive gives the child free rein, and promotes disrespect for rules and authority. In other words, you will have a job on your hands. Before going further, let's pay respect to those women who walk the line, right down the middle, assuming the role of mother and father, providing for their children financially and, with remarkable equanimity, teaching them self-respect, self-discipline, and self-confidence. In truth, many of these women do not need a man living with them—they just think they do!—because a man would probably disturb the equilibrium, which has been obtained after years of hard work and struggle.

Yet these type women are of the minority; many of today's women look to someone else to raise their children. This would not be so bad if they would have at least started on the job. Think about it: Junior, nine years old going on thirty-five, has been allowed to call his own shots, come in when he feels like it, speak his mind, and whatever else he feels like doing. This forces you, the new man in the house, to do one of two things: overlook Junior's behavior, or attempt to reform Junior—who, by the way, does not like you, remember?

The third factor, though not the least important: the transition—more specifically: Who's moving in with who? Ideally, if all possible, she and her children should move in with you, or, second best, you and she and her children move into a different home or apartment. This way Junior is more receptive to change. Moving in with her and her brood isn't necessarily a problem, but keep in mind that you are intruding—yes, intruding—on someone else's domain. Of course she doesn't see it that way; she invited you. But Junior does, and you should keep that in mind. The way Junior sees it, everything was going fine before you came and will continue to do so when you leave. Thus sudden rule changes instigated by you are unwise and more likely to exacerbate the problem. A good idea is to assume the role of visitor, which to an extent you are, and observe more than comment till you get a feel of the situation.

Don't expect much to change in the first year of so, and any attempt by you to speed things up will slow things down. For example, you expect Junior to come in at a reasonable time, so you demand he do so. "Hmmph! Who are you, my daddy?" he snorts. That night he stays out later than usual. Therefore don't demand; request or suggest, and be flexible.

Another big mistake many stepfathers and live-ins make is attempting to buy Junior's affection. This never works, and when Junior starts treating you like a bank, don't say, "All that boy wants from me is damn money!" You started it. Money cannot buy respect, which is what you and Junior need the most.

When Junior sees that you are in for the long haul and you have no desire to misuse him or his mother, he will come around. Again, this takes time—lots of time and patience. Simply reaching the level where Junior respects you—and you him—is a tremendous challenge, and reward. So, by God, if you reach it, don't mess it up, which is very easy to do. For example, verbally or physically assaulting Junior's momma—do this, and no matter what you do, you and Junior will always be at odds. Cheating on Junior's momma, lying on Junior's momma, and gawking at other women have the same effect. Yet notice if Junior's momma does the same thing to you, then that's not a problem, unless you react negatively to it.

Before even thinking about disciplining Junior, talk to his mother. It would be wise to let her handle corporal punishment. With any form of discipline, always ask yourself, "Is the punishment for his benefit or mine?" Remember, your ultimate goal is respect. Gain a child's respect and you have his cooperation. Once Junior's and your relationship slips into strategic warfare, it's over. This can be avoided by dealing with Junior directly. If you have a problem with something he's doing, especially if it's petty—usually it is—then by all means tell him, not his mother. Keep in mind that Junior loves his mother and she him. No shitsky, right? But often the stepfather, or live-in, and Junior wage war with Momma as the spoils. The root cause of this behavior: Petty Jealousy—on the man's part!

Unchecked, vying to gain Momma's affections and attention can get seriously out of hand. In other words, someone can get hurt. As childish as this behavior is, most men who get caught up in it cannot see it. Instead they continue to personalize everything that Junior does. "He did that to spite me!" A very sad state of affairs. Eventually drama will occur, usually over something unbelievingly petty, and the relationship, or the hope of having one, is dead. Think about it, how can you and Junior possibly form or maintain a relationship after you put him in a headlock, or choked him, or punched him, or kicked him?

This applies also if Junior puts you in a headlock, or chokes you, or punches you, or kicks you. The next time an altercation occurs, and there will be a next time, will be worse. A mature and self-confident man would not let the situation progress to violence, because he would not have participated in tit-for-tat with Junior. He knows that sort of thing is counterproductive, and he knows that that is no way to live—living in fear and contempt of Junior, or Junior living in fear and contempt of him.

Also, a mature and self-confident man doesn't bitch and moan about paying bills, and he understands that Junior has no concept of paying bills, so he doesn't expect Junior to be grateful for him doing so. This logic is lost on many a stepfather. In their minds paying bills is the true measure of a man, and that damned Junior should appreciate it!

Well, he doesn't, nor should he be expected to. His time to pay bills will come. And honestly, if paying a bill arouses much anger and resentment, don't pay it. Hell, shock everybody, keep your money in your pocket and refuse to pay anything. When Junior gets kicked out in the cold, he'll appreciate your efforts. Then you go live with your daddy, who bitches and moans about paying bills too.

A man who expects praise and reward for doing what he would have to do even if he were living alone has no business being a stepfather. Yes, the job is hard, with little or no "Thank you very much." But at the same time, a young man's or a young woman's life is at stake. His or her future depends on not only what stepfather does but also what stepfather says. Bitching, whining, fighting, name-calling, and sheer hating can cause a lifetime of guilt and hatred. Can you imagine someone hating you for life? Children by nature are quick to forgive, but they never forget intentional hurt. On the same coin, children intuit someone who has their best interest in mind—even though they rarely verbalize appreciation.

Regardless of your status, when you are in a child's life on a day-to-day basis, you are in effect a blueprint to how the child will behave as an adult. Depending on your conduct, the blueprint will be religiously adhered to, or used as a guide to "The Things I Will Never Do to a Child."

Check Yourself
Before You Wreck Yourself

You may have noticed that the pronouns and proper nouns have varied regarding certain issues. Why? Mainly to avoid the impression that African-American males are singularly predisposed to such issues. Most of the issues discussed here encapsulate all men, not just men of color. This is particularly true of the next subject matter, which is extremely ugly but needs to be addressed.

No joke, men can become sexually aroused by a slight breeze; it doesn't take much—the sight of a breast, the sound of a woman moaning, the smell of dirty underwear, the touch of something hairy, and the taste of something tangy. Often, the senses are not needed: a simple thought can achieve the same effect. This is an important point to remember—all sexual acts spring from thought. Thus the devil didn't make you do it; you thought about it and then you did it.

The exact number of stepfathers, live-in boyfriends, and fathers who rape their daughters and/or stepdaughters and/or young girls living with them is unknown. Yes, there are guesstimates, but no way can they fully include the unreported cases, which is no doubt significantly higher than the reported cases. In short, this tragedy happens more than you and the people who keep up with such information think. Of the reported cases it is also ambiguous to how many accusations are false, stemming from revenge, acrimony, and spite.

Still, whether you did it or you didn't do it but were accused of doing it—try explaining *it* to SCAN—you have a serious problem on your hands. A very serious problem! Bluntly: If you are doing it but have yet to get caught, chances are you will; but no doubt you are destroying a young child's life. Stop it, and seek help!

Fact: Never starting is a helluva lot easier than stopping—and avoids a tremendous amount of pain and frustration, not to mention jail time. All of the above is easily avoidable. First and foremost, if she is not your daughter, and she is not a toddler or younger—hands off!—and this includes spanking, touching, hugging, playing—basically all forms of physical contact. Yes, this sounds somewhat extreme, especially the ban on hugging, but this is the first step to checking yourself before wrecking yourself. In time, many years, when you and your stepdaughter have formed a respectable stepfather/step-daughter relationship, hugging might be considered. Keep in mind, with a young girl, that the mere appearance of impropriety alone can come back to haunt you.

Therefore you must conduct yourself in a proper fashion at all times. Frankly, pornographic material—magazines, tapes, books, movies—are definitely not a good idea to keep in the house when you have a young girl living with you. If you cannot part with your porn, at least take it somewhere else. Use the same sound judgment with television and music; even if her mother condones explicit entertainment, you shouldn't sit there with the daughter and watch or listen to such.

Avoid being alone, if all possible. In other words, when Momma hits the door, you should be a second behind her—or insist that Momma take her daughter with her. You wouldn't like it if your daughter was left in the hands of her momma's new boyfriend, would you? Of course not. So allow no one to put you in a situation you wouldn't approve.

Keep away from personal effects and private areas—bedroom (knock), diaries, books, clothes, notes, letters, etc. Plus, who she goes out with, and who her boyfriend is, should not be your foremost concern. However, if you have legitimate concerns about her safety with so-and-so, express them to her mother. Remember, you are a stranger to her, the daughter, and she will not be receptive to you telling her who to befriend.

"Yeah, but who's paying the bills? I am! If she cannot do like I tell her, then she needs to get her shit and get out!"

This is an attitude many men have, but it's a destructive one to maintain. This starts down the road to justification of stupid behavior. Maintain this attitude, and eventually the theme will go from "I can go anywhere in this house!" to "Anything in this house belongs to me!" to "She's living free off me without doing anything in return!" to "She can at least do this one thing for me…after all, I pay the bills!" to jail. And this negative "I pay the cost, so I'm the boss" attitude engenders resentment and argument—which can lead to a false accusation. Think about it, what man who calls himself a man gets into a heated argument with a little girl?

Finally, check your thoughts. There are very few men who have not looked at a young girl with lust in their heart. A fleeting thought is simply a fleeting thought. "Her breast are growing." The problem occurs when the thought surpasses fleeting. This is what separates the men from the pedophiles. A man will check his thoughts then and there—by channeling his thoughts elsewhere, which is not difficult to do. A pedophile, however, will entertain the thought, which leads to uglier thoughts, which leads to sexual fantasizing.The risk of this sickness increases when one is under the influence of drugs and/or alcohol since both make checking and dropping negative thoughts difficult.

When negative thoughts give way to sexual fantasizing, action often follows. And it's inexcusable! Listen to the sick attempts to justify sick behavior…

- "She tempted me!"
- "She put herself on me!"
- "I couldn't help myself!"
- "Someone had to teach her."
- "She wanted it."

Sodomy, oral copulation, inappropriate contact, molestation, fondling, and sexual assault all boils down to the same thing when a minor is concerned—rape!

A sad fact: The overwhelming majority of accusations of child rape are dead-bang true. Also, the damage doesn't stop when the abuse stops. Here is what typically occurs in these incidents: The child alerts the mother of the rape. The mother is mortified, shocked, hurt—but not to the point of alerting the authorities, or at least kicking the man out, or leaving. The man vehemently denies the accusation. Not wanting to lose her so-called man, the mother accuses the child of instigating the rape (notice how ugly this sounds, even on paper). Imagine the child's feeling…not only has she been raped but her mother assumes the side of her rapist. Often under such circumstances the child will run away or start participating in self-destructive behavior such as alcohol, drugs, or prostitution.

Imagine the love and joy circulating in an environment where the daughter is forced to reside with her rapist, or she is living on the street while her rapist still lives with her mother. Imagine the pain and scars this child will carry into her adult life.

Imagine the same thing happening to another child under this man's care.

Of course, you, a decent African-American man, would like to believe that most men do not stoop to this level of sordid depravity. And you, like all men who can stomach their image in a mirror, know that all men make mistakes, but the rape of a child is not a mistake but an evil, vile, deplorable, criminal act that causes a lifetime of pain and frustration on its victim, an innocent child.

Pet Peeves

Remember back in school, the one kid who the teacher flagrantly favored the most? Remember how this kid, in her eyes, could do no wrong? Remember how you wanted to strangle that kid? Men who have a biological child and a stepchild tend to totally forget about the latter. And they wind up doing exactly what that misguided teacher did: Play Favoritism. Outside of abuse—physical, verbal, and sexual—and sheer neglect, nothing causes resentments more than favoring one child over another.

Naturally, a man will love his own child more so than a child not his own, but it is unnatural to treat the other child or children in the same household like dirt, which happens more often than not in these type situations. Depending on the maturity of the man, favoritism can range from subtle slights to outrageous physical and verbal abuse. For example, Junior and biological Junior, both five years old are playing outside. A disagreement erupts, culminating with Junior pushing biological Junior to the ground. Hearing his son's wails, Daddy rushes out the house.

"What did you do to him?" he screams at Junior, who shrugs. Daddy slaps Junior, picks biological Junior up, and goes into the house—leaving Junior outside wailing like a banshee.

While this account is fictitious, it happens every day, with many incidents involving harsher physical assaults. Another example of traumatizing favoritism is when Daddy comes home with toys, snacks, and treats for biological Junior but nothing whatsoever for Junior. Often in these cases, Momma tries to compensate by favoring Junior with a little more attention. Thus instead of a cohesive family, you have opposing factions, with Daddy and biological Junior on one side, and Momma and Junior on the other. This can get very ugly.

All of this can be avoided if you simply ask yourself: "How would it make me feel?" This simple question can eliminate a lifetime of bitterness and resentment.

"How would it make me feel if in every conflict someone automatically assumed I was at fault?"

"How would it make me feel if someone treated my sibling like a king or queen while treating me like a pauper?"

"How would it make me feel watching my sibling play with new toys while I have nothing?"

"How would it make me feel if my sibling were taken fun places and I were left at home?"

The answer to each question: You would feel hurt, very hurt! Granted no one expects you to emulate Mike Brady, but why not simply buy something for every child—even if it is of unequal value, at least something. Otherwise you are telling a child: "I could give a damn about you!" What better lesson for your own child to learn than to treat others equally? He or she will never learn that if you, the father, are dishing out preferential treatment.

As stated from the beginning, if you for whatever reason feel you can not perform the duties of a stepfather, then don't. Actually it speaks better of a man to say he cannot do it than to do it grudgingly or contemptuously. While it takes a man to be a father, it takes a very special man to be a stepfather.

Here the emphasis is on the negative aspects of stepfatherhood, but there is an army of special men out there fulfilling the role of stepfather. You can detect many of these men in the eyes of their stepchildren, who look upon them with respect, admiration and, no doubt about it, love.

On the flip side, in the eyes of some stepchildren there is not anything a stepfather can do to gain their favor. Sometimes this is the result of biological Daddy dropping salt or mucking up the works. In some cases this is simply: "I just don't like you!" Regardless of reason, a special man will accept this, because his goal is not to be loved but respected, and he knows the only way to achieve this goal is to give respect.

Ten Creeds That Special Men Live By

1. I will never hit a child out of anger.

2. I will never call a child out of his name.

3. I will never disrespect a child's mother.

4. I will make an honest effort to treat all children under my roof the same.

5. I will encourage a child to be the best he or she can be.

6. I will never express my personal problems to a child.

7. I will never speak ill of someone else to a child.

8. I will respect a child's personal living area and personal effects.

9. I will not avoid communication with a child; nor will I engage in arguments with a child.

10. I will offer time and assistance to a child on a regular basis.

Chapter 11
Your Planet or Mine?

"Advice is like a suppository, easy to dispense, difficult to self-administer." H.H.

One woman, mind you, set the whole thing off. By no intention of her own, nor her husband's, she experienced an orgasm. So naturally she told her friends, and they told their friends, and before long everybody knew. Until then most women thought that orgasms were myths, romance novel fodder. But not anymore. Armed with new information, women started to expect orgasms. Meanwhile men, agreeable to anything that suggests more sex, happily agreed to help out.

Confusion replaced anxious anticipation when men and women both discovered that whereas women are concerned, those orgasms were slippery little fellows to catch. To add premature ejaculation to dissatisfaction, women magazines told stories of women having "Earthquaking Orgasms," "Apocalyptic Orgasms," and "Global Warming Orgasms." Then a woman in Homer, Louisiana, topped everyone with a shocking claim of "Multiple Orgasms." Well, as you can imagine, this news set women into a quiver, especially those who had yet to experience so much as a ripple. "Something's wrong!" was the cry that echoed across the land. Millions of formerly contented women, boiling hot! Mad as hell! They simply couldn't figure out why the much ballyhooed Mr. Orgasm couldn't find time to stop in their patch of town. If only they would have consulted an honest man, he would have told them: "The topic of sex generally elicits exaggeration." No doubt he would have added: "You cannot truly miss what you never had."

No one thought to ask, and the raging momentum swelled, and then the mantra changed. "Something's wrong!" was replaced with "Something's wrong with my man!" To men this came as a shock; after all, they were still doing what they've been doing for a long time—ejaculating prematurely, making ugly faces, and snoring loudly. This was unfair, not to mention mean-spirited. The least men could do was acknowledge the unfairness of it all. So once again, men played along, by tapping into their so-called "sensitive side." It didn't work. Mainly because He Who Could Cut Loose At Any Time was expected to share and express his feelings and then minutes later go out and remove the tarantula from the front walk.

To add an unexpected electrical surge to an electric sex toy, many women started faking orgasms, which is on the same par as faking employment—a helluva lot of trouble to fool your damn self.

In large numbers, women turned to the workforce. "Why work and slave for a man all day, cleaning house and watching his children," when you can go out and get a job—and basically do the same thing for a salary. As you well know, this arrangement dramatically changed the dynamics of relationships. Two or three paychecks later, many of these women decided that they could go it alone. Marriages disintegrated, shacks crumbled, and millions of Sugar Daddies scrambled to pick up the pieces.

All of this confusion could have been avoided with a simple question and a simple, honest answer. Then no one would have gotten upset, no one would have felt jealous, no one would have felt used or taken for granted, and no one would have felt misunderstood. Not to mention millions of trees spared—from all those books about saving, repairing, and enhancing a relationship. Speaking of which, does a couple really need Venus and Mars in every aspect of their relationship?

One problem with many of these type books—far too much to remember. Unless you take notes, and keep them handy, you probably will not remember to respond in the suggested manner: "Gee, honey, do you mean I'm toilet phlegm in a Venus and Mars sense, or am toilet phlegm because you are in your feelings?"

Always keep in mind that whereas relationships are concerned, as well as other matters, advice is simply advice—usually a course of action that worked for the one giving the advice. But what may have worked for someone else might be disastrous for you—for example, complete honesty, which most relationship eggheads say is the road to take; but a man whose significant other breaks the weight scale should never tell her she's big as a house, even if she is. The same reticence should apply to confessing infidelity: If she served time for killing her last philandering boyfriend, no way do you tell her that you committed a sexual transgression.

For the most part, African-American men do not run to the local bookstore when conflict arises between their mates; they run to family and friends, who can ditch out bad advice with the best of them. Notice the instruction always begin with "If I were you…" In heated issues the rejoinder is usually "I wouldn't take that shit!" Yes, while driving a fist through a brick wall usually works for your homeboy when he wants his old lady to comply, your doing the same thing could get you KISSed—or at the least, a broken hand.

When seeking advice, it's usually a good idea to seek out more than one source and then decide which is most favorable to you and your situation. Keep this in mind as you read on, because even though what is said here is credible, factual, indisputable, and the results of years of research, there exist reasonable alternatives.

Shacking

Even with no regards to moral implications, shacking is one area into which Brothers step with the wrong foot. At a glance, shacking appears the ideal situation: no pesky legal commitments; no marriage penalty; and in some cases, no substantial deduction in food stamps. Well, as you know, everything that looks good isn't good for you. This definitely applies to shacking.

Think long and hard and try to remember one couple you know who shacked blissfully and happily for a long term. Don't strain yourself. Now think of the Brothers you know who have been kicked out of the shack not once but several times. You can stop counting now. This tells you that shacking has an unusually high failure rate, far higher than marriage. Here's why…

Men and women think differently: women tend to think more in the long term; men, however, tend to think from one orgasm to the next. So when a couple decides to cohabit, it's usually the man, giddy with anticipation of the next orgasm, who moves in with the woman, who has given up on orgasms a long time ago and who has already figured out who moves out if things don't work out. For a time things do work out, and everyone is happy. But conflicts are almost surer than death. And when she says, "Get out!" you got to get out. Even a so-called good man, he who forks over his entire paycheck, will at some point hear: "Get out!" Those two words aren't as painful to a man who has not yet had the opportunity to program his favorite channels into the cable system, but to a man who has been around for a few years and has invested thousands of dollars, the words are daggers to his heart. Regardless, he, too, has to "Get out!"

Getting kicked out the shack once or twice can be chalked up to a misunderstanding, a disagreement that got out of hand, but three or more police escorts off the premises reeks of immature dependency and emotional weakness on the man's part. Even if she begs you to come back, chances are she will kick you out again…and again…and again…

Most men who subjugate themselves to this game suffer from low self-esteem, while others suffer from a mental illness called Sweet Peter Psychosis, or SPP for short. SPP generally occurs in men between their late teens and early thirties. Symptoms include a rash or nausea at the mere thought of work, an overly endowed penis, and an extraordinary fondness for satellite television. SPP causes bizarre delusions, specifically the belief that one can lay up on a woman forever, without a job, or money, or contribution to household chores, as long as Sweet Peter is applied daily.

While Sweet Peter might get you in the door, it will not afford your stay indefinitely. Money talks, Sweet Peter walks. The complete opposite is our friend, Sugar Daddy, that poor, misguided soul who believes that because he pays a bill he has a say on the hill. This logic doesn't even work in Washington D.C. When she gets tired of him—and she eventually will!—he has to go! "It's not working out," she tells him. "I need some time to myself. But…" And here's the catch. "…I still need you in my life." Translated: "Get out! But I still need you to paid my bills." You'll be surprised by how many men fall for this.

To avoid these pitfalls, simply insist she move in with you, or move into a new place, with both your names on the lease. If it's your place, in your name only, don't forget that women rarely play the Revolving Door game. So if you demand that she "Get out, and don't come back!" she'll probably do just that.

Moe Money

Male chauvinistic, sexist, egotistical, whatever, but money drives women out of their minds. Even with the most frigid of the fridgidest, a stack of bills can start a woman to trembling, shaking, shouting, eyes watering, and gnashing of the teeth. Yeah, yeah, yeah, many men also lose their minds over money. But think about it, how many men you know—and yes, there are a few—will cuddle up with an old hen, ten times their age, simply because she has money?

A smelly, grotesque-looking alien could come to earth, don a suit, and, as long as it had money, attract a gaggle of women. It would not be lonely. To be fair, and to avoid being sued or stoned, some women, a small minority living in the Florida Everglades, do not go into a seizure at the sight of money. If your significant other, wife, girlfriend, shack buddy, whatever, respects money, yours and hers, consider yourself truly blessed.

If not, pay close attention to the following greed mechanisms women use on men to make ends meet.

Denial: Two types, conscious and unconscious. When she says "No, I have not seen your money," and all the while it's in her purse, this is a classic form of conscious denial. Unconscious denial usually manifests itself when the man is headed out the door, and she cannot—and she does try—remember half the times she gypped him out his money.

Regression: After several weeks of adhering to the budget, she passes by a K-Mart and flips her lid, reverting back to her prodigal ways, buying things neither you nor she can afford.

Rationalization: "Your last girlfriend took your money," "I was only rearranging your wallet," and "Yes, the rent is due, but my nails deserved priority" are textbook examples of rationalization.

Displacement: You are angry because she blew the light bill, and she's angry because you're angry, but she takes it out on your friend Harry Hydrophobe, calling him "A serious threat to the ozone layer," and kicks him out.

Projection: Your sister borrows a few dollars from you, and she, your significant other, has a hissy fit, calling your sister a gold digger, a cheat, and everything but a child of God. Listen closely, she's describing herself.

Identification: She adores and praises femme fatales who dupe, trick, and connive men out of their money. Also notice that her close friends dupe, trick, and connive men out of their money.

Reaction formation: When her sister-in-law dupes, tricks, and connives her brother out of his money, she's ready to take a bite out of a bear. But for the life of her, she cannot connect her sister-in-law's duplicitous deeds to her own.

Sublimation: After many years of nagging and conniving you out of your money, she finally sees the error of her ways, goes to church, and gives your hard-earned money to the young, good-looking preacher who cannot sustain life without three Bentleys—one for him, his wife, and that pretty hot thang who sits the first pew every Sunday.

Fantasy: In a foolish attempt to turn a little money into big money, she goes to the casino or bingo hall, and comes home broke, as usual. When you—hungry and in the dark—try to explain the ills of gambling, she tells of the woman sitting right smack beside her who played three quarters on the Triple Diamond slot machine and won a million dollars.

Amnesia: Like the Clintons, she cannot remember monumental events that occurred just the other day. Everyone else can remember the day someone put large bills in their hands—but not she! "I simply cannot recall that happening," she says. Yet she can recall quite clearly and quickly every penny she has given you in the last twenty years.

Compensation or Substitution: The dealer had nineteen, she had eighteen. Poof!—there goes the car note money. Instead of telling you that she blew it, she tries to blow—you get the picture.

Undoing: Though an impulse buy, the designer clothes—with initials that mean Fleecing Us By Us—she bought for you and her were way too expensive. So she takes back only the items she bought for you and gets a refund.

Intellectualization and Isolation: After having far too much fun with someone else's money—yours—she intellectualizes that a safe, secluded, isolated place (her mother's house) would be the ideal place to stay for a few days, at least till you cool off.

Not mentioned in the above is "Borrowing," which is a concept, a simple concept: "Borrow, pay back." Again: "Borrow, pay back." As simple as that is, many women cannot grasp it. The first part poses no intellectual hurdles, and most women have it down pat. The second part, however, causes utter confusion. Amnesia cannot be cited here because the word *borrow* in itself implies "I'm going to pay you back." Phases such as "Gimme..." "Let me have..." and, though lacking in specificity, "Let me hold...", suggest that reciprocity is not to be expected.

Yet there is a plus side to women's fondness for money—mathematics. Search high, low, and deep, and you will be hard pressed to find a man who cannot count money. Men with no schooling whatsoever, men who cannot read, and men who go to the bathroom when the dinner bell rings, all know how to count money. At an early age, Momma, grandmother, uncle, neighbor, *somebody*, makes sure the young man can count.

This is done because everyone knows about the one man in a million who cannot count money—and what a tragedy that is: His wife or girlfriend tells him how much he makes. "Gosh, Harold, you made the same this week as last week. How much? Watch my fingers…one…two…three…four…Four dollars, Harold." Of course, all women are not like that—most would have stopped at three.

Money is yet another reason why it pays to take your time before committing to a relationship. If you and your mate are not on the same page on money matters, you will truly experience hell on earth. Even if she respects money while you blow yours, this will still cause serious problems. The status of the relationship also plays a big factor. In a marriage, men are more inclined to stew under the "one big pot" system, where the man's money is her money and her money, for the most part, is her money. In shacking and girlfriend/boyfriend relationships, men are less inclined to stew under the "one big pot" system, in part because of the Revolving Door game. Getting put out and having cab fare and your clothes neatly tucked away in suitcases is one thing; getting put out and having to walk with your clothes draped over your back in a Glad garbage bag is quite another.

Whether she handles the money, or you, or the both of you, doesn't matter as long as you both are happy with the results—which is quite rare.

Lying

African-Americans, in general, would rather be lied to than lied on. Most African-Americans know that everybody lies, so rarely are they shocked when someone confesses to lying. Notice that African-Americans rarely use the word liar, or the phrase "I can't believe he lied to me." Yes, they can believe it! Even when confronted with an outrageous liar, African-Americans seldom confront falsification but often skirt around it in such phrases as: "Sounds like some bullshit to me," "If you say so," "You sho' bout that?" and "Uh-huh." Amazingly, many African-Americans, even when highly agitated, still skirt around directly calling someone a liar, preferring such phases as: "You full of bullshit!"; "You must think I'm a damned fool!"; and "Your breath stank!"

Whenever you hear a Brother say, "You a damn lie!" it's best to seek cover, because drama is about to occur. Whenever you hear someone say, "I ain't lying," "I ain't quick to lie," "You're not going to believe this…" and "This ain't no lie," you can almost guarantee that he or she is lying.

No lie, everybody lies, some more than others, and some more foolishly than others. Let's agree that to a certain extent lying helps a relationship. For example, your significant other asks you if her thighs are getting bigger. Do you tell the truth? "Yes, baby, they look like elephant's legs." Or do you lie? "No, they aren't." Of course you lie, and you lie without hesitating.

This type of lying avoids hurting someone feelings. So when does lying hurt a relationship? Good question. The answer is rather tricky, but remember this: The best lie is the one you never get a chance to tell. Otherwise, if a lie causes you or anyone else guilt, pain, remorse, regret, frustration, anger, sorrow, then it is not only harmful to your relationship(s) but also your health.

This concept eludes the pathological liar, usually RRHOIDS and First-class A-Holes, who lie for the sheer sake of moving his or her lips. More often than not, the pathological liar has other social inadequacies such as stealing and cheating. Anyone who lies when the truth would suffice can be considered a pathological liar.

So who lies the most, men or women? Believe or not, both! Women tend to lie more often to other women about personal issues, age, family, and relationships. Men tend to lie more often to other men about masculinity issues, sex, money, and accomplishments. In relationships, men tend to lie more often than woman, usually to avoid confrontations. Ironically, lies about sex and money hurt relationships the most, and are the top two topics lied about in relationships. Women, by far, rationalize more than men. The old cliché "It's a woman right to change her mind," many women think, palliates fabrications.

If this isn't hypocrisy, nothing is. A woman changes her mind about a promise—usually about sex—and the man, she expects, should understand. However, a man isn't afforded this luxury. Women, more so than children, are devastated by failed promises. In their minds, if you promise it you better damn well deliver. This slams smack hard into the current trend in which many women expect a gift for every holiday, including Groundhog Day. Someone should get around to announcing to millions of women that Mother's Day was originally planned for mothers, not shack buddies and girlfriends.

"Gosh, baby, I'm sorry I forgot the mink coat you wanted for Flag Day," will not cut it in today's culture. Even if she says, "That's okay," you can bet good money it isn't. If you are shacking and it's her place, it's a good idea to mark all holidays, and don't forget her birthday, her kid's birthday, and her last boyfriend's birthday. The same foolishness occurs around Christmas. The man goes out and buries himself in debt for the next twenty years to clutter the Christmas tree with gifts, and for his efforts, what does he receive? Tube socks. Or the yearly favorite, V-necked T-shirts. A word of caution: If you have been maxing your credit cards out each year for gifts for your better half, don't try to suspend doing so dramatically; gradually wean her down; otherwise she might go into Sugar Baby psychosis.

Honestly, the most anyone should expect from their partner is a reasonable level of trust. This means sexual fidelity, telling the truth when it's blatantly obvious, and an independent willingness to right a lie. Expecting complete and total honesty from someone is a pipe dream. The true measure of a man or woman is not how often he or she tells a lie, but how often he or she admits a lie. Pathological liars, drunks, drug addicts, and other emotional misfits rarely, if ever, admit a lie. Being backed into a corner with the truth and then admitting the truth is not truly admitting a lie but having nowhere else to turn. For further clarification on this read Slick's grand jury testimony.

Trust in a relationship seldom deteriorates by "I'm going to cut the grass after the game" type lies, but by the heavyweight lies concerning sex and money. Occasional discrepancies with two's and fews (less than five dollars) barely register on the temper meter in most relationships. (Unless, of course, the couple are both crackheads and/or drunks, and then a mere fifty cents could instigate irreconcilable differences.) In most instances, the source of frustration stems from one party spending too much money. Men are more willing to forgive money miscalculations than women. Blow one too many paychecks, and most women are totally void of any understanding. "You can sleep where you spent all your money, but not here!" is usually the reply. Many women will forgive a man's philandering as long as it doesn't involve money. In other words, she can deal with him sleeping with the woman next door, but the moment he puts a dime in her hand, it's over. Men, however, can deal with castration better than dealing with infidelity on their partner's part. Even if the man has been sleeping with half the town, he cannot deal with a single act of infidelity on his mate's part.

Whatever the reason, once the relationship dips to zero trust, it's best to start thinking about doing something different. Yes, some couples work through major breaches of trust. But some cannot. The key to doing so is forgiveness. With the exception of Bobby and Whitney, there is no uglier pair than a couple who stay together but no longer have respect for each other. They are going through the motions, no joy, no passion, just suspicion—and plenty of it. Zero trust almost always causes one party to pick up a magnifying glass and play the role of detective. Though untrained in the field of investigation, an amateur sleuth in the form of a suspicious woman can make Colombo look like Barney Fife. First, she cross-examines: "Where were you at last night? What time did you leave? With whom? Were there any women there? Where did you stop before coming home? How long were you there? Where else?"

Then she collects the evidence. Lint, paper, receipts, pocket change, a single hair, photograph(s), letter(s), body scars—scratches, hickeys, bite marks—and phone numbers can all be used against you.

But that's not enough for a conviction. She interviews witnesses. Those phone numbers she found in your pocket, they will be contacted. Often, her friends and relatives are more than willing to conduct undercover surveillance. Dan Daily—remember him?—he too is more than willing to help out. Finally, the indictment comes—but here you are guilty till proven innocent. Think about it: Isn't this rather ugly, not to mention no way to live? Imagine coming home to a body inspection every day, your woman looking upside your head for nicks and hickies and such. Or imagine yourself conducting or thinking about conducting a body search. Ridiculous, right? Yet you would be surprised how many relationships stoop to this sort of foolishness. Once the relationship dips to zero trust, it's very difficult, and takes a long time, to regain even a semblance of trust.

Suffer one too many bad relationships, regardless of who was at fault, and you will become jaded. Hollywood figures talk of finding true love on the sixth and seventh try, but in real life that's pure bull. Think about it, how could you not become jaded?

You know from experience that relationships often do not work, and usually end bitterly.

So you hold back to a certain degree, thinking: "If I don't put all I have into it, I won't lose everything if it doesn't work out."

It's simple. If you want a reasonably trustful relationship, you put in a reasonable amount of trust in a relationship. It also never hurts to forgive, or ask for forgiveness. Again, some couples can overcome major breaches of trust; some cannot. If you think you can do so without feeling bitter or resentful, without playing detective, then by all means do so. The same logic applies to your mate; if she cannot forgive you, or she said she could but acts otherwise, then you and she should reassess the relationship.

It's Your Move?

Men and women both play games, but women rarely act out after losing. Yes, they cry and occasionally fall out, but they don't start breaking things and picking fights with the victor the way men often do. Considering this, it's reasonable to conclude that women are better game players than men, especially when it comes to head games. Men react more outrageously to head games than games where money is on the line. Therefore the following list of head games that women play offers advice on how not to play along, because no way can a man win by doing so. Keep in mind that the goal of most head games is to hurt or pay back, not to win.

Monopoly: This game is the favorite of women who have grown tired of their shack buddy or boyfriend. She declares everything—TV, bed, couch, chair, spoons, plates, dirt—hers. These women sum it up in one sentence: "You don't own shit here!" To argue this point is foolish. Even if the Internet is in your name, what good is that when you are out on the streets. Method to avoiding this game: Get your own shit.

Battleship: Many women who watched the movie *Waiting To Exhale* clapped and cheered when the woman burned her husband's clothes and sold his expensive car for peanuts. Apparently, destroying a man's property is more emotionally satisfying than selling it for a fair price and splitting the money. Perhaps the reason why so many women do this or approve of it being done is that so many men fall in love with their toys. If you hug your golf clubs more than you hug your significant other, guess what is going to be the first thing that goes up in smoke after a major disagreement? Uh-uh—not the V-necked T-shirts or the tube socks. Guess again. Method to avoiding this game: Hide favorite toys at the first sign of stormy waters.

Hide and Seek: The junior version of this game almost always involve car keys. The woman demands that you stay home, you say no way, then you can't find your car keys. Or she simply throws them where you will have a hard time finding them. The method to avoiding this game is quite simple: Make more than one set.

The adult version is far more complicated and often results in injury. Instead of throwing keys where you cannot find them, she goes where you cannot find her. This drives many men out of their mind, which, perhaps, is the reason why some women do it (this doesn't include if she's hiding out in fear of you). Say, for example, she caught you cheating on Friday night and then she disappeared Saturday morning. If she left anything, she will be coming back. If she took everything...well, it's time to subscribe to Better Homes and Gardens.

Method to avoiding this game: Don't ding out! Perhaps she needs a little time to herself. Regardless of her reason, this doesn't give you the right to launch a massive search and force her back. Also, remember this: Searching, begging and pleading are forms of stalking.

Trivial Pursuit: This game is by far women's all-time favorite. Here's the rule of play: Instead of telling a man what's really bothering you—for example, he stayed out late with his friends, which made you upset—you carp on the most trivial misdeeds you can think of. For instance, if he leaves the toilet seat up, you simply go ballistic. Method to avoiding this game: Ask her what the true problem is. "No, baby, my chest moving up and down is not really why you're mad. What is?"

Sorry: The first time—even though she forgot to say, "Sorry!"—she dropped a lamp onto your head may have been a mistake, but the second and third time definitely were not. Women who have a visceral need to get even play this game the most. They feel they must exact the same amount of pain inflicted on them—usually a case of infidelity. Their method of payback can range from sleeping with a man's close friend to having someone key his car. This is also the game of choice for women who like to sleep around but also keep a man at home. "Honest, honey, I'll never do it again" gets old after the third time.

Method to avoiding this game: Run! Remember, listening to noises? These type women usually have a history of related behavior, which means you are probably not the first. If she got a perverse delight out of dropping a electric curling iron in her previous philandering boyfriend's tub—while he was in it—chances are she told you about it not once but several times.

Clue: This game, though seemingly innocuous, wreaks much havoc and frustration. You don't have a clue to what's going on with her because she's not talking, or she's responding in grunts: "Uh-huh," or "Uh-uh." This is rather ironic; usually, when she isn't angry, you wish that she would give her lips a rest, but now that you can't get her to say anything, it's driving you crazy. Method to avoiding this game: Don't badger or plead with her to converse. Keep in mind that that she's expending a tremendous amount of energy keeping her lips from flapping—which can last but for so long. A better option: "I'm willing to discuss whatever is bothering you."

Aggravation: Like Clue, this game is very childish—but very effective in grating on nerves. When you and she were in a joyous state of oneness, you could say, "Sugar Pie, that noise you're making is getting on my nerves," and she would immediately stop humming, or whistling through her nose, or smacking gum, or sucking her teeth, or channeling phlegm through her nasal passages to her stomach and back again. But now that she's upset, all bets are off—and, to your horror, she has somehow increased the volume and frequency. Method to avoiding this game: Never, ever, let anyone who can produce a body noise that can drown out a passing train know you are uncomfortable with it. Doing otherwise almost always invites aggravation.

Scrabble: Finally a game that some men enjoy. Many women get so disgusted with their man that they decide not do anything, which means no more cooking and cleaning. With a woman who is an exceptional good cook this can be quite devastating. However, these type women are far and few between, not to mention that many of today's women specialize in one dish, usually grilled cheese or boiled eggs. So when she who cannot figure out how to roll ground beef into meatballs declares she's no longer cooking, thank your lucky stars. Method to avoiding this game: Red Lobster.

Mouse Trap: Originally this game involved a pregnancy and a man who desired to do the right thing, but that was then. Today's version involves a pen and a willingness to sign on a line that says CO-SIGNER. Here's how it works: Woman meets man, convinces man to sign contract, woman disappears, man forced to make payments on car, or furniture, or electronics, or whatever—it doesn't matter, he'll never see it again. Method to avoiding this game: Self-induced dyslexia.

Ouija: One month she's chanting, the next she's playing with snakes, then the next she's lighting candles and drawing weird hieroglyphics on the floor. Even worse, she insists that you, a heathen non-believer, join in. The word that best describes these women—confused! Method to avoiding this game: Run!

Operation: A man caught up in this game needs calm nerves and a thick skin. A wrong move to the left—*ding!*—and there are her friends, a wrong move to the right—*ding!*—and there are her family, each with a staunch opinion on how he should treat her, his woman. To add a missing billfold to a house full of company, she occasionally allows them to move in. Method to avoiding this game: Subletting.

What's Really Going On?

Many African-Americans eggheads have concluded that the African-American male is prone to domestic violence because of racism. This conclusion is a bit long. The average Brother during a heated argument with his mate isn't thinking about the redneck down the street; his sole focus is on his adversary at the moment—his mate. Plus there is no factual evidence that supports the claim that African-American men suffer more domestic issues than other groups. So the conclusion here is, African-American men engage in domestic disputes, including domestic violence, because of the same reasons that other groups do.

There are a multitude of reasons why men and women argue and fight, but the totality of reasons can be boiled down to either Unrealistic Expectations, Illing, or Clairvoyance.

Let's take a closer look at each, starting first with the last.

Clairvoyance: No one goes to a doctor and sits there mute expecting the doc to figure out their problem by psychic means. That's rather lame, isn't it? Not to mention the doc might guess wrong and create another problem. This is exactly what happens in many a relationship and causes almost as much frustration as a surgeon cutting off the wrong foot. Let's say, for example, you and your old lady were at a party and some joker cracks a joke at your expense, and your old lady laughs right along with everyone else. So now you're pissed off, extremely pissed off, not because of the joke but because your old lady laughed too. She, your so-called woman, you ruminate, shouldn't be laughing at you. On the way home, with her at the wheel, you make snide comments about her driving, then an argument erupts, choice words are exchanged. Now you're thinking: She doesn't give a damn about me! She's thinking: What an A-Hole!

Notice that nary a word was mentioned about the true problem, her laughing along with everyone else, which hurt your feelings. Face it, she hurt your feelings. And though you felt like she should have known she were doing so, it's quite possible she didn't. Think about it: If you had told her what was really going on with you, possibly you and she could have avoided a major argument.

YOU: "I really didn't appreciate you laughing at me."

YOUR OLD LADY: "I'm sorry. I really didn't mean anything by it."

Problem solved. Of course, this isn't implying that a Brother should go around sniveling and whining about his feelings all day, but if something hurts, or bothers you for that matter, by all means express what's really going on.

No doubt to some Brothers this sounds rather woosy, but check this out. Whether you admit it or not, you have a tremendous amount invested in your old lady (old lady sounds a trite tacky, but it beats *shack buddy*). She validates your self-worth, your self-esteem, your manhood, and she's your true partner. So what she says or does not say has a large effect on your physical and emotional well-being. Therefore it's to your advantage to communicate to her what's really going on with you, and she likewise, and then you and she can avoid much of the next topic...

Illing: Let's return to the exchange that took place on the ride home after the party. You don't mind yourself being used as an example, do you? What a sport.

YOU: You're driving too close to the centerline.
YOUR OLD LADY: No, I'm not!
YOU: Get a ticket, and I'm not paying it.
YOUR OLD LADY: Do you want to drive?
YOU: No.
YOUR OLD LADY: Then let me drive in peace, please!
YOU: You're too damn close on that man's bumper! If he stops suddenly you'll kill him and me both!
YOUR OLD LADY: Do me a favor, shut up!
YOU: You shut up!
YOUR OLD LADY: I'm not the one bitching!
YOU: You calling me a bitch now?
YOUR OLD LADY: I didn't call you a bitch! (Mumbling) But you're sure acting like a bitch.
YOU: Fuck you!
YOUR OLD LADY: Fuck you!
YOU: Stop the car! Stop the damn car!

Notice the escalating tension to the point of rage. You were already half-cocked before the argument started, because she laughed at you, and then the word bitch touched a hair-trigger, and then your old lady said it again, and then you clicked. Adrenaline and hormones flowed rapidly through your bloodstream, your heartbeat sped up, breathing became somewhat difficult, your muscles tensed, and your total concentration was on your old lady—and you were ready to fight or run like hell. If you had partaken any adult beverages or drugs at the party, you would have clicked a long time before she said the word *bitch* (she really didn't call you that).

Once you have clicked, practical reasoning is all but

impossible. Zero understanding. You cannot think clearly, and you're unreceptive to good advice—*"Why don't you chill...just chill!"* You're not trying to hear that, because your mind is totally centered on what you believe is a threat to your existence.

Men click more often on their mates than anyone else. Mainly because arguments, differences of opinions, and misunderstandings often segue into personal attacks. Once the name-calling starts, there's little hope of reconciling the disagreement peacefully. Always attack the issue, not the person.

Sadly, there exists a large population of men and women who have yet to realize that name-calling and harsh criticism is to a good relationship what arsenic is to good health.

Of this population, the women far outnumber the men. Still, this grants no excuse to click. Lacking in self-respect and social awareness, many of these women will continue a verbal assault long after a man has said, "Will you please leave me alone!" In some cases, when the man has made an honest attempt to remove himself from the situation, these women will crank up their car and go find him, primarily to continue the verbal assault.

In many relationships where the woman is a relentless termagant, the man does something completely opposite of clicking—though it poses the same harmful effects—he "locks up," becomes silent and withdrawn, often because he fears he might click. Interesting enough, often when a man locks up, the woman ratchets up the verbal assault. While she's ranting and raving, he's either contemplating leaving her or doing something to her. The risk here: After months or years of suppressing anger and resentment, he clicks because of her saying or doing something innocuous, such as "Hello," or bumping into him accidentally.

All of the above can easily be avoided. The following are three steps you can take to avoid clicking and locking up.

> **Step one:** *Check yourself.* You cannot control when you get angry, but you can definitely control the intensity of your anger. The very moment you sense yourself getting angry is the small window of opportunity you have to do something about it.
>
> **Step two:** *Look for the true origin* of the disagreement. This is often easy to detect if you search for it, but once you get emotionally bogged down, searching for anything is the last thing on your mind.
>
> **Step three:** *Listen.* Often a woman's goal in a disagreement is to be heard, so listen, without cutting her off, or attempting to end the disagreement too early. A good method, is to repeat back what she says. For example, she says, "You spend more time with your funky friends than you do me!" Then you say: "I spend more time with my funky friends than I do you?" Above all, this tells her that her perspective is at least being heard, which might open the door to cordial discourse. Put yourself in her shoes and look at the situation from her perspective; she may have a legitimate complaint. Avoid viewing the disagreement as a win-lose proposition. Think compromise. What good is winning if you're alone?

These three steps are easier said than done and take a fair amount of practice to perfect. But the rewards in doing so are priceless. Not only will all your personal relationships improve dramatically, but also your mental health and your ability to relate to others in all aspects of life—on the job, at play, in public. Additionally, you will never be the product of someone's else's anger. Since you know that getting angry in response to anger is akin to attempting to put out a fire with gas, you will not be at the mercy of A-Holes who delight in watching others click.

Another great idea is to study the relatively few couples in your area that actually have a loving relationship—not the couples who front until they escort you out the house. You can easily detect the difference. One couple strain at being loving, only attentive to each other when observed, but the other, the truly loving couple, act at ease with each other and everyone else. If you look closer at the truly loving couple you will notice some interesting habits. They follow a mutually agreed-upon set of rules. No going to bed angry. No disagreeing in public, or in front of friends and family members. No hitting, shouting, or cursing. Time-outs when the heat gets too hot. No broaching "Not Open for Discussion" topics—these are usually topics that trigger rage, such as character deficiencies in family members.

If they can do it, you and your significant other can too. If she's about having a loving relationship with you, she will be more than happy to adhere to a set of rules both you and she have agreed upon. Remember, though, rules mean nothing if not followed.

Unrealistic Expectations: Have you ever been given a dirty look or the finger by someone who was angered that *you* were driving the speed limit? Apparently the A-Hole thought you should have at least realized he was in a hurry and gotten out of his way. As ridiculous as this is, it's only a mild case of Unrealistic Expectations, which at its roots is the belief that others should not only allow you free access to whatever but should also fully comprehend the depth of your situation. Many men and women enter into a relationship with a wide range of unrealistic expectations. For example, many fatherless women, especially those who adopted a television Daddy, enter a relationship expecting the man to fill the void. On the same coin, many men enter relationships expecting the woman to fill the role of Momma—who, by the way, could roll ground beef into meatballs with one hand, one eye closed, while ironing clothes with her foot.

These men and women suffer when reality hits home, but often, instead of accepting reality, they continue trying to mold their partner into something he or she isn't, which causes more frustration.

The easiest and quickest way to get someone to comply to your expectations is to change your expectations. The more you expect from someone, the more you'll get let down. Say, for example, you hinted to your old lady that you wanted a weight set for your birthday, not once but several times. Your birthday arrives, but instead of a weight set, your old lady buys you a motorcycle, clothes, golf clubs, and a cell phone. Big deal!—you expected a weight set, and you're pissed off. On paper it's rather obvious how childish this attitude is, but in a real-life situation it's quite difficult to see, mostly because emotions take over. Now let's say you didn't expect your old lady to buy you anything for your birthday, and she bought you all the above. Of course you would be tickled brown—not to mention grateful.

No doubt in some matters—money, religion, moral values—it's best that you and your mate are on the same page, but in small, minor, insignificant issues there's no law that dictates you and she share the same opinion. This fact should be stamped on the forehead of men and women who inexorably rant and rave that their opinion is the right and only one in insignificant matters such as sweeping, walking, eating, sleeping, talking, driving, and a lot more. The common characteristic of these men and women is a quickness to call someone who holds a different opinion "stupid," "dumb," or "ignorant." What's truly "stupid, "dumb," and "ignorant" is stooping to name-calling and hitting when confronted with an opposing opinion. Remember, this is the mark of the racist, the A-Hole, and the extremely insecure.

If you and she both arrived at the mountaintop approximately the same time, though by different trails, is there really a wrong way or right way to come up? No, there isn't. If you and she are thriving for the same goal—to love each other, right?—why bicker over the small stuff? Why get upset if she holds an opinion different from your own? Think about it: If when you first met her, you had discovered that all her opinions were identical to yours, then you would not have continued the relationship, would you? Of course not.

Her being different from you is in part what attracted you to her. Keep this in mind the next time she says, "Ronald Reagan was the greatest president!"

Oops, Upside Your Head!

A very, very small group of august men can proudly say, "I have never hit, pushed, shoved, or verbally assaulted a woman." The majority of these men were fathered by men who never hit, pushed, shoved, or verbally assaulted a woman. Most of these men are self-confident, high achievers, drug- and alcohol-free, spiritually grounded, and reasonably honest. No, in case you are wondering, the author cannot be included in this group.

Now let's take a look at the other three groups, men who have verbally or physically assaulted a woman, starting with the First-class A-Hole first, then the Control Freak, and finally the Wimp.

The First-class A-Hole: This is the smallest group of men who abuse women, but by far they are the most pernicious abusers. The First-class A-Hole is a psychopath, void of empathy; he cannot comprehend that someone other than himself feels pain. Which is probably why many First-class A-Hole abusers do not experience an increase in heart rate during an assault, which is characteristic of the Control Freak and the Wimp.

Also uncharacteristic of the other two, the First-class A-Hole often takes his abuse outside the home.

Yes, he occasionally expresses guilt and sorrow for his deeds, but it's mimicry at its finest. This is another reason why the First-class A-Hole is the most dangerous. He's extremely charming initially, but eventually his true fangs show, and he attacks, viciously. His first attack is seldom the result of an escalation from verbal assault to physical assault but an out-and-out unprovoked blitzkrieg.

An important point to remember: The Control Freak and the Wimp can reach the same mental state of the First-class A-Hole via drugs, alcohol, stress—especially the loss of a job—or abandonment. Misuse of cocaine, amphetamines, anabolic steroids, and some prescription drugs, such as Talwin, often causes abnormal aggression and other antisocial tendencies, including symptoms identical to paranoid schizophrenia.

The Control Freak: The Control Freak is a Wimp who has graduated to the next level. He, like the Wimp, behaves one way at home and another way in public. Often his friends and family are shocked to discover that he assaults his mate—and often they refuse to believe it. "Gosh, Harold wouldn't hurt a fly!" Yet at home, alone with his significant other, Harold is a tyrant, a despot. His significant other cannot please him, because Harold keeps moving the goalpost; so she moves around delicately, trying her best not to upset him, her joy in life predicated by his temper tantrums.

The movie *What's Love Go To Do With It* is a case study of a Control Freak. However, this does not mean to imply that Ike Turner is a Control Freak. The movie didn't exactly jibe with the book. Plus no one thought to call Ike and ask his version of events, which, undoubtedly, would have been strikingly dissimilar to Tina's. Still, the movie's character exhibited the classic signs of a man out of control trying to control—jealous, insecure, low self-esteemed, and physically violent. He controlled his wife's money, her friends, where and when she went, everything. Any advancement on her part he saw as a threat—possible abandonment, and a serious affront to his manhood. When his wife, not he and his band, was invited to sing for a different venue, he clicked, sent everybody home, and brutally assaulted and raped his wife.

The eggheads have yet to clearly define the connection, but it appears that "clicking" hormones and hormones controlling sexual arousal intermingle at the peak of rage or the cooling-down period, which may be part of the reason why so many abusers claim an increase in sexual arousal during or after an assault.

The man succumbs to his base instincts, and becomes an animal, a monster. Think about it this way: Someone much stronger than you attacks you, brutally, yet that is not enough, he or she also sexually assaults you. Can you imagine the pain and suffering?

The First-class A-Hole cannot imagine this because the ability to empathize is not in him; the Control Freak can imagine this, but he completely blocks empathy out because he sees himself as the true victim in the relationship. Let him, the Control Freak, tell it—she's taking advantage of him, misusing him, treating him unfairly. Boo hoo! She, according to him, needs correcting time to time because if not she would get out of hand. He believes this with every fiber of his being.

Because the Control Freak can justify his abusive behavior with amazing ardor and sincerity, he distinguishes himself from the other two in one area—planning. It's not enough that the Control Freak's significant other follows all his orders quickly and performs his duties exactly as instructed. He will think of something to become outraged about. Most men find it emotionally unsettling to carry the thought of having a fight with the old lady after work around all day, but not the Control Freak; he enjoys planning the attack almost as much as he does the attack itself.

When the woman in his life finally gets fed up of being treated like a slave, she will leave; might take some time, but she will leave, or in some cases, injure or kill. Her leaving tells him that all he has done, all he has worked for, and all he has tried to accomplish were for naught. And he clicks, like he has never clicked before. Remember in the movie, the character portraying Ike Turner pulls a gun and demands that his wife come back to him.

The Control Freak foolishly thinks that he's being a man, taking charge, but he's playing a deadly game. He is not totally unaware of this fact, but he thinks he knows who to pull this crap with and who not to pull this crap with. This is why some men abuse their wife but not their girlfriend, or vice versa. This is also why every graveyard in the country is filled with men who thought they knew who they were fucking with. Profane? Yes, but so very true. Falling into this foolish behavior is akin to playing Russian Roulette: You might get away with it a time or two, but when you lose, you lose big.

The Wimp: He is in the largest group of abusers, and very few men can deny ever putting his shoes on. The Wimp hits on impulse. Something is said or done that touches a hair trigger, he clicks, then hits. But oh, is he so very sorry! "I didn't mean to do it!" "I will never do it again!" "Oh, baby, I'm so sorry—I don't know what come over me!" Yes, no doubt about it, the Wimp is the most remorseful—and if one or all of the above doesn't work he'll shed some tears. Still, his chances of doing the same thing are high, extremely high, even higher if he observed his father or anyone else abuse his mother. However, some Wimps wimp out only once. This is due to a variety of reasons, including unexpected death and unexpected quadriplegia. Also included in this group are men who can detect their own gas before expelling it. In other words, they sense themselves falling into self-destructive behavior and do something about it instead of pleading they will never do it again, such as seeking counseling.

The largest group of Wimps, also the largest group of abusers, are the men who click every so often, less than three times a year. Many of these men, and their significant other, do not see this behavior as abusive because it's irregular, but it has the same deadly potential. A good percentage of men in this group lock up in response to stress—not good—so when they do click, they click with a vengeance. Plus there's always something lurking around the corner, particularly an unexpected stress factor—loss of a job, illness, infidelity—that could easily turn three-times-a-year clicking to three-times-a-week clicking.

The final group of Wimps are simply Control Freaks in basic training. These men are not too sure where they stand yet, so they bide their time with insults, harsh criticism, and minor assaults—pushing, shoving, and snatching. The moment they get the green light, usually when the woman accepts the apology after the first major assault, they make the transition to Control Freak.

Don't get hung up on the classification; each group has representatives in every graveyard. You can avoid the whole lot if you keep one thing in mind: Physical and verbal assault do not work, and both are inexcusable. Physical assault seems effective because it immediately stops a person in his or her tracks. Everything stops—talking, shouting, whatever—and the focus of the attention is on the person who hit. Think about it: If someone bigger and stronger than you were to hit you, he would definitely have your attention, wouldn't he? No doubt. Yet while he may have your attention, he does not have your respect; in fact, you are ruminating over a way to pay him back, in spades. The same thing occurs when a man hits a woman; after being hit she does not look at him lovingly. Uh-uh. She, too, has murderous thoughts. If the abuse continues, she may very well act on those murderous thoughts.

Hitting basically says one of two things: "I cannot deal with what you are saying or doing!" or "I can make you do what I want you to do!" Never does hitting say… "I love you!"

"I cannot control myself."

"You made me do it!"

"It's all your fault!"

Finally some good news: You don't have to be a Wimp! Sounds rather simple, doesn't it? Well, it is. The only step it takes is to control yourself. Which includes, of course, controlling your anger. For the umpteenth time, because it cannot be emphasized enough, the ideal time to defuse anger is the first moment you feel it coming on—trembling, twitching, burning sensation, shortness of breath, rapid heartbeat, muscles tightening, whatever. This is the time to leave the scene, channel your thoughts elsewhere, take a walk, ask for a time-out, or whatever works for you, but take control early as possible, before the hammer comes down and you click. The more you practice defusing anger, the better you will get at it. Yes, no doubt, anger will occasionally get the best of you, but by practicing controlling it, seldom will it overwhelm you.

Let's return again to the acrimonious ride home after the party. When you said, "Stop the damn car," you intended to get out and walk home, because you sensed yourself getting angry beyond control. Right? Then, when you arrived home, you told your old lady what was really going on, and you and she apologized and laughed about the incident. Okay, but the average Wimp would have handled that situation quite differently. A Wimp would have walked home, too, but instead of defusing his anger, he simply intensified his anger by rehashing everything his old lady did to him in the last twenty years. A bigger Wimp would have walked to his friend's house, gotten drunk, and taken to heart the lies his friends told about how to control a woman, and then gone home and followed the foolish advice. The wimpiest of the Wimps would have gotten out of the car and proceeded to fight his old lady right there on the highway.

A man who controls himself controls his destiny.

Any questions before moving on? *What if the woman initiates the contact?*

Damn good question. A man worth his salt doesn't fight a woman; on the same coin, a man doesn't take more than one ass-whooping from a woman. Yes, as you know, there are some women who can do the job. Still, regardless of the situation—who was right, who was wrong—the second she lets you up should be the second you hit the door, never to return. Stay, and like so many men and women in abusive relationships, you will almost certainly get your ass whooped again. Then, numerous ass-whoopings later, your self-esteem and self-confidence will be so low, you no longer have the intestinal fortitude to leave.

Also avoid women who literally beg a man to hit them. "Punk! Hit me, then!" Often these women come from abusive relationships and expect abuse; it's all they know. Sad, but not your problem. Stay with this type woman long enough and eventually you will fall for the senseless rhetoric she's putting down—this is called Wimp building, and the results are the same, abuse with deadly potential.

One option that Brothers rarely consider with an aggressive woman is to call the police. Yes, in the African-American community this appears...well, wimpish, really. But it's not. Women, moreso than men, tend to comply with common sense after a few hours, or days, in jail. Another option that many Brothers never consider when confronting an aggressive woman is running, even if the woman is in clear possession of a gun or knife. Running is never wimpish when compared to gaping knife wounds and see-through gunshot wounds.

Love and Unhappiness

Let's say you won your state's lotto. A million dollars. Wow! Excited, you run home intent on telling your significant other the good news. Before you can start, she says, "I'm leaving you. Sorry, but I've found someone else...someone who will treat me right, who doesn't have a conniption when I laugh at him." Your mouth drops open, you start to cry, then laugh, then both simultaneously. She thinks otherwise, but those are tears of joy streaming down your face. You know that once the divorce papers are final, or once the Love Shack is disassembled, it's over. Then you'll call her up and relay the good news.

Now let's put a little reality in the supposition. You didn't win the lotto, or a two-dollar scratch ticket, but your significant other says the same thing. "I'm leaving you. Sorry..." Your mouth drops open, you start to cry—well, at least your eyes water, okay. But those are not tears of joy, but true sorrow, pain, frustration and hurt.

What's the difference between the two? Well, yes, the money, but the main difference is the way you perceived her leaving you. In the first scenario, no doubt you were hurt to some degree, but the thought of getting the last laugh diminished the hurt. In the second scenario you had no million-dollar cushion to bounce back on; all you had was what you brought in the door, your feelings and the clothes on your back.

Keep in mind that this type situation, and ones similar to it, has sent many a man to prison and the graveyard. Players, Sugar Daddies, pimps, millionaires, congressmen, professional athletes, preachers, janitors, and many more have succumbed to TNT (Tit and Nookie Trauma). Make no mistake about it, TNT is a very dangerous and explosive state of mind. Clicking pales in comparison to TNT because clicking, usually, lasts a very short time—anger progresses to rage, then subsides—but TNT can last a very long time, the anger progresses to rage, but never subsides. TNT is similar to picking at a scab because the wound is never allowed to heal; instead the constant picking at it causes it to bleed and hurt again.

Let's face some cold, hard facts. Divorce, shack disassembly, and girlfriend and boyfriend breakups hurt men and women both, but without a doubt, men have greater difficulty handling the ending of a relationship. Women, in general, express their emotions, which has been proven to reduce emotional stress. Men, however, tend to keep their emotions bottled up. It's the manly thing to do. But it's the unhealthy thing to do.

Men tend to view relationship failure as personal failure. Pure ego. To make matters worse, all the internal fears—fear of rejection, fear of abandonment, fear of being alone—kick in. On top of all this, the biggest fear of all kicks in, and this fear tends to supersede all others—the nookie fear! Don't misunderstand, this fear isn't a concern that the nookie might suffer mishap or injury. Uh-uh. The fear, the heart of TNT, is that some other man will come into contact with the nookie—and not just casual contact, either. At its core this is plain old jealousy—yet it is oh so powerful. Nookie fear can rob a man of the ability to eat, sleep, walk, work, think clearly, and, most importantly, move forward and let the relationship go. Yet nookie fear in itself does not constitute TNT. Many men have endured nookie fear without incident. TNT sufferers aren't so lucky; some type of drama usually occurs, in the form of violence.

Keep in mind that TNT can happen to any man, even to self-confident men. The moment you slip into one or more of the three R's—Righteous Indignation, Rehashing, and Reading—the fuse has been lit to TNT, and a devastating explosion is imminent.

Righteous Indignation: Listen closely: "I gave her so much, all I had to give, and she goes and treats me like this!" "She doesn't appreciate a good man!" "She doesn't give a damn about me! If she did, she wouldn't have done what she did!" "She left me for that sorry sonofabitch!" "He won't treat her half as good as I did!" Each of the above statements is reeking with victimization, the root cause of Righteous Indignation. Basically, the man feels that he has been wronged, terribly.

Everyone occasionally feels wronged from time to time, but in relationship breakups this feeling often intensifies to a dangerous level. Feeling victimized and/or righteously indignant provides justification for your hurt, anger, and rage…but robs you of self-respect and self-confidence.

In other words, you've been mistreated, so where do you go from there? Maintain a sense of victimization long enough, and you truly go to Victimhoodville, a very ugly place, populated by whiners who love to cry and masturbate.

To avoid this crippling state of mind, simply assume responsibility for the breakup. Even if she stole all of your money and ran off with your best friend, guess what? You are still complicit. Who chose her? Who should have detected negative aspects of her personality from the get-go? Blaming it all on her will keep you in a funk and lead to...

Rehashing: No doubt you know a Brother who bitterly talks about the woman who did him wrong thirty years ago. Sometimes you want to say, "Get over it, already!" Remember this: Once the initial hurt is over, everything else is picking and poking at a scab, which will never heal if picking and poking is continued. Rehashing is a thousand times more dangerous than picking and poking at a scab because often the emotional feelings are so intense, so volatile, that clicking to the extreme is sure to occur. In fact, rehashing is nothing more than self-induced clicking.

Let's say, for example, your significant other runs off with your worst enemy, number one on your DFW list. To say the least, you are upset. You cannot think clearly because you imagine him and her together, doing something that you thought was reserved only for you and her. Honestly, you want to hurt them both. Now here is where the whole thing can get tricky. Your initial emotional response to the situation is to be expected—damn right, you're angry!—but what happens afterwards? This is where the slide into rehashing occurs. To an extent a degree of rehashing is automatic in all breakups, but there's a danger point. This point differs in one man to the next, but the moment you can work yourself into the same heated frenzy you experienced initially, you have crossed the line. In other words, if the thought *"That heifer did me wrong!"* incites the same, or higher, sense of outrage as it did when you first discovered what happened, then you have slipped deep into rehashing.

This is a very easy slide to make, and is very dangerous.

Think about it: What happened happened—you cannot change that! So why beat yourself up? Why keep playing the same noise over and over and over in your head, working yourself up in a heated frenzy? Once the rehashing starts, all manner of sinister imagination comes into play. "She's been doing this all along!" "She got my partners thinking I'm a punk!" "The whole world thinks I'm a chump!" "Everybody knows!"

Tick tick tick tick tick...You see how easy this can get out of hand?

The best way to prevent rehashing is to be aware of rehashing—"Hey, this is the fifth time I thought about that. I'm rehashing." Stop it by simply thinking of something else. If your thoughts return to the noise, do the same thing each time. Yes, on some occasions, doing this is somewhat difficult. Still, keep aware of negative thoughts that keep playing over and over again. Ask yourself: Is my thinking helping the situation? Are my thoughts the true source of my anger?

Other lit fuses to look out for: family and friends. These people unwittingly promote rehashing simply because they are family and friends. Of course they'll agree with you that so-and-so "is a no-good slut who needs her butt kicked." They'll say anything if it might make you feel better. This never helps; often it makes the situation worse, a helluva lot worse. A wise friend or family members knows that it's best not to endorse rehashing, or name-calling, or character assassination; and he or she wisely knows that it's never a good idea to add anything. "Yes, she definitely needs her ass whooped." These type statements from family and friends have KISSed many a men.

Reading: Listen closely: "I do not want to be with you anymore." Nine words. Distinct, simple words. Yet someone suffering from TNT cannot comprehend those nine, distinct, simple words—or any word or phase or action that plainly states that the relationship is over. Usually when a woman makes a declarative statement such as the aforementioned, she's at her wit's end: at first she tried to be subtle, then, because the message apparently was misunderstood, she spoke bluntly. And still, the man doesn't get it. He's Reading.

Simply: Reading is twisting words and actions clearly stating rejection into a totally different meaning.

Thus "I don't want to be with you anymore" becomes "I might want you if you beg harder, plead harder, show your ass more." Yes, this is a self-induced psychosis, also the impetus to all forms of stalking. This is very ugly, and very dangerous. The woman says *"The relationship is over,"* the man calls her fifteen times a day. The woman says *"The relationship is over,"* the man keeps showing up at her house. The woman says *"The relationship is over,"* the man shows up at her job. The woman says *"The relationship is over,"* the man follows her wherever she goes. The woman says *"The relationship is over,"* the man beats her up. The woman says *"The relationship is over,"* the man kills her.

There's a lot at play here: fear, insecurity, low self-esteem, Righteous Indignation, Rehashing, delusion, jealousy, fantasy, and rage. The latter tends to dominate all others. Despite Reading, the man at some level understands he's being rejected—yet all the while he keeps putting himself in a position to be rejected again and again. Think about it: She couldn't reject him more than once if he stayed out her face and stopped contacting her. With each rejection, the rage intensifies. His answer to the dilemma: Try harder. Insanity in action. This is why so many TNT sufferers go quickly from presenting flowers to abusing and/or killing.

Men who are Control Freaks are more susceptible to Reading than any other group, because they honestly feel that they know what is best for the woman. The second highest susceptible group is men with very low self-esteem who think that their life cannot go on after a breakup—"I can't live without you!" and "If I can't have you no one else will!" The third group are young men in love for the first time dealing with a breakup, who feel that life is not worth living without their true and only love. The second and third group are almost identical, but the second group consists of men who have suffered TNT more than once.

However, don't put much stock in the classification. Reading is automatic after most breakups: "I wonder if that's what she really wants?" But you can avoid crossing the line by taking a woman at her word. Always! When she says no, accept no. Yes, it hurts like hell, but doing otherwise exponentially compounds the hurt.

A good idea is to put yourself in her shoes. If you told someone "The relationship is over," you would not want to be bothered with constant phone calls; you would not want to be feverishly begged "Please give it one more chance!"; you would not want unexpected appearances at your home and/or job; you would not want to be stalked; you would not want to hear threats of suicide or threats to your person; you would not want your property damaged; you would not want to be physically assaulted; and you damn sure would not want to be killed.

Relationships end, more often than not, bitterly. A sad fact of life. There exists no manual to handling a breakup amicably. "Get over it" is the most popular response. If only it were that easy. It takes time to "Get over it," as they say, and depending on your temperament it may take a lot of time. Hell, many men never get over it. Many men become jaded after the first breakup, never fully trusting a woman again, never giving all they have to give in future relationships because of fear of another breakup.

As sad as all that is, nothing is sadder than the level of violence many men resort to after a breakup: assault, rape, suicide, torture, kidnapping, and murder. Pick up any newspaper, hick town or big town, and you will find an article about some man who simply could not let go. How in the world, you ask yourself, does a man think he can gain his woman back by putting a gun to her head and holding her hostage? "Gee, Bob, I didn't know how much you really cared till you beat me, stabbed me, shot me—I love you!"

A good number of men are graveyard dead—suicide, killed—because they slid into a muck of Righteous Indignation, or Rehashing, or Reading, or a combination of all three. A good number of men are in prison for the same reason, a few regretting the fact. An even larger group of men are ashamed and embarrassed at the way they conducted themselves after a breakup—despite the ignominy, many will repeat the behavior.

But you, a specimen in self-control, are above all of this. You know that TNT can be avoided by simply acknowledging the truth: "The relationship ended, I'm just as much to blame as she, and it hurts like hell." You know that begging, pleading, whining, bitching, fighting, rehashing, sniveling, Reading, and stalking only prolong the hurt.

You also know that a woman would rather come back to a man who comports himself respectfully after a breakup than a man who dings out after a breakup. Oh yes, you definitely know that!

Another big mistake many men make after a breakup is to immediately seek comfort in the arms of another woman. Doing so is more preferable than turning to drink or drugs or succumbing to TNT, but the results are usually the same. Disastrous! Face the facts.

You are hurting. You need time to heal. The last thing you need at the moment is to embark on another relationship.

This is an ideal time to get to know yourself. An ideal time for reflection, forgiveness, and growth. When the hurt becomes overwhelming, immerse yourself in social activities with friends, family, or even better, religious activities. Volunteer work, any sort, is an excellent tool to chisel away the stress of a breakup, not to mention a great way to reinvigorate yourself and help someone else at the same time.

Lastly, keep your head up! You will eventually meet someone else. Though the next time around you will take your time, because you know what to listen for, the noises, yours and hers.

Chapter 12
Don't Hate the Player, Hate the Game

"The difference between a Brother in New York and a Brother in Los Angeles: approximately 2800 miles." H.H.

Professional sports players win; even if they lose the game, they still win. Yes, the team may not advance to the playoffs, but the players still win—every payday. Fat pay to the order of checks. Which is why some players—most don't—float through the season, doing only enough to keep a job. It's tempting to list a few names here, but most of these guys are rather large and hold grudges longer than they hold the ball.

Then there is the fan, a word derived from fanatic, which is an appropriate term for some fans. Unlike the professional sports player, the fan is not offered a win-win platter at the game. If the team does not make the playoffs, the fan loses a source of entertainment. The season is over; it's time to go home and rent some movies. This is probably why some fans take the ending of their favorite team's season harder than the players do themselves. Can you imagine Allen Iverson secluding himself in his bedroom all summer long because the Sixers didn't beat the Lakers? No, you cannot.

Therefore would it not be wise to put yourself in Allen Iverson's shoes? No, not his tennis shoes, or his car, or his mansion, but his position, a win-win position.

Yes, you, too, can put yourself in a position where even if you lose you still win. How? A playbook. Or, in other words, a strategic set of guidelines that will give you the upper hand in most situations and the ability to confront unexpected situations. You can devise your own playbook, of course, but every Brother needs the following two plays in his book—The Triangular Defense and The Nickel Defense. Let's take a closer look.

The Triangular Defense

The triangular defense consists of three components: Appearance, Confidence, and Attitude. Each compliments the other, and minus either one, you no longer have a triangle but a funny-looking shape that slopes downward. For example, a surfeit of confidence means little if your appearance is shabby, or your attitude is negative. The same negative-canceling occurs when you project a positive attitude but emit a smell that would cause a skunk to blush. Each component of The Triangular Defense must come together in order to achieve a win-win position. Okay, that understood, let's move on. But keep in mind: If the shoe doesn't fit, don't look for a match.

Appearance: Somehow many Brothers have translated "I work every day" into "I don't have to wash up ever again." To be blunt, funk is funk, and simply because you work a job that requires you to get dirty doesn't mean you cannot come home and wash up and put on some clean clothes. Your appearance speaks volume to who you are, what goals you have, and where you are going in life. Your appearance dictates what type women you attract. Your appearance determines what type people gravitate to you. Most importantly, your appearance goes hand-in-hand with your self-confidence.

This is not to say that a Brother should spend his last dime on expensive suits and what-not. But all the basic hygiene requirements should be addressed everyday: a shower or bath, clean teeth, and clean clothes. It takes little money to iron clothes and put a shine on shoes. If you can afford designer clothes, that's fine, too. Your clothing style is totally your choice, but keep in mind that there is a time and place for everything. For example, if you prefer to wear your pants down to your knees, exposing your underwear, no problem. But it would be unwise to do so at a job interview or at work. Keep in mind that the first impression is often the only impression.

While there's nothing wrong with keeping in step with the latest fads and clothing styles, you should always remember that these things change quickly. So think long and hard before committing yourself to something you might regret later. Yes, you may be the highlight of the neighborhood with an assortment of tattoos and body rings today, but what about ten years from now? Those holes do not fill up easily.

Honestly, only an idiot would tattoo his girlfriend's name on his body, anywhere. If the relationship ends, who pays for removing the tattoo? A greeting card can say *I love you* just as well.

Admit it, when you are smelling good and looking good, you feel good. Oh, yes! What more pleasing a sight than a Brother strutting his stuff? His chin is up, his shoulders are squared, his back is straight, and he walks and talks like a man, a highly confident man. Even if he does not have two pennies to rub together, he is still projecting…

Confidence: The Honorable Dr. Martin Luther King said, "If a man hasn't discovered something he will die for, he isn't fit to live." So very true. No doubt the

Honorable Dr. Martin Luther King saw the Stare, that look of utter defeat on so many Black men's faces. In his time, the Stare was the results of years of systematic racism. Now, today, the Stare stems from drugs, alcohol, and an abject lack of confidence. You notice that racism was left out. Yes, and that's part of the problem. No one—White, Black, or Blue—has figured out how to tell an African-American that being African-American means dealing with racism, prejudices, and inequities, without—and here's the rub—undermining the African-American's confidence. How can you tell a young Brother to thrive for his dreams, to challenge himself, to be all he can be, and at the same time tell him, "A Black man has a hard row to hoe in a White man's world"?

This is why racism cuts the African-American two times on one glancing blow. Cut one: Racism and prejudice do exist. Cut two: Contrary to what many African-American demagogues preach, not all African-Americans' problems stem from racism—and to preach such definitely undermines confidence.

Subtle or overt racial paranoia is equally as damaging as subtle or overt racism in that each kills confidence. More than anything else, including money and education, a Brother needs confidence. No confidence, no motivation. No confidence, no desire. No confidence, no willpower. No confidence, no self-discipline. No, confidence, no passion. No confidence, no life. You see it everyday. Brothers who stay on dead-end, paltry-paying jobs, never once thinking to move on and up. Brothers with college degrees working entry-level jobs, never thinking to move on and up. An even sadder sight, Brothers with marketable talents—singing, drawing, painting, writing, storytelling, rapping, acting—who simply stop for whatever reason, never thinking that what they used to love to do is a possible vocation.

Gaining confidence is very simple: You make it

happen. That's it. Make it happen. Each time you make it happen, your confidence grows. This is why it's best to build your children's confidence at an early age—with each accomplishment, set the post a little bit higher. Outside of an elephant breaking wind, no sound is more disturbing than a Brother saying, "I should have done this, I should have done that." It makes no sense—if he could have done it, why the hell didn't he? Is it too late now? No risks, no rewards.

Nothing is more pleasurable than making it happen—not sex, not money, nothing. If you've ever set a difficult goal, and then passionately committed yourself to achieving that goal and eventually accomplished that goal, you know the above is true. Nothing compares to it—absolutely nothing! Plus you will discover that working to achieve the goal is equally as exciting, if not more, as accomplishing the goal. In other words, you can't lose.

Attitude: Ugly people should not have a bad attitude. Yet people with bad attitudes are always—not sometimes but always—ugly! Everyone has a bad day now and then, but there are many people who are simply stuck on stupid. Yes, stupid. Maintaining a negative disposition is very stupid. Even more stupid, many people with bad attitudes cannot understand why people avoid them. "Gee, George, perhaps, you think, if your attitude wasn't so funky that wouldn't be the case." Who gravitates toward someone who frowns, bitches, whines, moans, groans, and snivels far more than he smiles or laughs? No one does.

This is yet another issue where many African-American men sign their name above the line titled DUPED. The guy who said that African-American men are stuck on rage was full of himself. Actually he was full of shit. Yet many Brothers actually believe that they are supposed to go through life angry all the damn time.

This type of BS also undermines confidence.

That said, let's say you and another guy were competing for the same promotion. You both have the same qualifications—time on the job, same skills, same educational background. The only difference between you and he is that he has a…well, let's say, a less-than-positive attitude. He never clicks or anything, but he never smiles or laughs either. Guess who gets the promotion? Yes, you do. (Bet you thought you would be the bad guy once again?) No, this is not being an Uncle Tom, or a Skinner and Grinner for that matter. This is simply attracting people to you. A smile tells people you are approachable and friendly, and says, "I like myself. I like people."

No doubt you've visited a friend or relative who was watching television and they continued to do so while you were there. During commercials was the only time they would speak, but still their eyes never left the television. Worse than that is to be in a conversation with someone, and then the guy who is glued to the television turns the volume up louder, a tacit way of saying, "Be quiet! I can't hear the television!" Yet a loud way of saying: "I enjoy television more than I enjoy people!"

To truly enjoy life you must enjoy people. Yes, people—regardless of color, regardless of financial status, and regardless if your favorite sitcom is on. People are far more important than anything you might see, feel, or experience. Therefore to succeed in life, you must do what? Yes, you are so right. You must enjoy people. How do you go about doing that? A good question. Simply: You attract people to you—and the way to do that is to convey a positive, approachable, winning attitude.

The Nickel Defense

Two Brothers, Buck Short and Moe Green, work at the same job and make the same hourly wage, $12.50 an hour. Both men are single, both drive the same type of car, a Honda Accord, and both live in the same apartment complex. This is where the similarities end. Unlike Moe, Buck is constantly in need of money. He borrows from friends, coworkers, family, and when those don't pan out, he hits the local Check Cashing company, where they hold his personal check until next payday and charge an arm and leg in interest.

No, Buck is not a crackhead. In a nutshell, Buck's problem lies in his method of budgeting. He utilizes the Cash In Pocket method of budgeting. The goal of this method of budgeting is to keep as much spending money in the pocket as possible. Each payday Buck pays the most current expense—rent, car note, utilities, whatever—then he pockets the rest. A problem occurs when two expenses bump heads, so to speak, on the same payday, which happens to Buck quite often. This is when the borrowing starts. Then, the next payday, he has another expense plus the expense of paying back the borrowed money. This entails more borrowing and more borrowing and on and on and on…

Though Buck has never tried drugs in his life, he certainly knows how a drug addict feels—miserable and depressed! You would, too, if you worked week after week and instead of moving ahead financially you found yourself deeper and deeper in debt. Ironically, Buck truly believes that if only he made more money his problems would be solved. Apparently he hasn't heard the old cliché: If you cannot manage $500 a week, you damn sure can't manage a $1 million a week.

On the flip side of the coin, Moe utilizes the Nickel Defense method of budgeting. Moe knows where every nickel of his money goes, every week, every month, and every year.

How? He simply writes it down. Here's how his monthly budget looks:

EXPENSES
RENT: $350.00
CAR NOTE: $300.00
UTILITIES (ELECTRIC, GAS, AND WATER): $250.00
FOOD: $300.00
INSURANCE: $75.00
GAS: $100.00
MISCELLANEOUS: $75.00
SAVINGS ACCOUNT: $100.00 (A DAMN GOOD IDEA!)
TOTAL EXPENSES: $1,550.00
INCOME
MINUS MOE'S MONTHLY TAKE-HOME PAY: $1,575.00

LEFT AFTER EXPENSES
$25.00

Yes, Moe's budget is rather tight, and he knows it. So he doesn't buy impulsively, nor does he borrow money. When an unexpected expense arises, he uses the money from his savings account. Of course, Moe desires to make more money, so he keeps his eyes open for a job that'll pay more than his present salary. If one comes along, he'll take it at the drop of hat, because he knows that take-home pay and benefits are more important than relationships at work.

The Nickel Defense, or any other budget for that matter, is a win-win proposition. You know how much you have to spend and what you can afford. And this eliminates borrowing, which is a short road to debt frustration. Control! Why have it any other way?